The Execution Squad Fraud

Bum Beefed

STEPHEN DOHERTY

The Execution Squad Fraud: Bum Beefed

"Grand jury hears Walpole Testimony" reprinted with permission of the *Boston Herald*.

Published by Wheatmark®
610 East Delano Street, Suite 104
Tucson, Arizona 85705 U.S.A.
www.wheatmark.com

International Standard Book Number: 978-1-60494-163-0
Library of Congress Control Number: 2008933783

introduction

I n November 1998, the first National Conference on Wrongful Convictions and the Death Penalty was convened in Chicago—ironically, on Friday the 13th. Among those present were thirty out of a known seventy-five former death row inmates who had been exonerated of the crimes for which they had been convicted. In less than four years, that figure rose to over one hundred individuals who were exonerated after having been sentenced to die. The numbers continue to rise.

As astounding as some people might find that figure to be, the number would have been far greater if it had included those who had been wrongfully convicted of capital crimes in states that do not have the death penalty and had been sentenced to life in prison instead.

Such as the wrongful convictions in the notorious *Execution Squad* case that came out of Walpole State Prison, in Massachusetts, in 1977.

I know, because I was one of them. If we had had the death penalty in Massachusetts back then, I'd most likely be dead by now, executed for a crime that I not only had nothing to do with, but a crime for which I was framed by the Massachusetts justice system.

CASE BACKGROUND

In 1976, I was doing time in Walpole for a bank robbery and was about to be transferred to MCI Framingham to be placed in a work release program. This is the last step before actually being released back to the street. However, on the night of December 2, 1976, at the instigation of a politically ambitious district attorney named William Delahunt, (now a United States Congressman), myself, and eight other inmates were dramatically whisked out of Walpole at midnight and placed in the segregation block (a.k.a. "the hole") at MCI Bridgewater—a combination prison and insane asylum.

The next morning, the *Boston Globe* ran a bizarre story, under a dramatic front page headline, that claimed that the police had uncovered an inmate execution squad at Walpole State Prison. This case is a textbook example of how the system can be manipulated and abused through the combined efforts

1

of an ambitious prosecutor/politician, unethical or overzealous police work, and certain elements of the media who find it to their advantage to parrot what the prosecutors, or the cops, tell them and report it as fact. Of course, the suppliers of the information are usually identified as "informed sources" and the "facts" are always prefaced with "allegedly." The midnight transfer of the fictitious *Execution Squad* from Walpole to Bridgewater was made strictly for publicity purposes, as we were returned to Walpole the very next day and placed in the segregation unit—the infamous Ten Block—where we could have been placed right from the start, minus all of the fanfare. However, then they wouldn't have gotten their headlines.

one

O n Thanksgiving Day, 1976, an inmate named Robert Perrotta was found brutally murdered in his cell. His penis had been torn from his body, *while he was still alive*, and stuck in his mouth.

My first indication that I was even considered a suspect in Bobby Perrotta's murder came on the night after it happened. I was in my home cellblock, block A-2, when I heard another inmate being paged over the loudspeaker. "Arthur Keigney, please report to inner control. Keigney, report to inner control."

That was generally not a good sign. After the evening meal, everything was pretty much recreation and relaxation. To hear your name over the loudspeaker at that time of night usually meant bad news, possibly notification of a death in the family at home.

A while later I heard, "John Campbell, please report to inner control. Campbell, report to control."

This definitely caught my attention and changed my perception of the calls. Two guys from my block—both from my hometown of Charlestown—being called out on the night after a murder had occurred in our block was not a good sign. I came out of my cell and looked around. I noticed that other guys were doing the same thing.

A little while later, Jackie Campbell came down the back stairway. I lived in cell 12, the last cell on the right-hand side of the bottom floor (the flats). The stairs were right next to my cell.

Jackie stopped at my door. He asked, "Did ya hear them call me?"

I nodded, "Yeah. I heard them call Arthur earlier. Is he back yet?"

Jackie shook his head. "No. I checked his cell before I came down."

Jackie and Arthur both lived on the third tier. So hadn't Bobby Perrotta.

"That's not a good sign," I said.

"I know," he said.

I asked, "If you're not back by lock-in, you want me to call someone for ya in the morning?"

He nodded his head, "Yeah."

As he walked away, I said, "Good luck."

A little while later, I heard, "Stephen Doherty, please report to inner control. Doherty, report to control."

My hair stood on end. I had never even considered that I would be called. A few weeks earlier, I had been okayed for a transfer to MCI Framingham to be let out on work release. Framingham was a coed (but mostly women's) prison. It was just a question of waiting for the paperwork to come back from the main office of the Department of Correction (DOC) in Boston. In the meantime, I had been doing my best to keep as low a profile as possible. There was no way that I was going to get involved in anything. Once you're that close to getting out, you don't even like to come out of your cell. In a place like Walpole, in the seventies, you never knew from one moment to the next what was going to happen. Fights, murders, riots, and lots more were commonplace. They were just part of the environment.

I came out of my cell, went up the back stairs to the third tier, and walked over to Campbell's cell. He wasn't there.

There were guys standing on the tier, leaning on the railing. I asked, "Did Jackie come back?" Even though I already knew the answer, I had to ask. They just shook their heads.

I said, "Arthur?" Same response.

One of the guys standing there was from Charlestown. I called him off to the side and said, "If I'm not back by count time [10 pm, when they locked us in our cells for the night and took the count], I want you to call my lawyer for me in the morning."

"Sure," he said.

I gave him my lawyer's number. "His name is Alan Caplan. Thanks."

I then went to the cell of another guy from Charlestown and repeated the process.

I went back down to my cell and got dressed. Even though inner control was just down the corridor and did not require me to go outside, I dressed warmly, taking a winter coat and gloves. I even put on my sunglasses. It was almost December, and Keigney and Campbell had yet to return. Who knew where I was going to wind up?

As I came out of my cell, I had another thought. So far, they had called three people—all from Charlestown. The two guys that I had arranged to call my lawyer were both townies. How did I know that they weren't being called next? I went back upstairs. I gave Al Caplan's number to two other guys, neither of whom were from Charlestown.

When I got to inner control, one of the correctional officers (COs) behind the bulletproof glass said, "They wanna see you out in counseling."

Inner control is a large, circular, and secure room at the center of Walpole from where certain gates and solid steel doors were controlled. These doors included two on the left of control, which led out to the visiting room, and two on the right that led to the counseling area.

I went through the doors and turned right, into the counseling section. It consisted of an open area, maybe thirty square feet, which was surrounded by about ten small offices. The offices were about seven or eight square feet. At this time of night, they were all empty, except one.

There were two large guards, probably about three hundred pounds each, standing outside one of the offices. They waved me over and into the office.

I walked into the office and realized that there was barely room for me. Sitting behind the desk was the warden, Fred Butterworth. He introduced me to the two suits sitting next to him. One was an assistant district attorney (ADA) named John Prescott. He introduced the other as a chemist. There were two or three others standing off to the side. One of them was a state police detective named William Bergin.

Fred Butterworth was one of the last wardens to actually start as a guard and work his way up through the ranks. He was a small guy. Picture James Cagney with a totally pockmark-scarred face and a high-pitched voice. He was a pretty harmless-looking guy, but looks can be deceiving.

After the introductions, Fred said, "Steve, we're going to do a test on you. The chemist is going to scrape under your fingernails."

That was fine with me. I had been nowhere near Bobby Perrotta on the day he was murdered.

I said, "Sure, but I wanna call my lawyer first."

Fred said, "No lawyers."

I asked, "Why not?"

He just shook his head and repeated himself. "No lawyers."

That got my hackles up. I looked at the prosecutor and said, "You're a lawyer. Is this legal?"

He didn't respond, at least not verbally. He obviously hadn't expected the question, immediately glanced at Fred, and then looked down at the desk.

"I said, 'No lawyers,'" Fred reiterated.

I thought for a minute. Then, removing my sunglasses and handing them across the desk, I said to the prosecutor, "Here, would you mind holding these for a minute?"

He looked startled but automatically took my glasses.

Stepping back from the desk, I folded my arms and placed my hands under my armpits. I said, "I have nothing to hide. But, if you're not going to allow me to speak to my attorney, I can't cooperate."

We all stood there for a long, silent minute.

Finally, Fred said, "Get him."

The two over-nourished guards grabbed me from behind. I didn't fight back. I simply resisted. After a few minutes of squirming contention, they had me lying on my stomach, across the desk. Both of them were lying on top of me. One of my arms was twisted up behind my back. The other was stretched out in front of me while the chemist scraped under my fingernails. They reversed arms, and then it was over. They released me, and I stood up.

I held out my hand to John Prescott for my glasses and said, "Thank you."

He looked befuddled.

Fred came out from behind the desk, walked out of the room, and said to me, "Come with me."

I followed him out with one of the guards lumbering along behind me. He walked into one of the empty counselor's offices. I followed him. The guard followed me.

Fred turned around and, seeing the guard, waved him out of the office. "Wait outside," he said.

The guard hesitated for a minute. He said, "Are you sure? You wanna be in the room alone with ..."

Fred cut him off; waving his arm again, his voice rising, "Get out, I said. Get out."

The guard quickly stepped out and closed the door.

Fred held up his hand and said to me, "Don't say nothin'. You know you've got a lawsuit, an' I know you've got a lawsuit. We'll deal with it when the time comes. My question is can I put you back in population?"

Surprised, I quipped, "Have I got a vote?"

Impatiently, he asked, "Are you gonna start your shit?"

Confused, I asked, "What shit?"

"You know," he said. "That riotin' and protest shit."

When I had first walked into Walpole, back in February 1973, it was right in the middle of the Porelle lock down. The whole joint was locked down for seventy-nine days—no showers, nothing. It was also the peak of the burgeoning national prison reform movement that was a direct result of the massacre at Attica state prison in New York about a year and a half earlier. I wound up in the middle of it as the National Prisoners Reform Association (NPRA) representative of the New Man's Block. The notoriety stuck, and Fred had a long memory.

I said, "Hey Fred, that stuff's fun, but you're talkin' about a murder here. This is for real."

"You give me your word that you won't start any of that shit," he said.

I asked, "Can I call my lawyer?"

He nodded his head. "Give me your word," he said.

"You've got my word," I said.

He opened the door and said to the guard, "Take him to my office, and let him use the telephone."

Fred had been a hard, old-time guard, but his word was good. It was one thing we had in common. In all the years I knew him, I never saw him break his word. He'd kick your ass and throw you in the hole if he felt like it, but he wouldn't break his word.

The guard took me to Fred's office, and I called Al Caplan at home and told him what happened. After we spoke, I was returned to my block. Arthur and Jackie were both back in the block. They had had their fingernails scraped too.

two

The following week on Thursday night, December 2, 1976, I was watching the eleven o'clock news. All of a sudden I heard noise out in the block. I got up and peeked out. There were a whole gang of screws (a.k.a. guards), a move team, removing a guy from his cell on the third tier. It was Paulie Z, who was a nice and quiet guy, a Vietnam veteran from South Boston. They took him out of the block in cuffs, turned right, and headed down the corridor.

The view from the angle of my cell allowed me to see all the way down the length of the block, across the corridor, and into block A-3. I could see a large group of screws milling about in the corridor, which was definitely not a good sign.

A few minutes later, the move team returned. They didn't come back into A-2, which allowed me a sigh of relief. Instead, they went across the hall into block A-3.

A little while later, they emerged with another inmate in cuffs. I recognized him. It was Myles Connor.

After a while, they returned again. But this time, they came back into A-2. I could see a gang of them coming down the tier toward my cell. I stepped back away from the window and sat down on the bed. Then I heard them going by my cell. I thought, "Yes, they're going back upstairs," or so I thought. A hand reached in through the window and pulled down the little curtain that covered it.

As the door started to open, a voice said, "You wanna step out?"

There were about a dozen guards surrounding my door. They took me out and strip-searched me. As I was putting my clothes back on, a guard that I got along with said to me, under his breath, "You better dress warm."

As luck would have it, it happened to be the coldest night of the year.

I said to the cop in charge, a senior officer nicknamed "Chicago Al," "I don't suppose this is my Framingham move?"

He just grimaced and said, "Not hardly."

When they took me outside, Myles Connor was already there. They chained us together and placed us in a van. Nothing against Myles, we got along just fine, but I was not happy. I could not imagine why I was being locked up with him. I had enough heat of my own. I certainly didn't need his, and I'm sure that he felt the same way.

A little while later, the van door opened and in came three more: Ronnie MacDonald, Arthur Keigney, and Jackie Campbell. By the time the dust settled, there were nine of us in two vans.

A while later, we got to our destination, Bridgewater State Hospital. Bridgewater was an ill-famed monument to barbarism, whose only positive contribution was as a classic example of how a mental institution should *not* be run. They treated people so horrendously at Bridgewater that, when movie director Frederick Wiseman exposed them with a film documentary in 1967 titled *Titicut Follies*, the politicians in Massachusetts got the Massachusetts Supreme Judicial Court to order the withdrawal of the film from circulation. They fought it so hard that the ban lasted for twenty-five years.

We were immediately taken to their segregation unit, an antiquity that was aptly named The Fort.

They gave us these skimpy little thin jumpsuits to wear. Nothing else. No socks, no underwear, nothing. They locked us in separate cells.

The cell that they put me in had a bed and a sheet, but no blanket—*and no heat*. It had a high ceiling, maybe twelve feet high, with a metal grating covering the cell at about seven feet. It also had a window. Unfortunately, the window was out of reach above the metal grating, and it was broken!

I curled up in a ball under the sheet and tried to go to sleep. I couldn't. My feet were so cold they were hurting. I sat up and looked around the cell—nothing, except a pillowcase on the floor. I picked it up and crawled back under the sheet. Then I reached down and slid my feet into the pillowcase. It came up about halfway between my ankles and my knees. After a few minutes, my toes began to thaw out a little, and I drifted off to sleep listening to the others talking back and forth between their cells. My last thought before I fell asleep was, "How the hell can they stay out of bed in this cold?"

I was awakened by two guards serving breakfast, coffee, and corn flakes. I said to the guard, "Say, do you think you can do somethin' about the heat in here?"

"What's wrong?" he asked. "Is it too hot?"

"Not really," I answered. "There ain't any. On top of that, the window's broken, and I'm freezing my balls off."

"I'll see what I can do after I finish feeding," he said. Then he moved on to the next cell.

Myles was in the next cell, and I could hear him asking the guard if we could call our lawyers.

I was talking to David Weichel, who was across the hall from me, at his door. However, as soon as I got my coffee, I told him that I was going to go back to bed, because I was freezing.

He looked surprised, and said, "You're cold? I'm roastin.'"

The cell doors were solid, with just a small window, maybe six inches by eight inches, around face level. I hadn't realized that David wasn't even wearing the jumpsuit. Now I did.

I said, "Listen, if you're really hot, how about letting me have your sheet? And your pillowcase?"

He laughed and said, "Why don't I just give you the blanket?"

I said, "You got a blanket?"

He laughed again. "You ain't?"

Calling the guard over, David said, "Excuse me, could you give him my blanket? He's freezin', and I don't need it."

The guard said, "Nothin' gets passed."

David said, "Hey, it's just a blanket. He ain't got one, an' he got no heat."

The guard repeated himself. "Nothin' gets passed."

I said, "All right. Nothin' gets passed. Then can you just get me a blanket?"

He looked at me and, without saying a word, walked away.

All the while that this was going on, everybody was asking the guards why we were locked up and what was going on. Their immediate refusal to answer any questions sparked an outcry of demands to be allowed to call lawyers. In the midst of all this, I went back to bed. It was just too cold to stand barefoot on that stone floor. Moreover, my lower back was killing me. It had been screwed up since the morning after they scraped my fingernails.

When the guards had finished feeding and gone back downstairs, Myles called out, "Listen, everyone. I asked the screw if we could call our lawyers. He says that they've already been notified. Let's take a vote. Everyone who believes that raise their hand." This brought on about two seconds of silence, followed by a gale of laughter and a burst of catcalls.

"They don't even know who my lawyer is," yelled Weichel.

"Me neither," someone else yelled back.

The outburst of noise brought the guards back upstairs, wanting to know what was going on. That got me back out of bed.

The first one asked, "What's the matter?"

Arthur Keigney asked him, "Did you call my lawyer?"

"I didn't," the guard replied. "But the Department of Corrections did."

"You fuckin' liar," Arthur laughed. "I don't have a lawyer."

Everyone started laughing again, and the guard got red in the face.

"You wouldn't be lying to us there, would ya, sport?" Arthur asked him.

"Of course he's not," someone called back. "You know Fred's officers don't lie."

"Yeah," someone answered, "but this is Bridgewater, so these ain't Fred's officers."

Everyone laughed. At Walpole disciplinary hearings, whenever undeniable "discrepancies" (a.k.a. lies) showed up in a CO's testimony against an inmate, the issue was invariably settled by Fred Butterworth's standard response: "My officers don't lie."

The guards retreated down the stairs to a barrage of laughter and insults.

|||||||||||||||||||||||||||||||||||||||||||||||||||||||||||||||||||||

LATER ON, THE same guard showed up at my door and called my name. Thinking that he had finally gotten me a blanket, I got out of bed and went to the door.

"If you want to call a lawyer just give me the message, and I'll call the lawyer for you," he said.

I was incredulous. I asked, "You're gonna make my attorney call? What am I, a moron?"

"Nobody is allowed to use the telephone. But if you want to call a lawyer, just give me the message, and I'll make the call," he said.

"That ain't good enough," I said. "I got something that I want to tell him, and I know you ain't gonna do it."

He raised his hands and showed me a pen and a pad of paper. "Just write down the lawyer's name and number and whatever message you want to send him. We've got orders to read exactly what you write down to the lawyer."

Then, with a hard look, he said, "But that's all you're getting."

I thought for a minute, then said, "Okay, gimme the pen an' the paper."

I wrote down Alan's name and number, and then I asked, "You're gonna give him this message, word for word?"

"That's right," he said.

I nodded, and then printed my message on the pad of paper, in large and clear letters. I wrote for a few minutes, quickly jotting down a copy for myself. When I was finished, I handed the pad of paper back to the guard. While I'd been writing, he had collected numbers and messages from some of the others. He placed my note with the others without looking at it.

"Gimme my pen back," he said.

"Sure," I said, without offering it. "But first, I'd like you to check the message to my attorney to make sure that you can read it."

Impatiently, he glanced down at the pad that I'd just given him. As he read, I watched his face. For a moment, there was no response. Then, his face turned dark red. He looked up from the paper and glared at me. He was hot. He stormed away without another word.

As he walked away, I called after him, "Could you read that okay?"

After he walked off of the tier, Keigney called over to me, "Hey, what happened with that cop? He was bullshit."

"I don't know," I said. "I just gave him a message to read to my lawyer. All I wrote was:

"Alan, I want you to get down here as soon as possible. I have no idea what's going on. All I know is they've got me in a freezing cell with no heat, no clothes, no blanket, and a broken window, and the fucking asshole who's reading this to you won't even give me a blanket."

A while later, they moved me to a cell with heat—and a blanket!

||||||||||||||||||||||||||||||||||||||||||||||||||||||||||||||||||

BEFORE THEY MOVED me, around lunchtime, we were standing at our respective doors talking. As I said, David was across from me. Myles was next to me, and Ronnie MacDonald was across from Myles, next to David. The four of us were kicking it back and forth, trying to figure out just what the hell was going on. Nobody had a clue.

Then Ronnie said, "Hang on a minute. The news is on. There's a little hole in the floor by the pipe, and I can hear the guy downstairs' TV."

About five minutes later, he came back to the door and said, "They just had a thing on the TV about an execution squad."

Someone said, "That must be about that nut Gilmore out in Utah that wants to die. He's supposed to go Monday."

Gary Gilmore was the first person to be executed in this country after the reestablishment of the death penalty that the United States Supreme Court had abolished in 1972. As luck would have it, the same day that they snatched us out of Walpole, the Supreme Court had granted Gilmore a stay of execution, a stay that he did not want. His story was on the news that day.

Ronnie said, "No, listen will ya? They were talking about *us*! Wait a minute. Everyone shut up. They're talkin' about it on another station."

For the next few minutes, you could hear the proverbial pin drop. Then Mac came back to the door. He said, "You ain't gonna believe this shit. The guy on the news just said that they moved nine guys out of Walpole last night, because they were an execution squad. *That's us*. We're a fucking execution squad. He said we killed five guys this year."

This was how we found out that we had been designated as an execution squad.

Later that afternoon, they returned us to Walpole. We were taken straight to the Departmental Segregation Unit (DSU), the notorious Ten Block.

three

Oddly enough, we were all happy to be there. Bridgewater is a scary place. While beatings and lock downs were pretty much the norm in Ten Block, they were a lot better than having your mind tampered with, physically. Over the years, forced chemical treatment, electric shock treatments, and lobotomies were only part of the arsenal of weapons that the state found useful in dealing with residents at Bridgewater. So, as crazy as it might seem, we were all relieved to be back at Walpole, even if it meant Ten Block.

Ten Block consists of four separated tiers, two upstairs and two downstairs. Each tier has fifteen cells. Each cell has two doors. The first is a regular barred grill, the kind that you see in the movies. Outside of that is a solid steel door. The solid door is usually left swung wide open, back to the wall, unless you are doing board time (a.k.a. isolation), where they remove all of your property and lock the solid door, usually for fifteen days at a time.

We were all placed on the lower tiers. Campbell, Keigney, David, Paulie Z., Ralph Petro, Mickey Donahue, and I were placed on the right tier. Myles Connor and Ronnie MacDonald went on the left.

They took us in one at a time. I was last. We walked all the way down to the second to last cell. It was a strip cell (a.k.a. a blue room).

The last two cells on the tier were blue rooms. A blue room had one advantage over a regular cell. It is much roomier. Not to say that it's a larger cell, just that it is unencumbered by those things usually found in a regular cell—like a bed, a sink, a desk, a toilet, or anything else.

A blue room's furnishings consisted of a mattress on the floor—sometimes. It also had a round hole in the floor, maybe eight or nine inches in diameter, in the back of the cell. The purpose of the hole, of course, is to allow the inmate to urinate and defecate (and, if necessary, regurgitate). This "toilet" can be flushed by the guards—*at their convenience*. Unfortunately, it sometimes had a tendency to flush in the wrong direction, disgorging large amounts of filth into the cell. Consequently, even if you got a mattress, it was not the most sanitary of sleeping accommodations.

A blue room also provided an inmate with the opportunity to cultivate a pet—provided, of course, that you have a fondness for rats. Ten Block rats were a particularly hardy and independent breed. Upon popping out of the hole in the floor and finding the cell occupied, they might, depending upon their mood, either retreat back down the hole or decide to stand and do battle for the room. Which, through long occupancy, they rightfully considered theirs—squatter's rights, so to speak.

I took one look at the blue room and said, "Hey, wait a minute. What's this shit? Why am I gettin' put in a strip cell?"

One of the guards said to me, "There's no regular cells left."

I said, "So, I'm gonna sleep on the floor an' shit in a hole in the floor? I don't think so."

He said, "Look Stevie, it ain't us. There's nothin' we can do about it tonight. There just ain't no other cells. I think we can find you a mattress tonight, but that's all we can do. The day shift'll get you a bed in the morning, an' you'll get ya property as soon as they go through it."

As pissed off as I was, I wasn't up to starting a major confrontation just then. My back had been out for a week. It had been a long week. Occasionally, over the years, I'd had sciatic nerve problems but never anything like this. For the first time in my life, I had actually damaged the sciatic nerve on *both* sides of my lower back at the same time.

The morning after the fingernail scraping, I had been unable to get out of bed. I didn't leave my cell for the next day and a half. On the second day, a medic that I got along with showed up at my door. He came in and said, "I hear your back is out?"

I just nodded and said, "It's killin' me. Worse than it's ever been. Both sides."

"Ouch," he said, making a face. "I don't think I ever knew anyone who threw out both sides at the same time."

He took out a bag of white football-shaped pills and said, "Here. There's really not much you can do for sciatica, but these'll help. They're muscle relaxers. Start off with two; then wait a while. If two don't work, take 'em one at a time after that till they kick in."

That was what I'd been doing for the past week. Now here I was, in a strip cell with no bed to lie down on—and no muscle relaxers. The ones that I'd been taking had worn off at Bridgewater, and the pain was back to page one.

So I said to the cop, "Okay, just get me the mattress then. My back is killing me."

My back was so bad that I had to stand holding onto the bars till the mattress came. When it finally did come, I had them put it on the floor about a foot inside the bars, running parallel with the door. That way I could lie on my right side, facing the door. After I got it in place, it took long and tense minutes to lie down on it, carefully lowering myself down the bars.

Later on, around midnight, I was lying on my side facing the door. I wasn't asleep, but my eyes were closed and I was miles away. Suddenly, something lightly bumped the left side of my neck. My eyes flew open, just in time to see the tail end of a rat scurrying under the bars and out the door. A rat had just run across my throat.

I instantly went from the prone to the standing. It's quite possible that I didn't even bend my knees. All I know was that one moment I was lying there, and the next moment I was on my feet, cursing loudly.

Jackie Campbell, who was in the next cell, hollered over, "What's a' matter?"

I yelled back, "*A fuckin' rat just ran over my fucking neck!*"

Which he, and everyone else, thought was hilarious.

The truth is that I've always hated rats—two-legged and four-legged. After a couple of minutes of cursing and growling, I grabbed the mattress and pulled it to the back of the cell. I put it over the hole in the floor. While sleeping on a "toilet" was not my idea of the ideal way to spend the night, it beat having rats run over me. After moving the mattress, I turned to go back to the door. Midturn, out of nowhere, the sciatic nerve suddenly said, "*Hello.*" I literally dropped to my knees. It took all I could do to roll over and squirm onto the mattress. Adrenaline only lasts so long.

The next morning, after we had breakfast, I told the day shift that I wanted to be moved to a real cell—one with a toilet. They told me that there were none. Ten Block was full. They said that the only other empty cell was the other strip cell, the one right next door to me.

I told them about the incident with the rat the night before. Then I said, "There's no way I'm gonna use that hole for a toilet an' have some rat bite me on the ass."

The guard said, "I understand what you're sayin', but there's nothin' I can do about it.

Then I told them how bad my back was bothering me—that there was no way that I *could* use the hole in the floor as a toilet with my back the way that it was.

"There's nothin' I can do," he said.

"Let me use the guard's bathroom. The one just off the tier, out by the visiting room," I said.

There was a toilet about fifteen feet from the end of the tier, their toilet, which was also used by visitors.

"Look, Stevie, it's nothin' personal, but I can't let you do it," he said.

As he was walking away, I said, "OK, but you just remember that when the shit comes down, it's nothin' personal."

That caught his attention. He came back to my door. He asked, "Whatta ya talkin' about?"

"If I'm gonna have to put up with this shit, so will you," I said.

He asked, "Whatta ya mean?"

"There's no way I can shit in that hole with my back as fucked up as it is. I'll have it all over me. So any time I have to shit, one of you will wear it too."

"Oh man," he said. "C'mon Stevie, don't start that."

"What choice have I got?" I asked. "You got a toilet right out there, an' I can't use it? I gotta shit in the floor? Fuck that."

He walked away.

Ten minutes later, he was back. He asked, "You gotta go the bathroom?"

"Yeah," I said.

He cracked my door. "C'mon."

We went out to the visiting room/guards' rest room. After I was done, he brought me back to my cell. "You should have your property before the day's over," he said.

four

Shortly after lunch, a screw came to my door. He told me that I had
an attorney visit.

Al Caplan was already in the visiting room when I got there.
Ten Block's visiting room was about eight feet by ten feet. It was divided by a
counter about three feet off of the ground. On top of the counter was a metal
screen that ran up to the ceiling. They put me on the smaller of the two sides.
Alan was on the other side of the screen.

He asked, "Are you okay?"

As they closed the door behind me, I said, "Yeah, I'm okay, but I hope you
know what's goin' on, because I don't."

"Well, I don't know much more than you," he said.

Getting out of his seat, he said, "I'll tell you what I do know in a minute.
Hold on."

He went to the door, and, through the bars, said to the guard who was
watching us, "Listen, I have confidential matters to discuss with my client.
Also, there are papers that we have to go over together and some that he has
to sign. Is there any reason that we can't be on the same side of the screen?"

The guard replied, "It's against the rules."

Alan asked, "Could you tell me why that is?"

The guard said, "Security. Inmates in Ten Block are too violent to be allowed on the same side of the screen as the visitor."

Alan nodded his head apparently agreeing with him. "I can understand
that and appreciate your concern for my safety, but in this case, it's not necessary. I have a long-standing relationship with Mr. Doherty. I can assure you
that it's never been anything but pleasant."

Clearly at a loss for words, the guard said, "Well, I don't know what … I
mean, I can't … It's against the rules."

Alan nodded, "All right. I think I understand. Would you please notify
your supervisor that I would like to speak with him?"

Alan came back to the screen as the guard walked into the supervisor's
office. He took the front page of the *Boston Globe*[1] and another newspaper

18

clipping from a folder and laid them on the counter, side by side, facing me, so I could read them through the screen.

"This is what started it all. It came out yesterday morning. It's what got you sent to Bridgewater," he said.

As I started to read, I heard the supervisor's voice say, "I'm the supervisor. My officer tells me that there's some kind of problem here."

I tuned the voices out and read the newspaper.

The top of the front page was covered with a headline that said that they had discovered an execution squad at Walpole state prison. The article said that, while investigating Bobby Perrotta's murder, the State Police had uncovered an inmate execution squad. They said that State Police Det. Lt. William Bergin, of the Norfolk County District Attorney's office, claimed that Perrotta's murder was an execution that was ordered from the outside by a prisoner in another institution and was carried out by a gang of murderers from Block A-3 who thought that Bobby had given up a series of bank robberies to the cops. They claimed that there were at least nine members of this execution squad, who they said had also killed John F. Stokes and James Aloise. They said that all of the inmates in Walpole were terrorized. That they were afraid if they were even seen talking with a guard or cop they'd be branded as a stool pigeon and executed.

One of their most ridiculous lies was that the whole problem existed in the three minimum blocks, A-1 through A-3, and that some guy who represented each block of seventy-two inmates, reported to someone in A-3 who controlled this made-up execution squad.

But the classic lie, which ostensibly documented all of the lies that they were printing, was their claim that, before his murder, Perrotta had given the Walpole Superintendent a letter outlining the scheme to kill him, and that he named his potential killers. They quoted Bergin as saying that the inmates who Perrotta named were the prime suspects in his murder. The unavoidable insinuation being that Perrotta had identified me, Arthur, and Jackie as his killers. They just went on and on with false garbage.[*]

When I finished the article, I looked up. Caplan was staring at me.

I said, "I wouldn't have believed you could put that much bullshit into so little space. How the fuck can they print that shit?"

---

[*] I tried to include the entire article, but the Globe told me that I couldn't print it unless I paid them to do it. No way. I find it ironic that they can print lies for Big Brother, but you have to pay them to show that they printed those lies.

He replied, "Well, they didn't mention any names and…"

I interrupted, "So what's that supposed to mean? Nobody knows it's us?"

He held up his hands and said, "Whoa. Take it easy. Yellin' at me's not gonna do you any good. I'm just tellin' you how they get away with it."

He was right, of course. "I'm sorry. It just pisses me off, is all. The fuckin' thing reads like somethin' outta *The National Enquirer*. Except it's not the *Enquirer*. It's the *Boston Globe*. People believe what they read in the *Globe*."

I realized that I was on my feet and yelling again. So I shut up and sat down.

Caplan asked, "Feel better?"

"Not really," I said. "Don't worry, I'm okay. Go ahead."

"All right, let's go over the article and see exactly what it says," he said.

Turning the newspaper sideways so that we could both read it, he said, "First of all, it says that the murderers came from block A-3. Says it three different times. Did you ever live in A-3?"

"No," I answered. "Only A-2. Ever since I came to the minimum end I've lived in A-2. And it says that some guy from A-3 runs the whole show and everyone has to report to him. That's so stupid it's almost funny, for Christ's sake. Like, your gonna kill someone an' then go rat on yourself."

Then, I said, "Listen, fuck the rest of it for now. Read the last two paragraphs on the first page."

As Alan read them, I said, "It says that Perrotta gave them a letter naming the guys who were gonna kill him. Then it says that the guys that he named are the prime suspects. I want a copy of that letter. There's no way my name's gonna be in it. Bobby an' I weren't what you'd call close, but we got along okay. I don't know nothin' about him talkin' to a grand jury. I ain't sayin' he didn't. I just don't know. I do know this; I never knew him on the street. So even if he was talkin', I had nothin' to worry about. There's no way my name's gonna be in that letter."

"All right," he said. "I'll try to get a copy of the letter."

"By the way, have you got the results of the fingernail scrapings yet?"

"No," he answered. "I'll ask for them first thing Monday. They wouldn't have waited a week to lug you though if the tests had come back positive."

"Look Alan, there's no way those tests can come back positive. I was nowhere near Bobby's cell the night he got clipped."

We talked for a few more minutes about the rest of the newspaper story, but he didn't know any more than I did. We were both curious about the identity of the prisoner in another institution who was supposed to have sent the execution order.

Alan said, "Well, I'm sure we'll find out soon enough. Now, listen, I've been talking to the other guy's lawyers, Tom Troy and Richard Vita. We're going into federal court on Monday to try an' get you all moved back to population or at least to find out what you're being charged with. You know, it's pretty outrageous, considering what they've put in the newspapers, that they won't even tell you what you're being moved for."

"Do you think they'll move us back to pop'?" I asked.

"I don't know," he answered slowly. "It might depend on what judge we get. By law, they're supposed to give you a hearing. It could go either way, but I wouldn't count on anything."

He was putting his papers back in his briefcase and getting ready to leave when he said, "By the way, did you happen to overhear my conversation with the supervisor while you were reading the article?"

"No. What did he say?"

"He says that all visits in Ten Block have to be conducted on opposite sides of the screen."

"Is there anything we can do about it?" I asked.

He smiled and said, "Maybe. I don't know. Lawyer/client confidentiality. I'll know more when I come back down."

When I got back to my cell, my property was there, including a bed! Now all I had to do was to keep the hole in the floor blocked.

five

That weekend, after being questioned about the authenticity of the so-called "execution squad," Lt. Bergin went on television to deny that he had ever used that phrase.

However, in response to Bergin's denial, John Cullen, the reporter who wrote the initial article exposing the execution squad (or inventing, depending on just which one of them you choose to believe), specifically stated, "I did not use the term 'execution squad.' After going over the details I had, I had a long conversation with Bergin, and it was he who used the term." [2]

Coincidentally, Cullen had also been a state trooper.

Shortly after that, Delahunt and the commissioner of corrections, Frank Hall, both denied knowledge of any execution squad. They also both disclaimed any responsibility for the dissemination of the fraudulent label.

Their disclaimers only lasted a couple of days, though—until Federal Judge Joseph Tauro ruled that they had to at least tell us what we were being charged with and grant us a hearing at which we could respond to those charges.

They quickly filed an appeal. In their appeal, they reversed their position. Once again, they claimed that we were being kept in the hole because of the existence of an execution squad. Then, to add fuel to the fire, they stated that there just might be more members of the evil execution squad than those in segregation.

Until the appeals court ruled in their favor. Then they went back into disavowal. Once again, they didn't know anything about any execution squad.

||||||||||||||||||||||||||||||||||||||||||||||||||||||||||||||||||||||

By this time, it was common knowledge that their stool pigeon was Tommy Carden, a weasel junkie who happened to be Bobby Perrotta's ex-brother-in-law. Bobby had been married to Carden's sister, but they had been divorced a few months before Bobby was killed. As a result, problems developed between them, because another girl was visiting Bobby; so Carden's sister wouldn't let him see their kids.

||||||||||||||||||||||||||||||||||||||||||||||||||||||||||||||||||||||||||||||

ABOUT A WEEK after we got to Ten Block, Mickey Donahue (a.k.a. Knot-head) was out on the tier for his shower. He came to my cell. Knothead was about five-five, maybe five-six, around a hundred and twenty pounds with long, black, stringy, and greasy-looking hair. He always looked like he was about a week overdue for a shower—even after he took one.

He said, "Hi. Got a smoke?"

I got up and gave him a Kool. He lit it and coughed. "How can you smoke these things? They're terrible."

I shrugged, "Don't smoke it."

He ignored that and asked, "D'ja find out anything new from your lawyer?"

"Not really. We're still waiting for the federal court to act. He doesn't think they'll put us back in population. He says there's a shot, because the move was against the DOC's own rules and regulations, but that the courts don't like to fuck with the DOC. He said we were lucky we got Judge Tauro."

"Why?" he asked. "Is he a liberal?"

"Not really. Actually, he's hard as nails. I had him on a bank trial a couple a' years ago. He scared the shit out of one lawyer, flattened an uppity prosecutor, an' totally destroyed a federal marshall who was out of line. The thing is, he goes right by the book. But, in this case, that's to our advantage. We're in the right, and we need someone to stand up to the DOC. One thing Tauro's got is balls."

"You bet your ass we're in the right," he said. "This is all a frame, an' everyone knows it."

Then, lowering his voice, he said, "I was just talking to [deputy superintendent] Tom McLaughlin down at the grill. He was half stiff, an' he was tryin' a pump me for information. You know they're tryin' ta get you for the Perrotta thing?"

"Well," I replied, "nobody's said anything to me, but I got an idea that's what it is, since they scraped my fingernails the next night."

He bobbed his head again, "Yeah, yeah. Well, I think they're gonna try an' nail me for "Mousy."

That surprised me. Mousy was Jimmy Aloise's nickname. He had been killed in A-2, and Knothead lived in a different block, A-1. Now, when someone's being charged with a crime—especially a murder—it's not a subject that you want to ask too many questions about. There are some things that you just don't want to know. So, I kept my response simple.

"You got any problems? They got anything on ya?"

He grinned and said, "I ain't got a fuckin' thing to worry about. These assholes are so hot to bust someone. I guess they ain't checkin' what their stool pigeon's tellin' 'em ."

"Whatta ya mean?"

The grin got larger. "Man, I was on a visit when he got killed. Shit, I didn't even know about it till the next day."

I asked him slowly, "Are you sure?"

"Fuckin' right I'm sure," he said, still grinning.

"Did you tell McLaughlin that?"

He shook his head. "Nah, I ain't told no one."

I let my thoughts run for a moment. Then I said, "Listen, I got an idea."

I could feel the excitement growing inside of me. "I'd like you to do something for me—actually, for everyone. Don't say anything about being on a visit."

Looking at me rather skeptically, he asked, "Whatta ya mean?"

"When you go to the d-board, don't tell them you were on a visit." The d-board was a disciplinary board, which consisted of three staff members, who would rule on any disciplinary infraction that an inmate was charged with.

Looking absolutely incredulous, he said, "Why would I do that? They'll find me guilty."

"I know. But they'll have to use Carden's statement. He'll be on record for having falsely accused you. Once they find you guilty at the d-board, you have your lawyer ask for the visiting room records for the night that Mousy was killed. As soon as they see that you were on a visit, they'll have to drop the charges, but we'll have Carden on record for having lied about you."

I paused for a second, staring at him. "Will ya do it?"

His grin was back. "Yeah, yeah, I get it. Fuckin' right I'll do it. I'd love to bust these pricks. They been fuckin' us for years with that 'reliable informant' bullshit, an' gettin' away with it," he said.

"All right," I said. "But ya gotta keep your mouth shut about it."

Mickey wasn't a bad kid, but he was a terrible gossip, the original town crier.

"Hey, don't worry about it, man. I can keep my mouth shut when I have to. Lemme have another smoke," he said.

I handed him a Kool. "I'm sure you can. I just want you to realize how important it is. If they even get a hint that you were on a visit they won't charge you. You do realize, by not sayin' anything, you're probably gonna have to spend a couple a' months in Ten Block?"

He nodded his head, grinning and, with a shrug, said, "Yeah, I know. Fuck'em. What's a couple a' months? Hey, did you see that thing in yesterday's paper where they said that there's gonna be guys from Walpole testifyin' at the grand jury in the Perrotta thing?"

"Yeah, I'm dyin' to see who they got, besides Carden."

I heard the key click in the grill lock at the end of the tier.

"Hey Donahue, times up," the guard yelled.

"Okay," he yelled back.

Then to me, "Lemme have anotha' smoke before I go in, will ya?"

"Sure," I said. "Here, take a pack."

"Thanks," he said.

Then, as he was walking away from my cell, he called out, "Anybody got a pack a' smokes they wanna trade for a pack a' Kools?"

Looking over his shoulder at me, he said rather sheepishly, "These things really suck."

I was still laughing when they locked his door.

六

The following week, on December 15, 1976, Delahunt, along with eight assistant DAs and twenty state troopers, invaded Walpole in the middle of the night. They forcibly questioned over two hundred inmates, in the "A" blocks, from 10 pm to 7 o'clock the next morning.

The resultant publicity was great for Delahunt. The next day, the Globe reported that "Delahunt ...called the surprise move 'very productive.'" And that, "Delahunt...'was well pleased with the results' and termed the effort 'worthwhile.'" Finally, he specifically stated, "We uncovered a lot of new information".[3] The real truth is, not one scrap of evidence was gleaned from those forced interviews. At least, I'm assuming that there wasn't, as not one iota of the very productive, worthwhile, new information that Delahunt claimed to have uncovered was ever used at our trial.

Unless, of course, the evidence that he supposedly uncovered was evidence that might have helped the defense. But, as we were never allowed to see the results of the interviews, we really don't know now, do we?

What we do know is that for about nine hours that night, twenty-nine of Massachusetts' top law enforcement agents engaged in wholesale, concerted attempts to coerce, bribe, or extort information from men who were physically forced to meet with them.

They had at their disposal the most tempting inducement possible—and the most frightening threat—a man's freedom. Moreover, they were able to do all of this secure in the knowledge that they would not be disturbed by such annoying distractions as lawyers—or the law, every cop's dream.

This shameful rape of the U.S. Constitution was planned and executed by three of the highest holders of public office in Massachusetts: Commissioner of Correction Frank Hall, Commissioner of Public Safety John Kehoe, and District Attorney William Delahunt.

||||||||||||||||||||||||||||||||||||||||||||||||||||||||||||||||||||

THE NEXT NIGHT, after the evening meal when the guards were handing out the mail, I received a notice to appear in court on the following day.

After the guard had finished handing out the mail and had left the tier, I called out to the others, "Who else got a court slip?" No one answered.

So I repeated my question, a little more loudly. "Don't fuck around. Who else got a court slip for tomorrow?" The response was an echo.

So I called for the guards. "Hey *guardhouse.*"

One of the guards responded from off of the tier. "Yeah, whatta ya want, Stevie?"

"I'd like to make an attorney call."

He replied, "No phone calls tonight."

"Listen, I just got a court slip for tomorrow, and I have to talk to my lawyer."

"Sorry, we got our orders. No phone calls tonight," he said.

I thought about it for a moment, and then called back. "Okay, will ya leave a note for the transportation people for the morning?"

The guard said, "Sure, whatta ya want."

"Tell 'em when they come to get me for court in the mornin' to come heavy, 'cause we're gonna roll all over this fucking cell and all over this tier, an' then we're gonna roll all over the van an' all over the fuckin' courthouse when we get there."

It's not that I wanted the beatings, but sometimes you just don't have any other choice.

After a couple of minutes of silence, one of the guards yelled down the tier, "Hey Stevie, we just called out front. They said to let you call your lawyer."

After they cracked my cell door, I went down to the front of the tier, and the guards passed me the telephone through the bars. I called Alan Caplan at his home. I told him about receiving the court slip and asked him what it was about.

"I have no idea. They never notified me," he said.

That was slightly in apropos, as they were well aware that Alan was representing me in this case.

I asked him, "Is there a grand jury sitting in Norfolk County?"

"Wait a minute. Let me check," he said.

He was back a minute later. "Yup," he said. "Sure is."

"I'm not going. I'm not testifying in front of any grand jury."

Alan said, "You've got to go. They'll make you."

"Really? You watch what I gotta do. They may get me there, but by the time they do, they'll know I got nothin' to say."

Alan said, "No, listen Stevie, I want you to go. I'll meet you there, and we'll talk about it then."

I reluctantly agreed.

In the morning, they let me out of my cell early to shower and shave. After I was done, I stopped at a few guys' cells to say goodbye and to let them know what I thought was happening. The last one that I stopped to talk to was Arthur Keigney.

I said to him, "You know this is a kidnapping. I probably won't see you again till trial."

He asked, "Whatta ya talking about?"

"C'mon Arthur, there's nine of us in here for this execution squad shit. I'm the only one on the verge of hittin' the street with my Framingham move, and I'm the only one bein' called in front of a grand jury. Figure it out," I said.

He shook his head, grinning, "No way. You'll be back."

"We'll see. I hope you're right."

I said goodbye and, as I was heading off of the tier, he called after me, laughing, "You been a paranoid since we was kids. I'll see ya at supper."

When I got to the Norfolk County Courthouse, in Dedham, Alan was waiting for me. "You're right. It's a grand jury," he said.

"No way am I goin' in front of a grand jury," I said.

"Listen, hear me out. I want you to go in. I'm going to give you a pad of paper and a pen to take in the room with you. Every time the prosecutor asks you a question, write it down on the pad; then tell them that you want to speak to your attorney. I can't go in the room with you, but they have to let you come out and speak to me. When you come out, just rip off the sheet of paper and give it to me. Then go back in and take the Fifth Amendment. At the very worst, maybe we'll learn something," he said.

In my gut, I still didn't like it, but it made sense. So I did it.

There were a total of eight questions. I really only remember the last one. The prosecutor, John Prescott, asked me, a little heatedly, "Are you gonna keep doin' this?"

I wrote down on the pad of paper, "Are you going to keep doing this?"

I then said, for the eighth time, "I'd like to confer with my attorney."

Prescott shouted something to the effect of, "That it. Get out. That's all."

I left the grand jury room and was taken back upstairs to the cage where I was being held.

Alan Caplan showed up shortly afterward. He was on the other side of the screen, but he seemed a little hesitant. He said, "Listen Stevie, don't get mad at me, but I have to do something. This is my job. Okay?"

I said, "Go ahead."

He took a deep breath and said, "Okay, Delahunt says that if you'll testify against Keigney and Campbell—that they killed Perrotta—he won't charge you with the murder. You can get out today, and they'll relocate you and give you a new identity. On the other hand, if you won't testify, he's going to charge you with the murder."

Alan and I were standing at the metal screen, which was about seven or eight feet from the wooden door that went out to the corridor. The door had a little window about a foot square, maybe five to six feet from the floor. Looking over Alan's shoulder, I could see Delahunt's profile. He just happened to be standing outside of the door, with his left profile to the opening, ostensibly talking to someone just to the other side of the opening.

Alan said, "What do you want me to tell him?"

I said, "Well, as far as not being charged with the murder goes, I didn't have anything to do with it. So that's nothin'. As for goin' home today, I've already been approved to get out on work release. So that's no big deal. And as far as a new identity goes, I might not like *where* I am, but I do like *who* I am."

Alan just nodded; nothing that I'd said surprised him.

Then, I said, "I'll tell you what, though; if he really wants me to be a rat, okay, I will, but I get to pick my own new identity."

I watched Alan's eyes widen in shock. We'd known each other a while, and one thing that he knew for sure was that I wasn't a rat.

I continued, "Tell him if he wants me to be a rat, okay, but I get to pick what rat I'm gonna be. If I can be Clark Kent or Patty Hearst, I'll take the job. Outside of that, he can go an' fuck himself."

At that point, my control just went out the window, as I yelled over Alan's shoulder, "YOU HEAR THAT YOU FUCKIN' COCKSUCKER, DELAHUNT. YOU FUCKIN' YADAYADAYADA …"

Delahunt's profile disappeared from the window as Caplan, between laughs, tried to shush me.

Afterward, I said to Alan, "You know I'm being kidnapped. They ain't takin' me back to Walpole."

Alan seemed surprised. "Wait a minute. Let me go check," he said.

He came back about five minutes later. "No, you're not going anywhere. You're going back to Walpole," he said.

"Okay, we'll see. I hope you're right," I said.

A little while later, the transportation cops came to get me. When we got outside, we got into a plain unmarked car. There were two of them in front, and the third one got into the back seat with me. With one car in front of us and another car behind us, we pulled out.

I knew the guy in the back seat with me. He had been a guard in Walpole before he moved to transportation. He'd always been a straight shooter, and we got along pretty well.

After we got out on the highway, he said, "Listen Stevie, this ain't got nothin' to do with us, but you ain't goin' back to Walpole."

I said, "Yeah, I figured. Where we goin', Bridgewater?"

His reaction was priceless. Eyes widening, he gawked at me for a second or two, and then said, "How the fuck did you know that?"

I just shrugged, "Where else ya gonna stash me?"

Gleaming with paranoia, his eyes swept back and forth along the highway. I could almost read his thoughts, "If I knew, who else knew?"

When we got to Bridgewater, they took me to the same building that they'd held us in two weeks earlier, The Fort. The Fort was the oldest building in Bridgewater. I don't know what they used it for, the hundred or so years before, when it was just a mental institution, but when I got there, they were using it as their "hole."

After they brought me inside and removed the handcuffs, waist chains/ shackles and leg irons, I asked the Bridgewater screw who was in charge if I could make an attorney call.

He responded in a belligerent tone, "You ain't makin' no call."

I repeated my request and attempted to explain the situation.

He interrupted me. "I said you ain't makin' no call. Now shut the fuck up."

I said, "I'm not going in a cell until I call my lawyer."

To which he responded, "We'll kick your ass."

I nodded my head and said, "Yeah, you all might, but *you* won't. You're a fuckin' coward and a weasel."

Stepping backwards and turning slightly so that my back was against the wall, I raised my hands and gestured him to me. I said, "C'mon, tough guy, let's do it. You come first."

It was obvious from the look on his face that he wanted to, and that he intended to, but before moving, he looked at the other guards.

There were three others beside him: two of the transportation cops who'd brought me and another Bridgewater guard.

At this point, one of the transportation guys stepped in and said to the one that I was arguing with, "Hang on for a minute. Let's go in the other room and talk."

They stepped into the office. They were maybe ten feet away, and I could hear parts of their conversation. The transportation guy was filling him in on what was going on.

After a few minutes, the Bridgewater cop picked up the telephone from the desk and called someone. He talked for a minute or two and then hung up.

They came back out, and the guy I'd had the problem with said, "The superintendent says that you can call your attorney."

Nodding his head toward the phone, he said, "Go ahead."

I called Alan Caplan. After he accepted the call, he said, "Hi. Everything okay?"

I said, "Swell. For someone that's sitting in Bridgewater."

His voice was somewhere between flabbergasted and disbelief, "Are you serious?"

I said, "Uh huh. In the hole of course."

He burst out laughing, and then said he was sorry. Then he burst out laughing again and then said he was sorry.

He also couldn't stop laughing.

Finally, he got himself under control and said, one last time, "I'm sorry, Stevie. I just couldn't stop laughing. Not at you. *At me!* How fucking stupid could I be? They told me that you were going back to Walpole and I *believed* them."

We talked for a few minutes, and then Alan said he'd be down to see me over the weekend.

seven

After I hung up, I came out of the office. They strip-searched me, took me to my cell, and locked me in. It was probably the largest cell I had ever seen. It turned out that all of the cells in the fort were that size. For some reason, this one seemed larger than the one I had been in upstairs, two weeks earlier, maybe ten feet by fifteen feet with a solid wooden door.

After a few minutes, one of the inmates in another cell called out, "Who's the new guy that just came in?"

I answered, "Who's askin'?"

"Ray LeBeau," he said.

I yelled back, "Hey Ray, it's Stevie Doherty."

I knew Ray from Walpole. We'd been in the hole in Nine Block together. I used to call him "Brussels sprout," because all of the time that he was in the hole with me, the administration kept him so well medicated that whenever he came out of his cell, he walked to the shower like a vegetable.

As soon as I identified myself, he yelled back, "Stevie, don't say nothin' else. All they got on this tier are rats. I'll talk t' ya in the mornin' when I come out for my shower."

I immediately yelled back, "What are *you* doin' here, Ray?"

He burst out laughing. "Oh, you son of a bitch. I shoulda known you'd ask me that. They just brought me back from an escape. They're holding me here till they send me back to Walpole."

I said, "OK, I'll talk to you tomorrow."

He said, "I hear ya. Did ya bring anything with ya? You know, clothes, soap, toothbrush? Ya got all that stuff?"

"Nothin'," I said. "They snatched me right from the courthouse. I'll tell ya about it when we come out for exercise tomorrow. How do they run the exercise?"

"We come out in the hall one at a time. You get a half hour to take a shower an' exercise," he answered.

"Okay," I said. "We can talk then."

A few minutes later, the guard came to my door and said, "Here, Ray sent these down."

There were potato chips, cheese, a bottle of olives, a couple of candy bars, a toothbrush, and toothpaste.

I yelled, "Thanks," and sat down to eat.

For the next couple of hours, I just sat on the bed pondering my situation. The more that I thought about it, the madder I got. It was bad enough that they were trying to frame me for a murder that I had nothing to do with, but then they were trying to turn me into a stool pigeon. Now it's even worse. They were going to try to make everyone think that I was a stool pigeon. Subjectively, I was instinctively infuriated. On the other hand, looking at it objectively, I understood their logic. It was an old trick. If they can make everyone believe that you are a rat, then maybe you'll become too scared to face people, and you'll turn into one. The problem was, sometimes it worked. Sometimes guys broke. From their point of view, on a purely objective level, I suppose that I was a likely prospect. Not only was I innocent, I also had one foot out the door with my impending work release program. Still, it aggravated me that they thought that I was weak enough for it to work on me.

After a couple of hours of sitting there aggravating myself with the above thoughts, someone suddenly knocked on my door. Then I hear the key turning, and the door swung open. There were two uniformed guards and a guy in a suit standing there smiling. The suit has a pizza box in his hands.

He said, "Here, Steve. We got a pizza for ya."

Without even glancing at the pizza, I said, "Who are you?"

He told me.

I didn't recognize his name so I said, "What are you bringing me a pizza for?"

"It's from the superintendent," he said.

I stood up and said, "You better get away from my door."

He looked bewildered. "Look," he said. "It's just…"

I started walking toward the door. "I said get away from my door."

He immediately stepped back. The guard closed the door.

I could hear them talking, loudly, "What the fuck's wrong with him. Is he nuts?"

I, on the other hand, was furious. My first thought, when he told me that he had a pizza for me was that I must have had a friend down there who'd heard that I'd come in, and he'd asked them to bring it in to me.

The minute that he said that it was from the warden, I lost it.

Who else would a warden send a pizza to, except for a rat? In my state of mind at that moment, I had no doubt that it was part of their plot to make me look like a rat.

I could still hear the guards talking, but they were farther down the tier. After a few minutes, I heard Ray LeBeau laughing. Then he called me. "Hey Stevie. What's the matter?"

"I don't know. Some guy just came to my door an' told me he had a pizza for me from the warden. I don't know what the fuck that's all about."

He said, still laughing, "The pizza ain't just from the warden to you. Everyone's gettin' one. They're havin' a Christmas banquet out in the camp tonight an', 'cause we can't go, the warden sent everyone in here a pizza instead."

The guards were decent enough to bring it back to my cell. Then they had a conversation outside of my door and decided that they really didn't want to open my door just then. So they opened my food slot, folded the pizza box in half, and passed it through, which I understood.

After they passed it in, I thanked them and said, "Listen, I want to apologize for what happened. I took it the wrong way."

One of them responded, "I guess the fuck ya did, but that's okay; enjoy it."

The next morning, Ray got out for his shower and came to my cell door. He confirmed what he'd told me the night before. The tier was filled with stool pigeons in protective custody (PC)—a good portion of PC's check into protective custody, because they have some sort of a sin on their soul, e.g., stool pigeons, skinners (rapists), diddlers (child molesters). These are things that make them less than popular in the general population.

A couple of years later, Ray was killed in Walpole.

eight

Alan came down over the weekend. As I came into the visiting room, he looked up from the papers he'd been reading and smiled, "Hello there. You're looking pretty good for a kidnap victim. Getting to make a habit of it though, aren't you?"

I was in no mood for our usual banter. I said, "Did you read this fuckin' thing?"

He glanced at the newspaper clipping that I'd just handed him and nodded.

The morning after I appeared in front of the grand jury, they had printed the story in the *Boston Herald*.[4] The article was probably the epitome of "yellow journalism." It was mostly factually accurate, yet totally misleading. Pure Hearst.

"Grand jury hears Walpole testimony"

A Walpole state prison inmate and a State Police detective testified before a special Norfolk County grand jury yesterday in connection with a series of murders in the prison.

The evidence was presented by Asst. Dist. Atty. John Prescott little more than 24 hours after all-night interrogation of 225 Walpole inmates by Dist. Atty. William Delahunt, eight of his assistants and 20 State Police officers.

Det. Lt. William Bergin, attached to Delahunt's office, testified for 10 minutes before the grand jury.

He was followed by inmate Stephen J. Doherty, 36, of Charlestown, who wore a blue, wool stocking cap. He was manacled [and] accompanied to the chamber by his counsel, Alan Caplan, who remained outside. His client emerged from the chamber eight times to confer.

Doherty is one of nine inmates who have been kept in isolation since shortly after the Thanksgiving murder of Robert A. Perrotta, 31, in his cell. The nine have appeals to the United States Supreme Court on the ground that their civil rights are being violated.

Doherty was not returned to Walpole after his Grand Jury appearance. He was taken, instead, to the Bridgewater correctional institution. The transfer was not explained.

The answer to the strangling of Perrotta was one of the primary targets of the all-night interrogation of the Walpole inmates. The investigators also sought information about the murders of two more inmates -- the Oct. 26 strangling of James D. Aloise, 21, of South Boston, and the stabbing of John F. Stokes, 24, of Jamaica Plain, on June 14."

As a final touch, just so no one would be mistaken, they put a picture of me next to the article.

The only conclusion that could be drawn from the *Herald's* story was that I was testifying. As I said, it was a classic example of yellow journalism—totally misleading. It was obviously printed to assist Delahunt in his attempts to pressure me into testifying.

Besides the *Globe* and the *Herald*, Delahunt also had a television reporter, named Ron Gollobin, parroting his lies. Essentially, they had all of the local daily media.

The only impartial, fair coverage came in two alternative weeklies, *The Boston Phoenix* and *The Real Paper*. Both looked into, and beyond, the lies being told by the DA's office and came up with a number of discrepancies. They even came up with a difference of opinion as to just who made up the "execution squad" fairy tale—the *Globe* or the cops, who both pointed a finger at each other. The *Globe's* writer, John Cullen, initially attributed his story to Bergin, but then admitted to the *Phoenix* that he'd gotten it from another source He did stick to his story that it was Bergin who came up with the "execution squad" label, even though Bergin denied it. The *Phoenix* also disclosed that the real source wasn't even in Walpole. He was in a house of correction— which he got out of for telling his story—and had a personal grudge against at least one of the guys he identified as being a member of the execution squad. It turned out that Cullen's "reliable source" was a known stool pigeon named Robert Fitzgerald, who later committed perjury at a murder trial and got an innocent man executed.

The Real Paper's headline told it all.

THE EXECUTION SQUAD MYTH
A FRAME-UP AT WALPOLE?[5]

I asked Alan, "What can I do about this bullshit?"

"Not much," he said.

"Whatta ya mean, 'not much?'" They lied about me testifyin'. I didn't testify. I refused to testify. Then, that shit about being transferred to Bridgewater, but the DOC won't comment on why. They did everything but come right out and say that I'm a stool pigeon."

"You're a hundred percent right," he responded. "And the operative phrase is 'they did everything but.' It's just so typical of the Hearst papers—that's where the phrase "yellow journalism" came from—although, in this case, the Globe's been just as bad. But the point is, they didn't actually say that you were a rat. They may have implied it, but that's not the same thing."

"Here," he said, picking up the clipping. "Look at exactly how they said it. They never said that you informed on anyone, just that you testified in front of the grand jury. And you did. Even though you only gave them your name."

"But you see how cutely they linked you with the state police, by saying that you and a state police detective testified?"

"Then, the implication that you were questioned by the state police one day and taken before a grand jury the next day."

"We know that you weren't there when they questioned all of the other inmates. But the people outside, that read the paper, don't know that. They just put two and two together and figure if the cops questioned you one day and took you before a grand jury the next day that you must've told them something during the questioning."

"The part about your being transferred out of Walpole after you testified, but that they wouldn't explain why you were transferred, is a nice touch. It's exactly what they would've done with a real informant. But—and it's a large but—they never actually come out and say that you are an informant."

He went on. "I suppose what we can protest is that the story appeared in the newspapers at all. Grand jury proceedings are supposed to be secret."

"Well, what can we do about that?" I asked.

He shrugged. "As I said, not much." I called the DA's office and talked to John Prescott. He was all apologies. He swears he had nothing to do with it and that he has no idea who gave the story to the Herald."

I said, "He's full 'a shit. They had a piece in the Herald last week sayin' that guys from Walpole were gonna be testifyin' in front of the grand jury."

I just stared at him for a minute. Then I said, "That's it? That's all he has to do, just say he don't know nothin' an' he's off the hook? We can't do anything about it?"

Caplan looked disgusted. "Realistically? I'm afraid not. That's one of the prices we pay for a free press."

"What the fuck does *that* mean? Free to say anything they want? Even if it's a fuckin' lie? Those cocksuckers are tryin' to get me killed or put me in a position where I have to kill someone.

"No," he said quietly. "They don't want you dead, although they are willing to risk it on the chance that the pressure will get to you. It's dirty business, but it's worked before. They put you in a position where your life is in danger, because people think you're a rat. What better way to get you to testify? They want you to think that you've got no options and, 'What the hell, if you've got the name anyways, you've got nothin' to lose and you might as well testify.'"

I said, "So it comes down to a choice between not testifying and staying in prison for the rest of my life, for somethin' I had nothin' to do with, with people who think that I'm a rat, or testifying and getting out, with a new identification and nobody knowing I am a rat?"

Nodding his head, he said, "That's what they figure. From their position, it's a good idea. We both know it's worked before."

"I know. I knew what they were doin' as soon as I saw the story in the paper. In a way, I knew it when I found out I was the only one goin' in front of the grand jury. The newspaper just confirmed it. I told Keigney before I left, I didn't think I'd be back."

Neither of us said anything for a minute. Then I said, "Like you said, from their point of view, it's a good plan, at least on paper, but they forget about the mirrors."

Alan cocked his head, looking slightly baffled. "Mirrors?" He asked. "What mirrors? What are you talking about?"

"You know." I said. "Those fuckin' mirrors you see yourself in every morning. How do you get up every morning for the rest of your life and look in the mirror and see a rat looking back at you?"

He laughed and then said, "You're taking it well. I expected you to be chewing the bars."

"Yeah. Well, if you really wanna know, I feel like chewing someone's face. They know I didn't do it, but it makes no difference. They need a conviction after all that publicity. They fucked up an' bought a bum story an' overreacted to it. Now Delahunt knows he'll lose face if he admits he was wrong, especially after they fucked up the DeSalvo case," I said.

When Albert DeSalvo (a.k.a. The Boston Strangler) was murdered in Walpole, the Norfolk DA's office tried to frame the wrong guys for killing him, just to get a conviction in a highly publicized case. It didn't work, and they had to drop the charges after trying them twice

"I think you're right. He never would've offered to put you on the street if he had any kind of a case," he said.

"Look," I said, "how about getting me transferred back to Ten Block? If I'm gonna be charged with a murder, don't I have a right to prepare a defense with my codefendants?"

"Well, you haven't been indicted yet. So, technically, you don't have any codefendants, but I'll see what I can do. I don't think they'll move you, though, unless you get indicted. Who knows? They might not even indict you," he said.

"Yeah, I know. In the meantime, I just sit an' wait," I said.

Then I said, "Do you realize I would've been out on work release in another week or so?"

He nodded. "I was thinking about it over the weekend. I think you might be right. I think that might've had something to do with them pulling you in, threatening you and then making you the offer. They might be figuring where you're this close to getting out, and where you've been planning on it for a while, that you might be in the right frame of mind to make a deal if they took it away from you."

I just smiled sourly. "Great minds think alike."

"In the meantime," he said, "there's really not too much we can do. The next move is theirs. I'll arrange for you to call me later on this week. Maybe I'll know some more by then."

As he was getting up to go he said, "Oh yeah, I almost forgot. I got a phone call from a guy at Norfolk named Joe Rego. Isn't he one of the guys who got moved out of Walpole the day after Perrotta got killed?"

Along with Carden, Joe Rego, Tommy McInerney and Bernie Battles, who all lived in A-2, had been taken out of Walpole on the morning after Bobby Perrotta had been killed.

"He sure was," I said. "What did he want?"

"I don't know," he answered. "I was in court when he called. He left a message that it was important that he speak to me. He wouldn't say what it was all about on the phone."

"That's interesting," I said. "It's no secret at Walpole that you're my lawyer. Especially since this shit started. I'm sure he knows it. He lived in my block. Also, he hung around with Carden and Perrotta."

Caplan said, "What kind of a guy is he?"

"Quiet guy," I said. "Never bothered anyone, minded his own business. I think he's got about six or seven years in on a life bit. I never heard any bad stories about him. When are you going to Norfolk again?"

Alan said, "I'll make it a point to get down there this week."

I said, "Tell him I was asking for him."

nine

The next time that Alan came down, it was almost eight o'clock at night when the guard came to my cell. "Get dressed," he said. "You've got a lawyer's visit."

"Son of a bitch," I said.

Not that I wasn't happy to see Alan, just the opposite. In fact, I'd been expecting him since suppertime. I had finally decided that it was getting too late for him to show up and had just gotten undressed.

He was already in the visiting room when I got there. He stood up, and as we shook hands, he said, "I know I said I'd be here about supper time but when you hear why I'm late you'll be happy I am."

"No problem, long as you got here."

"Well," he said. "I've been here since six o'clock. I've been talking to Tommy McInerney."

"How's he doing?"

"He's doing okay; he's working in the bakery."

"I know," I said smiling. "He comes by here every morning and yells 'hello' in the window. The first time he came by he yelled in, and when I yelled back he said, 'I saw that story they wrote about you in the paper. What a lot of bullshit. You know no one bought it.'"

"I yelled back, 'I know that.'

"He yelled back, 'An' don't you believe any of those stories they started about me, either.'"

"I laughed and yelled, 'Don't worry, Tommy. I don't.'"

Alan said, "He was worried about it, you know. He was afraid people were going to believe it."

I nodded, "Yeah, I can see where he might. I mean, the DOC did everything they could to make people think he was a stool pigeon in this case."

Caplan said, "They sure did. But let me tell you what he told me. A couple of days after they brought him here from Walpole, they called him to the superintendent's office. But instead, when he got there, they took him to an empty room. Then Carden came in the room and told him that he was going to testify and asked him if he'd back him up.

"McInerney told him that he hadn't seen anything."

"Carden told him not to worry about it—that he'd tell him what to say."

"McInerney told him that he couldn't do something like that."

"Then, Carden told him that if McInerney would just back him up on his story, McInerney could get out behind it. But McInerney wasn't goin' for it. McInerney said that it really got weird then. He said Carden started begging him. He said he actually got down on his knees and begged him. He thinks Carden was on something."

"Then Bergin came in. I guess him and McInerney know each other from before, and Bergin asked him if he could help them out with the Per-rotta case. McInerney told him that he didn't know anything that could help them. So, Bergin said that Carden saw this, and Carden saw that, and if McInerney would be able to corroborate Carden's story, it would be a big help."

"McInerney asked him straight out, 'Do you want me to lie?'" (An obviously rude question. Everyone knows that cops can't actually *tell* you that they want you to lie for them. That sort of thing is only done properly with a wink and a nod.)

"Tommy said Bergin got all fucked up. He said 'No, no, I don't want you to lie. We just thought you might know something that could help us out.'"

"Tommy told him, 'The only way I can help you is if I lie.'"

"Bergin called him a fucking asshole and walked out."

I was laughing. "Go ahead, Tommy."

Caplan said, "That's not all. When McInerney went back to his cell—they had him right here in The Fort—they put Carden in the cell next to him. He said Carden spent the whole night trying to talk him into testifying. He kept telling him, 'Don't be a fucking asshole. Those guys ain't nothin' to you. What did they ever do for you?'"

"Carden told him that if he would testify that they'd make a deal with him and that he could get out from under his life bit. Carden kept telling him that he'd never get another chance like this and that if he didn't take it, he'd be in prison for the rest of his life. Then he said, "If you testify, they'll give you another identity.'"

Smiling, Alan said, "Sound familiar?"

I made a face. "You're fucking right it does."

Then I said, "This Delahunt's a real sweetheart. Think of all the offers he's made to guys to testify in this case. I know that there's at least a half a dozen guys doin' life that they made offers to. Fucking politicians. He milked the execution squad for all the publicity it was worth, and now when he finds out it's all bullshit, he'd rather frame us than admit it."

"Well," Alan said with a shrug, "as you said, he's a politician. Forget about him, for now. I've got something else for you."

He was shuffling through the papers that were spread out on the table in front of him. "Here it is," he said, picking up a piece of yellow legal paper. "I talked to Joe Rego at Norfolk."

I perked up. "What did he have to say?"

"Not a hell of a lot, but enough," he said.

"First off, he's in the RB [the Receiving Building, a.k.a. The Hole) in protective custody, but he says he never told them anything about the murder. He says he doesn't know anything about it. He says that he didn't ask to leave Walpole—that they took him out. He says he knows that Carden is the one doing the talking but that the cops are making it look like he is too. One thing he did say is that, on the night of the murder, they took him out to the counseling area to talk to him and that Carden was out there and that Carden told him that he had no idea who killed Perrotta."

"Mostly, he wants people to know that he's not a rat. He says that when they took him out of Walpole, they took him to Norfolk. They kept him in the RB over the weekend, and then they let him out into population. He stayed in pop' for a couple of days, and then he got word he was going to be killed, because he was a rat. He says the cops started the rumor. Then they locked him up as an 'administrative' PC."

Alan paused, and then said, "For what it's worth, I believe him. Anyway, he'd like you to let people know that he's being bum beefed. Y' know, I got the feelin' that there was more that he wanted to say. He was definitely uneasy with me, but I can understand that. He doesn't know me. I'll tell you something. I felt bad for him. He seemed sort of lost, as if he couldn't understand how he got in the position he was in."

"I guess when the cops questioned him they told him that Carden told them that he could help them. When he told them that he didn't know anything, they got pissed off at him."

I shook my head. "That poor bastard. I'll bet ya they made him an offer, too."

Alan said, "He didn't say. I think he was really too nervous to trust me that much. By the time I left though, I do think he felt better."

ten

I was sitting cross-legged, on my bed, reading, when I heard the key click in the door. It was the guard, Frank, delivering the mail.

I said, "Hi Frank."

He responded, "How ya doin', Stevie?"

I thought he looked a little uneasy. Then I saw the two tickets (disciplinary reports) in his hand.

I said, "Are those for me?"

He nodded his head, "Yeah," and gave a half a shrug as if to say sorry as he handed them to me.

I glanced at the first one and realized why he seemed uncomfortable. It was for murder. As bad as it was, I'd been expecting it since the day they took me in front of the grand jury.

The second one was a complete shock. It was for extortion. I couldn't believe it. I sat back down and reread both tickets. Then again. Then I was on my feet pacing back and forth. I've always been able to think more clearly while I'm walking.

After about ten minutes, I called the guard. "Hey Frank, I want to make an attorney call."

"All right," he yelled back. "I'll have to check it with the deputy first."

About five minutes later the door opened. "The deputy said okay on the phone call."

By the time that I got to the telephone, Caplan was already on the line.

"Hi," I said. "I just received a d-report for the Perrotta thing."

"I know," he said, "A lawyer called me from the DOC. The hearing's set for January."

"Did they tell you that they gave me a ticket for extortion, too?"

"Yeah," he said. "What's that all about?"

"I don't know," I replied. "But I'll tell ya somethin', when I first got it, I thought it was bullshit. But after I thought about it, I started to feel better. Let me tell ya why. First off, ya gotta understand somethin'. The guy they say I extorted, Bobby Hutchinson? We got along fine. I've known him since I first come to Walpole. We started the bit in Five Block together when it was the New Man's Block. Anyway, the point is this: the ticket is a dead-up frame, and I don't believe he's involved. I mean, Hutch and I have never even had a disagreement. You know how I told you that Bobby Perrotta and I were friendly without being close? Well, that's how it was with me and Hutch, except I've known him longer. He took a PC sometime last summer. I never got the whole story. I heard he owed someone some money an' they were leanin' on him. Anyways, even though he's in PC, I don't believe he'd pull this kinda shit. But I know who would. When he checked in, his next-door neighbor was Tommy Carden."

"How convenient," Alan remarked.

"My point is this, for them to go to this extreme to frame me shows that they know just how bogus the murder beef is. I mean, if they figured that the murder charge was gonna stand up, they'd never bother to pull this shit."

Alan asked, "Where's Hutchinson now?"

"I don't know," I said. "The last I knew he was in A-6. [the main PC block in Walpole] I want you to get a statement from him for the d-board hearing."

"I intend to," Alan said. "All right, look, I'll be down to see you tomorrow night, and we'll discuss the d-board."

eleven

O n the cold January morning that my disciplinary hearing was scheduled, the guard called me just before 8:30 am, "Hey Stevie, the
transportation officers from Walpole are here for you."

I was still getting dried after my shower, so I yelled back, "I'm gonna be a
couple of more minutes. Tell 'em to sit down and have a cup of coffee."

I called them about fifteen minutes later. By nine o'clock, I'd been searched,
dressed, chained, and we were on our way.

We arrived at Walpole about 9:30 am. I had been looking forward to
seeing some of the others. I figured that I'd at least get to see Keigney and
Campbell. Wrong. I didn't even get inside of the walls. They were so paranoid
about people seeing me, or me seeing people, that they were holding me outside of the walls—*downstairs in the guards' locker room.*

I was there about a half an hour when Caplan showed up. We shook
hands, and he said, "I don't believe this. They're actually going to hold your
hearing down here."

I was surprised myself. Up till then I had thought that I was merely waiting there until it was time to go inside. I said, "Where are the others having
their hearings?"

"Ten Block," he answered. "You're scheduled for ten o'clock down here.
But I was just talking to the DOC lawyer, and he says that we're going to be
starting a little late."

"That's okay with me. It'll give us a little time to go over things. I'd still
prefer to have my hearing inside though. Isn't there something you can do
about it?"

"Like what?" he asked.

"I don't know. I mean, they are my codefendants. Don't I have a right to
talk to them?"

"Not according to the DOC," he said. "I already asked."

"Are the other lawyers here yet?"

"Yeah," he said. "They went in before I got here."

47

Al Nugent was representing Campbell, and Kevin Keating was handling Keigney.

"Have either of them ever done a d-board before?" I asked.

"No," he replied. "I've been trying to tell to them what they're like."

Smiling, he said, "Even so, I figure they're in for a surprise."

I knew what he meant. Especially for lawyers who were used to some sort of due process. At a Walpole d-board, being charged was tantamount to being found guilty. They had the usual ways of introducing evidence against you. But when all else failed, they had one that was right out of *Catch-22*. It was called "unidentified informant information."

Of course, that's what they were using in this case. The way it works is like this: The d-board chairperson tells you the offense with which you are being charged. Then, he tells you that the evidence against you, upon which this charge is based, is the statement of an informant who claims that you committed this offense.

In response, you ask them to produce their informant.

They tell you that they do not have to produce the informant.

Then, you ask them to identify the informant.

They tell you that they do not have to identify the informant.

Then you ask them just what this informant said.

They tell you that they do not have to tell you just what the informant said.

The board then leaves the room. A few minutes later, they come back in and tell you that they have heard the evidence and that they have determined that the informant is reliable.

Not that they have talked to the informant himself. In fact, the board doesn't even have to know the identity of the informant. The reporting officer who has brought the charge against you does not have to tell them.

Then, after not having told you what was said about you, they ask you if you would like to respond to what was said about you.

Then, they find you guilty.

As Yossarian said, "That's some catch."

|||||||||||||||||||||||||||||||||||||||||||||||||||||||||||||||

WE WENT OVER the paperwork for a while and discussed the impending hearing. But, the truth was, there really wasn't that much to discuss. It was going to be a routine boilerplate star chamber, and we both knew it.

After a while, we were both getting bored. The only thing in the locker room, besides all of the lockers lining the walls, was a ping-pong table. Alan picked up a paddle and said, "You play ping-pong?"

I said, "Yeah, a little."

Smiling he said, "C'mon, I'll give you a game."

And that's what we did for the next couple of hours.

||||||||||||||||||||||||||||||||||||||||||||||||||||||||||||||||||||||||||

WHEN THE D-BOARD still had not appeared by 1 pm, Alan said, "I'm going inside to see if I can find out what's holding things up. I've got a couple of other clients that I've got to see in there anyway."

He was gone about an hour. When he returned, he said, "You won't believe this shit. The d-board is still in Ten Block. They're doing Keigney and Campbell's cases now. I was talking to Keigney's lawyer. They hadn't even started yet when I got there. By the way, Kevin couldn't make it. His partner, Charlotte Perretta came down in his place, and before you ask, she's good."

"She's been here since nine o'clock this morning. You won't believe what the bastards told her the delay was. They told her that they were waiting for me to show up. Can you believe that?"

"I had to go down to Ten Block to see another guy. When I came in the door, I saw her. I said 'Hey, what's happened in here so far?'"

"She said, 'Nothing'. And I could see she was pissed off at me."

"She said, 'I've been here since nine o'clock this morning waiting for you to show up. Where the hell have you been'"?

"I said, 'What are you talking about? I've been sitting out front since nine-thirty waiting for the d-board to finish with you people in here. They won't bring Doherty inside; they're making him see the d-board outside, in the guard's locker room.'"

"I asked her who told her that they were waiting for me and she said, 'A Mr. Leppart.'"

"I said, 'Oh really. Let's go see him.'"

"You wouldn't believe his face when he saw me with her. I said, 'What did you tell these lawyers that you were waiting for me for? You know I've been sitting out front since nine-thirty.'"

"He tried to cop out by saying that she must have misunderstood him, but she wasn't having any of that."

"She said, 'I didn't misunderstand you. You told me that we've been waiting for Caplan to show up. Now what the hell is going on?'"

"Leppart didn't know what to say. At least he had the decency to be embarrassed."

"Anyway, they're doing Keigney's hearing now, so it's a good thing that I went in."

I was actually laughing by the time that Alan finished. I said, "I wish I could have seen Frank Leppart's face, but I'm not surprised. These bastards will do anything they can to discourage lawyers from coming here, especially in Ten Block. They've never really accepted the idea that a con has a right to a lawyer."

Alan nodded in agreement. "One good thing is that it gives the other lawyers a good introduction to Walpole. Neither of them ever really had to deal with the DOC before. It's just as well that they both know, up front, what they're up against."

The d-board came out of Ten Block at five o'clock.

My hearing took over two hours. It could have been over in two minutes.

In essence, what happened was the d-board chairman read the charge. "I have received informant information that Stephen Doherty was involved in the murder of Robert Perrotta."

We asked if they would produce the informant.

They said that they didn't have to.

We asked if they would tell us his name.

They said that they didn't have to.

We asked if they would tell us what the informant said.

They said that they didn't have to.

We asked what they did have to tell us.

They said, "Guilty," which was, all in all, a typical Walpole disciplinary hearing.

Incidentally, the sanction was fifteen days isolation and a hundred and fifty days loss of good time.

We also requested, for the umpteenth time, that we be allowed to see the letter that Bobby Perrotta had allegedly written—*the highly publicized, front page, letter in which Bobby supposedly identified the people who were going to kill him.* Up till now, they had totally avoided our requests to see the letter. Finally, when confronted face to face, they claimed that there was no such letter. Right. Except on the front page of the newspaper.

I wonder whom the letter actually named. Obviously, it wasn't us. Otherwise, "Front Page" Delahunt would have had it all over the news.

There was one other matter. They dismissed the second ticket, the one where they said that I had extorted Bobby Hutchinson—probably because Caplan had requested to speak to him.

|||||||||||||||||||||||||||||||||||||||||||||||||||||||||||||||||||||

ON THE WAY back to Bridgewater, I was sitting in the back seat of the car. The two Walpole transportation guards sat in front. Dick Falk was driving the car. Dick was a senior correctional officer on the night shift.

He was also the unofficial head of the "goon squad," not that that made him a bad guy. Actually, he was pretty much of a straight shooter, but every prison has a goon squad—which, admittedly, is sometimes necessary. The problem was, if the wrong screw was running it, they would use it to abuse and intimidate inmates. Dick Falk wasn't one of those guys. If they had to roll on somebody, he would. But he didn't abuse it.

At one point, he said to me, "Whatta ya gonna do now, Stevie?"

"Whatta ya mean?"

"Well, you know, ya can't go back to Walpole."

This was an obvious reference to the rumors that the false article in the *Herald* had started—that I was testifying in the case, that I was a rat.

I said, "I'll tell ya what, Dick. Turn the car around, take me back to Walpole, throw me in any block you want, and leave the cuffs on."

He glanced back at me in the mirror and said, "Look Stevie, you know you ain't a rat, and we know you ain't a rat, but what about the other guys?"

"What other guys?"

"Well, what about Keigney and Campbell."

"Hey, d'ya know what they said when they saw that shit in the paper?"

"No. What'd they say?"

"They said, 'Whew, better him than me,' which is just what I woulda said if they'd done it to one of them instead of me."

He laughed, and we continued on our way back to Bridgewater.

twelve

At three o'clock in the afternoon, on February 3, 1977, my door opened. There were seven or eight men standing there—some in uniforms. One expensively dressed, well-tanned, and light-haired suit stepped forward and introduced himself as Sheriff Marshall.

Sheriff Marshall then read off an indictment charging me with taking part in the murder of Robert Perrotta. He then presented me with a notice of indictment.

One of the other men held out a pen and a piece of paper. "Here, sign this," he said.

When I made no move to take it, he said, "It's just a …"

I interrupted him with a wave of my hand and said, "I'm not signin' nothin'. I wanna call my lawyer."

The superintendent, who was standing beside the sheriff, nodded and said, "All right. In a couple of minutes."

After they closed the door, I sat on my bed and read the paper that they had given me. I was scheduled for arraignment on the next morning. I wondered who else was going to be there. Because of the d-reports, I figured Keigney and Campbell would be there. I wondered if anyone else was going to be there.

The guard came back and opened my door. "All right," he said. "You can make your call now."

I went down to the office and sat in the chair in front of the desk while the guard placed the call. He handed me the receiver and left the room. A polite, albeit, meaningless gesture as another guard was certainly listening in at the switchboard or on another phone.

Alan wasn't in, so I left him a message that I was going in for arraignment in the morning.

||||||||||||||||||||||||||||||||||||||||||||||||||||||||||

AS THE SIX o'clock news began, I stood in front of the television with my hand on the channel selector rapidly snapping it between channels four, five, and seven. It was the lead story on five, right where I had expected to find it.

The headline "Death Sqaud" blazed out at me as I sat back on the bed to watch. The picture on the screen was of the Norfolk County courthouse in Dedham. I immediately recognized the voice-over as belonging to Delahunt's parrot, Ron Gollobin. (I always thought of him as "Gollum.")

Gollum's coverage of the case was so prejudiced that I was inclined to believe that he and Delahunt were close friends. Or, maybe not, maybe it was just a business arrangement; quid pro quo—favorable coverage in exchange for exclusive leaks from Delahunt and the DOC.

Gollum was saying, "Three men were indicted today for the brutal Thanksgiving Day murder of Robert Perrotta. The men were identified as Stephen Doherty, 36; Arthur Keigney, 35; and John Campbell, 23."

As he recited the names, three men were led through the courthouse doors. They were being led down the stairs to the waiting cars. The first one was Tommy Carden. He tried to hide his face, but I made him out immediately. As Carden entered the car, the camera shifted back to the top of the stairs. It was Joe Rego. He didn't try to cover his face. In fact, he looked lost. Then, they repeated the process. This time, it was Bernie Battles. He didn't try to hide his face either.

"The lousy bastards." I said out loud. "They staged the whole performance."

If you didn't know better, you would automatically assume that the three men who were just led down the stairs were Keigney, Campbell, and me—a misimpression, which Gollum did nothing to clarify in his subsequent, "non-partisan," interview with Delahunt.

thirteen

The next day, I was taken into the Dedham courthouse to be arraigned. I was, of course, still being kept separate from Keigney and Campbell. Alan Caplan then filed a request with the court that we either be allowed to confer with my codefendants, in order to prepare for the upcoming trial, or else that the cases be severed. Motion denied.

As I was being taken out of the courthouse, I was taken out the back door that led to the steps, which expanded to maybe fifty or sixty feet wide at the bottom. On the sidewalk at the bottom of the steps were two television cameramen from Channel Five, one on each side of the steps, with their cameras pointing up at me. Also on the sidewalk was Gollum.

As luck would have it, Alan Caplan happened to be walking out with us. He was walking beside me on my left side. The two transportation officers were walking behind me holding onto the chain connected to my waist shackles. Even though my hands were cuffed to my waist chain, I was holding a large manila envelope, containing legal papers. Instinctively, I raised the envelope blocking the right side of my face.

I said to Alan, "Try to stay between me and the camera on your side."

Alan moved up a little and off to the side, keeping himself between me and the camera. We continued on that way down the stairs until I was in the car. Concentrating on blocking the other camera, I never looked in Alan's direction again.

That night when I was back in my cell, I had the television on and was watching the news. Sure enough, there we were—a quick glimpse of me in the distance, then, mostly Alan walking toward the camera, swaying back and forth and waving his arms.

The cameraman was obviously having difficulty focusing, trying to aim his camera around Alan. All of a sudden, the picture was swirling. Then, we were looking at the sky.

Apparently, there had been some sort of a minor collision between Alan and the cameraman, which resulted in Channel Five filing an assault charge against Alan. Alan, in turn, filed a counter charge. I guess the cameraman allegedly hit Alan with the camera. Shortly after, Alan received a telephone call from Gollum. Gollum told him that they would drop their charges if Alan would drop his charges.

After they agreed to do so, Gollum told him, "And you better not get any of your wise guy friends after me."

Alan was as pleased as punch when he was telling me this. "I didn't know I had any wise guy friends," he said.

I told him. "Neither did I. Please keep 'em away from me, too."

fourteen

I was on a visit when the guard came into the visiting room and told me that he'd have to end the visit early, because they were short of help and had to transfer the visiting room officer to another part of the institution. I started to argue, but my visit calmed me down and said that it was all right.

The first thing I saw as I returned to the cell area was two guards from Norfolk Prison. One of them had a set of chains in his hands.

I looked at the guard who had just ended my visit and said, "Jesus, Frank, I hate to see ya get lying on your record at this stage of the game."

He got an embarrassed look on his face and said, "Better get your stuff together. You're leaving."

"I wanna make a phone call. I got a visit scheduled tomorrow, an' I don't want my people driving all the way down here for nothing," I said.

"Listen, we can't let ya make a phone call right now because of security. Lemme have ya number. I'll make the call for you after you're gone," he said.

"All right. Thanks," I said.

It was almost time for supper when we pulled into the parking lot at Norfolk. We went through the three steel doors, crossed no-man's land, and entered the administration building. We turned right and headed for the receiving building (RB).

The RB was to Norfolk what Ten Block was to Walpole and what The Fort was to Bridgewater, at least the third floor. It's a three-story brick building. The first two floors are used as a reception area to house new arrivees while they are being classified. The third floor is the hole.

I was taken to the third floor, strip-searched, and placed in their version of a strip cell. In the RB, that's a cell where everything has been removed except the bed, sink, and toilet. At least their strip cell had a toilet. While I was being searched I told the guard that I'd like to call my people to inform them that I had been moved, as I had a visit scheduled for the next morning at Bridgewater.

He told me that it couldn't be done until morning.

56

I said, "That'll be too late. They'll be leaving the house by eight o'clock in order to get to Bridgewater by nine."

"There's nothing I can do about it. All phone calls have to be approved by the day shift deputy, and he's already gone home," he said.

I asked, "If I give you the number, can you guys make the call?"

"Sure. I can do that," he said.

One of the two guards who had brought me from The Fort said, "Didn't the officer at Bridgewater say that he'd take care of it?"

"Yeah. But that's no guarantee. Out of sight, out of mind," I said.

The other guard said, "Gimme the number. I'll make sure someone out front makes the call."

I said, "Okay, thanks," and gave him the number.

The next morning, after breakfast, I heard a knock on my door. As I got off of my bed, a face appeared in the food slot. The food slot is an opening in the solid door about three feet from the bottom.

It was Joe Rego. "How ya doin', Stevie?"

He was smiling, and I could tell that he was genuinely glad to see me.

I laughed and said, "About the same as you, Joe. I saw you on TV."

His face tightened up. "The bastards tried t' get me killed," he said.

"I know," I told him. "I know just how you feel. You musta' seen that piece they put in the paper about me, the day after they took me in front of the grand jury?"

"Yeah," he said. "But you know nobody bought it."

"Some people did," I said. "The ones who wanted to believe it."

"Fuckin' assholes," he said, waving his hand dismissively. "PCs, weasels, stool pigeons, and fuckin' jerks that don't know you and just want something to talk about. Nobody pays any attention to assholes like that. But there's good guys that think I ratted on you an' Arthur an' Jackie."

I stared at him, surprised. "Still?" I asked.

He nodded his head.

I thought for a minute. Then I asked him, "Do they still allow the camp chairman to talk to guys in the RB?"

Again, he nodded his head. "Yeah. I think anyone who comes into the RB can talk to him once."

There was an elected inmate council at Norfolk that represented the inmate population in dealing with the administration. The camp chairman was the head of the inmate council.

I asked, "Is Frankie Salemme still the camp chairman?"

"Yeah."

"Can you get a message out to him?"

"Yeah," he said. "I can yell out my window."

"Tell Frankie that I'm up here and that I wanna see him."

Just then, the guard came over and said, "Ya gotta keep goin' Joe."

Joe looked up at him and said, "Okay."

Turning back to me, he said, "I'm out for a shower. I'll send that message out as soon as I'm done."

A little while later he was back. He was coming from the shower, and his hair was still wet. "I meant to tell you," he said. "Bobby Hutchinson is up here."

I immediately said, "Tell him I want to talk to him."

He nodded his head and said, "He already knows you're here. He seemed kinda nervous, but at least he stayed."

I said, "Whatta ya mean?"

With a big grin on his face, he said, "We've known you were comin' since yesterday. They came around to everyone's cell and told us you were on your way here. They wanted to know if anyone had a problem with you."

I said, "Are you shittin' me?"

Grinning even wider, he said, "Uh uh, an' three guys said they did. They got them outta here."

As he was walking away, I yelled, "Hey, send me somethin' t' read."

A while later, I was sitting on the bed reading a magazine that Joe had sent down to me when someone said, "Hey you."

It was Bobby Hutchinson at my food slot. He was smiling and trying to act casual, but the strain was showing. He was nervous. He had had a run-in with Jackie and Arthur at the courthouse, when they were "coincidentally" brought there on the same day. Jackie had received the same kind of "extortion" d-report that I'd gotten. I gather that some sort of brouhaha developed between them at the courthouse. So, he had no idea what to expect from me.

I got off the bed. As I approached the door, he said, "We gotta talk."

I said, "We sure do."

I handed him the d-report that they had given me charging me with extorting him.

He read it quietly, then said, "That fuckin' Vose. Stevie, so help me God, I never said any of that shit. Why would I? We both know it ain't true. You an' me an' Jackie been friends since Five Block, an' I don't even know Keigney. I told that fuckin' Vose that too. He knows you had nothin' to do with me takin' a PC. I tried to …"

"Wait a minute," I cut him off. "Did you say that you told that to Vose? When?" George Vose was the DOC staff member who had signed both of my d-reports. Up till then, Vose had been some sort of a counselor or social worker. I was told that, when the deputy warden, Dennis Brown, refused to sign the d-reports for Perrotta's murder, he was transferred to another institution and Vose was promoted to deputy warden.

"A couple a' months ago," he answered. "He came down to question me right after they lugged you guys. I told him that we were friends and that you had nothin' to do with me takin' a PC. In fact, when he asked me if it was you that I owed the money to, I told him that I wished the fuck it was, 'cause then I coulda' worked somethin' out, without havin' t' PC I tried to tell Jackie and Arthur that, that day in court, but they didn't gimme a chance."

"Yeah, I heard about it," I said.

Then, I added, "Will you put everything you just told me down on paper?"

"Sure," he said. "Whatta ya want me t' say?"

I said, 'That's up t' you. Just tell the truth. They already dropped the ticket, but I wanna be able t' prove that they were willin' to go that far in order t' frame me. An' I wanna show what a liar Vose is. He signed my d-report for the murder, too."

The guard came over and said, "Okay, ya gotta keep movin.'"

Hutch nodded, "Okay."

He was still holding the d-report in his hand. He said to me, "Can I take this back to my cell for a while? I never saw it before."

"Go ahead," I said. "Just don't lose it."

fifteen

T he guard came to my door about eleven o'clock and said, "The camp chairman wants to talk to you."

I put my shoes and sweater on and said, "I'm ready."

They took me down to the RB visiting room, and Frankie Salemme came in about a minute later. I hadn't seen Frank in almost three years—since July of 1974, when I'd gotten shipped out of Norfolk. I could tell from looking at him that he'd just gotten out of bed.

As we shook hands, I said, "How ya been, Frank. I appreciate your comin' up so soon."

"I didn't even know you were here. A guy just woke me up an' told me. Jesus, Stevie, we heard about the indictments. I don't know what t' say. What a lousy deal," he said.

As we sat down, I said, "You know it's a bum beef?"

"That's what we heard. Jesus, I heard you were gettin' out. Then this shit came down. I couldn't believe it."

"Yeah, I know," I said, "That's about how I felt."

"I can imagine," he said.

I said, "Listen, do you know a kid named Joe Rego?"

"Yeah," he said with a frown. "A fuckin' rat. He's upstairs in the RB."

"That's the problem, Frank. The kid's no rat. They set it up t' make him look like one."

He looked absolutely flabbergasted. "Are you sure? We heard he was tes-tifyin' against you an' Arthur an' Jackie."

"I know," I said. "That's what they want people t' think. They did the same thing t' him that they tried t' do t' me with that shit they put in the paper about me when they snatched me t' Bridgewater."

"Yeah, we read it, those fuckin' creeps. Ya know nobody bought it."

"Well, that's what they did t' Joe Rego. The worst part is, the kid's doin' life, an' they offered him a deal. He could hit the street if he'd go along with them. He turned them down cold."

"I'll tell ya somethin'," he said. "I'm glad t' hear that. I've known him for a while, an' I always liked him. He was a quiet kid, an' he always minded his own business. I felt bad when I heard he was rattin.'"

I said, "You know what they're tryin' t' do? They figure if they put enough pressure on him, he just might get scared enough that someone's gonna whack him for bein' a rat that he might as well become one."

Frankie, said, "Do you know who it is that is talking?"

"Yeah. A lying weasel named Carden, Tommy Carden. D' you know him?"

"No," he said. "But I heard his name. The story we got down here is that Carden, Rego, and a guy named Tommy McInerney were all testifying against you and another guy, Bernie something."

"Bernie Battles. Except he's gettin' bum beefed too, so's Tommy McInerney. You gotta hear this shit t' believe it. The only one they got is Carden. He told the cops that the others would back up his story. So they snatched them outta Walpole. They put Rego down here, McInerney in Bridgewater, and Battles out in Worcester. After Carden left here, they brought him down to Bridgewater, an' he tried to get McInerney to go along with him. He wouldn't. Then, when Rego wouldn't, they started the story that he was rattin' and then stuck him in the RB to make it look like he was."

Frankie said, "Those fuckin' creeps. And if someone did whack Rego, they'd say that you guys had it done to him so that he couldn't testify against you."

"Yeah. Well, that's one of the things that I wanted to see you about. I'd like you to let people know that he's not a rat. It ain't right that he has to stay in the RB as a PC."

"Don't worry about that," he said. "I'll tell them. Anybody in particular?"

"Well, basically, I want everybody to know, but maybe you'd better tell the Charlestown guys first. Between me, Jackie, and Arthur we've got a lot of friends down here."

"I was thinking the same thing," he said. "Anyone in particular?"

I gave him the names of a half a dozen guys. Then I said, "Make sure that they let everybody else know. Joe's kind of a small fella', and I wouldn't want some phony half-ass tough guy lookin' to impress people t' give him a beatin'. Or worse. You know how that goes."

"Yeah. I know what you mean. It'll probably take a couple a' weeks for word to get all around the camp," he said.

We talked for another fifteen minutes or so. Then he left, and I went back to the RB.

It took almost another month before they would allow Joe Rego to go back out to general population. It took a lawyer to force the issue. In the end, though, they had to let him out.

As he walked out of the hole, Frankie Salemme and three guys from Charlestown were waiting for him. They walked him around the camp taking him to each unit. At each one, he was introduced to anyone from Charlestown or anyone who happened to be a friend of ours.

The next day, when I was out on the roof in a recreation cage, Joe walked by the building. He called up to me, with a big grin on his face. "Hey Stevie, everything's all straightened out. I'm doin' okay."

Just then, two guards walked over to him and told him to keep on moving. Whenever I was out on recreation, they had two guards stationed by the building to prevent people from yelling up to me.

Joe exploded. "You go an' fuck yourself. You cocksuckers tried to get me killed. Then ya put me in PC. If it ain't for him, I'm still sittin' in there. You go an' fuck yourself. You wanna lock me up? Go ahead. Lock me up."

The guards obviously weren't bad guys. It was common knowledge what they had done to Joe, and they knew that he was right. Instead of busting him, they were trying to calm him down.

I yelled down to him, "Hey Joe. I hear ya, man, but let it go."

He looked up at me. Then back at the cops. Then back at me. Then he smiled, and nodded his head. Turning to walk away, he waved at me and yelled, "I'll be seein' ya, man."

sixteen

A few days after I got to Norfolk, Al Caplan came down to see me. He was already in the visiting room when I got there. We shook hands and sat down.

We traded amenities. Then he said, "I've got the grand jury minutes."

As he handed them to me, I said, "Beautiful. I've got some stories for you too. You're really gonna like a couple of them. What a mistake they made putting me here. It's Bridgewater and McInerney all over again, only more so. Let me read the grand jury minutes; then I'll tell you about them."

"All right," he said. "But just read Carden's testimony for now. His is the only one that matters. You can read the others when you get back to your cell. It starts on page eight."

I turned to page eight and started to read.

In essence, Carden's testimony was that he and Perrotta were brothers-in-laws and best friends, with Perrotta being married to Carden's sister. That, around 4:45 pm on Thanksgiving Day, 1976, Carden was walking from his cell, on the second tier, in cell block A-2, to Perrotta's cell, on the third tier. That, he came up the back stairs where I stopped him by placing my hand on his shoulder and offering to sell him marijuana in a loud voice, thereby preventing him from going to Perrotta's cell. That, Perrotta's solid steel door then opened and that Perrotta, Campbell, and Keigney came out of the cell. That, I then stopped talking and allowed Carden to proceed to Perrotta's cell.

Carden further testified that he was with Perrotta, in Perrotta's cell, around seven o'clock that night. That, he left Perrotta and went to another cell block, A-3, to place a bet. That, while in A-3, he heard Perrotta being paged for a visit. That, he returned to A-2 and, upon entering the block, looked up to the third tier and saw me leaning over the railing in front of Perrotta's cell. That, he proceeded up the front stairwell to the second tier, looked up, and saw me walking along the third tier toward the back of the block. That, Campbell and Keigney came out of Perrotta's cell. That, he then proceeded to Perrotta's cell and found the body.

63

||||||||||||||||||||||||||||||||||||||||||||||||||||||||||||||||||||

BY THE TIME I was finished reading, I wanted to bite someone's nose off, preferably Carden's.

I said, "That lyin' fuckin' degenerate. That shit about me bein' outside Perrotta's door at seven-thirty is a cold-blooded lie. So is my stopping him at five o'clock. That's another lie. Except that there's a little bit of truth in it. I did talk to him on the back landing about five, but it didn't happen the way he said it did. First off, he didn't come up the back stairs. He came up the front stairs, and he wasn't *going* to Perrotta's room when I talked to him. He was coming from it."

"And this other shit," I said, as I riffled through the pages. "Here, on page thirteen. He says he didn't know me, and we never talked before. That fuckin' asshole! I used to play ping-pong with him all the time, a whole crew of us. You know how many people I can get to testify to that? Not just cons, either. Guards used to watch us play too. I know a half a dozen screws alone that would testify, and I couldn't tell you how many cons. In fact, two of the guys who used to play with us are here at Norfolk."

"You know about Joe Rego? How they tried to set him up? They nearly got that poor bastard killed. Well, he's still in the RB with me, but he's goin' out to population soon. Anyway, he told me…"

"Wait a minute," Caplan interrupted, laughing. "One thing at a time, you can tell me that afterwards. Right now stick with Carden's testimony. What were you saying about talking to him at five o'clock on the night of the murder?"

"I was leaning on the railing, up on the third tier at the back of the block, just before the five o'clock count. I'm talkin' to Jackie Connolly. Anyways, here comes Carden traipsin' along the second tier. The reason we notice him at first is that he's drunk as a skunk. Then we see that he's come around from his side of the tier to the outside, an' he's heading for the front stairs. We're laughin' 'cause we think he's so drunk; he's headin' out of the block, an' it's almost count time."

Caplan broke in, "Wait a minute. How did you know he was drunk?"

"Well, for one thing, the way he was walking an' holding on to the railing. Besides, they'd been drunk all week."

"Who's they?" Caplan asked.

"Carden and Perrotta," I said. "In fact, I think they got written up for it down the church. Might even have been that morning."

"Anyways, I thought he was heading out of the block. You know how drunks like to roam around, and he was heading in that direction. But he didn't. Instead, he went *up* the front steps and headed for Bobby's room. Bobby lived in the second room from the front."

"Me an' Jackie Connolly were still talking a couple of minutes later when Carden came down the back."

"First he asked me if there was any grass around."

"I told him, 'Not that I know of.'"

"Then he asked me if I wanted to do anything with the game that was on that night. We used to bet personal sometimes, instead of betting with the bookie. Ya get a better line that way. In fact, we'd already bet the two games that had been on that day. I won. Just then, they called count. I told Carden I'd see him after count. I had to go right to my cell. I lived on the flats and they locked up my side first."

Caplan asked, "Did you talk to him again after the count?"

"Yeah. During the count, I checked the papers. I found out that like, Rutgers and Colgate, or someone like that were on TV."

"First off, I don't even like to bet college. I mean, at least with the pros, ya got a little consistency, but college, ya never know. At least, I don't. On top of which, I wouldn't even wanna watch Rutgers and Colgate. If it's Oklahoma an' Nebraska, or maybe B.C. or Notre Dame an' one of the Big Ten schools, or Southern Cal, all right. But outside of that, I pretty much stick with the pros."

"So anyways, Carden comes down to my cell when they open the doors at six. I tell him I don't wanna bet the game. He ain't too happy about that, an' he starts snivelin' about how he already owes me a couple a' crates [cartons of cigarettes] an' I'm supposed t' give him a shot t' get even."

"So I tell him, 'Look, stop your weepin'. It's Thanksgiving weekend. There's gonna be about a dozen more games on, before it's over. You'll get plenty a' shots to get even.'"

"So, he said, 'All right,' and he left."

"He still wasn't too happy. But he wasn't drunk enough to make an issue out of it either, just enough to let it show a little. He was kinda full a' shit. The only reason anyone had anything to do with him was because of Bobby."

Caplan said, "I remember your saying that. Okay, so he left your room. Did you talk to him again after that?"

I said, "Nope. That's the last time I ever spoke to him."

"Okay," Caplan said. "Now he says on page thirteen that he didn't know you and that it was unusual for you to stop him at five o'clock, because you'd never talked before. What's this about ping-pong?"

"We used to play ping-pong," I said. "Me, Carden, Bobby Perrotta, The General, Joe Rego, John Wilkie, all kinds a' guys. There was about a dozen of us that used t' play regular. Lots a' times we'd play doubles. In fact, the guy who was my partner most of the time is down here now. He knows Carden and Perrotta from the street. He sent me a message that he had some information for me. He told me to have you call him out when you come up—him and a couple of other guys. Those were the names I gave you on the phone the other night. Did you put them on your list?"

"Yeah," he said. "I've got three names on my list besides yours. Two of them are guys you wanted called out, Joe Rego and Robert Lee. Oh, 'The General,' I get it. Is it Robert E. Lee?"

I said, "Yup. That's why they call him The General.

Alan asked, "Which one do you want called out first?"

I said, "You might as well call The General."

Caplan went over and told the visiting room guard that he was ready for Robert E. Lee.

At first, the guard wanted to send me back to the RB before he called The General. But Caplan explained that we had to see him together, as he had information relating to my case. Alan came back and sat down as the guard checked with his supervisor.

While we waited, Caplan asked, "Were you serious about there being guards that will testify that you used to play ping-pong with Carden?"

"Sure," I replied. "Plenty of them. Well, three or four that I can think of offhand. On top of that, he played monopoly with us a couple of times. On top of which, you realize we both worked in the computer room. In fact, so did Perrotta."

Alan perked up. "You never told me that," he said.

I said, "It never came up. I never knew he denied knowin' me. What a stupid thing to do. I wonder if he was still drunk when he did it?"

Caplan smiled and said, "Two months later? C'mon, you're reaching."

"Not really. The last thing that he did before he PC'd was to go to the guy who was holding Perrotta's pills and get them. They were bootleg Quaaludes," I said.

Alan just stared at me. "How in hell did you find out something like that in lock up, in a different prison?"

I just shrugged. "Word travels. On top of that, they brought him here to Norfolk, from Walpole, on Friday, the day after the murder. He stayed in population till Tuesday when he went into PC. I figure he must've made his first statement by then, an' he was loaded the whole time. He also sold his diamond ring for drugs over the weekend."

Just then, Bobby Lee came into the visiting room. He handed his pass to the guard and looked around. When he saw me, he came over. We shook hands warmly.

"Man, I don't know what to say. I didn't believe it when I read they indicted you," he said.

"That makes two of us," I said.

"Bobby, I'd like you to meet my lawyer, Al Caplan. Al this is The General."

They shook hands, and we all sat down. Bobby lit a cigarette and said, "That fuckin' weasel."

Then, turning to Caplan, he said, "You know Carden's lyin', don't you?"

Caplan nodded.

Bobby continued, "They put him in my house, Seven-Three, the weekend he was down here. He was loaded the whole time he was here. We spent about seven straight hours in my room one night just talkin' an' smokin'. Look, Mr. Caplan, I'm tellin ya somethin'. Tommy didn't know who killed Bobby. I've known Bobby since I was a kid. I mean like, his mother and my mother are friends an' all that, ya know? We grew up in the same neighborhood, an' we were friends for a long time. Tommy knew that. We talked a lot about Bobby that weekend. Believe me. He had no idea who killed him."

I said, "Tell him about the ring."

Bobby said, "Okay, he got down here Friday, but I didn't run into him till Saturday. I didn't even know he was here till I saw him waiting to use the phone on Saturday morning. So I go over, an' I said, 'Hey Tommy, when did you get down here?'"

"He said, 'They brought me in last night. Did ya hear what happened to Bobby Perrotta?'"

"I said, 'Yeah. There's all kinds a' stories goin' around, but nobody really knows anything except what was in the papers.'"

"He said, 'Man, it was heavy. I'll tell you all about it after I get off the phone.'"

"The guy who was usin' the phone got off, an' Carden made his call. He talked for about ten minutes. Then he hung up, an' we went upstairs."

"He told me that he'd called Bobby's mother. He said she was all fucked up about Bobby. He was all fucked up too. He was on downs. He told me that he was out of the block when it happened and that when he came back, he found the body. He said that when he first saw him, he didn't believe it. He kept sayin,' Man, his prick was in his mouth. Who coulda' done somethin' like that? I couldn't believe it.'"

"He said the reason they moved him outta' Walpole was because him an' Bobby was so close and that they moved a couple of other friends of theirs too—Joe Rego, Bernie Battles, an' Tommy McInerney. He said they all got moved, because the cops figured they were Bobby's friends and that they were either gonna get hit themselves or go after whoever whacked Bobby."

"He was lookin' for more downs, but he had no money 'cause he just got there; so, he went to a guy that had some and showed him this diamond ring he had. The guy liked it, so he bought it for an ounce of grass and some more downs."

"We spent the whole weekend talkin,' an' he had no clue who killed Bobby. He didn't know why it happened or how it happened or who did it or anything about it. He said that none of the other guys who got lugged had any idea who killed Bobby either."

Caplan asked, "Did he say that in front of anyone else?"

Bobby shook his head, "Not that I know of. If he did, it was when I wasn't with him. Maybe he talked to somebody else about it; I don't know."

Caplan asked, "Did he tell you he was going to take a PC.?"

"No. I found out about it after he was gone."

I said to Bobby, "D'ya know what he told them? He told them that him and I had never spoken before."

Bobby said, "He said *what?* Jesus, you an' him musta played ping-pong a hundred times."

Turning to Caplan, he said, "We used to play ping-pong all the time, a whole crew of us. How the fuck could he say somethin' like that? That's just stupid. There's even screws that used t' come over an' watch us."

Alan nodded, "Stevie told me that. Do you think any of them would testify to that?"

Bobby said, "Yeah, there's a couple of 'em I think would."

Bobby looked at me and said, "Whatta ya think?"

I said, "I agree. There's a lot of 'em that wouldn't. But I think there's a couple that would, unless the administration leaned on them."

Bobby said, "Yeah, Fred might. He's hard as nails."

Alan said, "Listen Bobby, I'd like you to do something for me. Could you write down everything you remember about that weekend? Everything that Carden said. There's no rush. I'll be back down in a couple of weeks."

Bobby said, "Sure. No problem."

I stood up. "I wish we could spend some time talkin', but Al's pressed for time, an' he's still gotta see a couple of other guys. We'll have some time to talk the next time he comes down. Okay, Bob?"

Bobby got up. "Sure. You take care of yourself."

|||||||||||||||||||||||||||||||||||||||||||||||||||||||||||||||||||||

JOE REGO CAME in about five minutes later. He shook hands with Al, and we all sat down. Joe told Alan everything that he'd told me. If he had gone along with Carden and corroborated his story, he could have walked out the door with about seven years in on a life bit. He was a stand-up kid. He also told us that his appearance in front of the grand jury was a sham. The prosecutor never asked him anything about the murder. He never even mentioned it.

seventeen

On the second to last day of April, some four and a half months since I'd last seen my codefendants, I was brought to the Dedham courthouse for a pretrial hearing on discovery motions. The motions were being heard by Judge Mazzone. Once again, I was not placed in the room where the cage was, where the defendants were usually held. Instead, this time I was taken to a DA's office, which was right next door to it.

It wasn't that big of an office, maybe fifteen feet by thirty feet, if that, with three or four desks. John Prescott was talking on one of the telephones. A secretaryish-looking lady, around forty, was talking on one of the other phones. The only other person in the room was a guy around thirty in a brown suit who was doing paperwork at one of the other desks.

I put my manila envelope and the book I'd brought with me on an empty desk. The transportation officer then removed the waist chains, cuffs, and leg irons. I took my coat off, and he replaced the cuffs.

Prescott hung up the phone and nodded to my escort. Turning to me, he said, "Hi Steve. How's it goin'?"

"Swell," I answered. "What am I doin' in here? Why ain't I in the cage?"

He looked uncomfortable. "I can't answer that. You'll have to ..."

I didn't find out what it was that I'd have to do, because a court officer stuck his head in the door and said to Prescott, "Can I speak to you in the corridor for a moment?"

As Prescott left the room, I walked over to the boarded-up door that separated the office from the bullpen—a wire cage in the room next door where the incarcerated were usually held while waiting for a court appearance. I pounded loudly on it a couple of times and yelled, "HEY JACKIE, AR-THUR, YOU IN THERE?"

I got no answer, but the brown suit who was sitting at the desk next to the door came halfway out of his chair. The startled suit squawked, "Knock that off. You don't pull that stuff in here."

I ignored him and said to John Prescott who had just stepped back in, "Any particular reason I can't wait in the cage?"

"Look, Steve, it's not me that's keeping you separated. We've got orders from the DOC."

He even said it with a straight face. I just smiled.

When Caplan came in, I said, "Listen Al, there's gotta be somethin' you can do about this shit. If Campbell and Keigney are gonna be my codefendants I wanna be able to talk to them. If I'm not gonna be allowed to talk to them, I want my case severed from theirs."

He turned to Prescott. "What about it, John?"

He replied, "You're gonna have to take it up with the DOC, Alan. It's outta my hands. They don't want Doherty in with Campbell and Keigney. They say it's for security."

Alan turned back to me and said in a soft voice, "I'm gonna take a walk across the street. Judge Mazzone is over there. I'm gonna ask him to put you in with Keigney and Campbell. I'll be back in a little while."

Prescott left the room shortly afterward. The only ones left with me were the lady, the brown suit, and the cop at the door that they had watching me.

I heard the sounds of approaching prisoners. Clanking chains and court officers yelling, "CLEAR THE CORRIDOR. CLEAR THE CORRIDOR. COMING THROUGH. PRISONERS COMING THROUGH."

As a small knot of people went by the door, I thought that I saw Keigney going by, but I wasn't quite sure. I waited about five or ten minutes till I was sure that they were inside the bullpen, then I said to the cop, "I'm thirsty. I need a drink of water."

"Wait a minute," he said, as he looked out the door into the corridor.

"All right," he said. "C'mon".

He took my arm as we stepped out the door and turned left toward the water fountain. We had to walk by the door to the bullpen on our way to the fountain. The bullpen door is solid wood. However, it has an opening, about a square foot, right at face level. The window where Delahunt had been standing when he had Caplan offer me the street if I would testify. As we passed the door, I simply turned to my left and was looking into the bullpen, maybe eight feet from the door.

Campbell and Keigney were standing there. I yelled, "HEY."

They both looked at the door, and their eyes widened. "HEY," they yelled back.

I just smiled and, as the cop was pulling on my arm, I said, "I'll be back."

I got my drink of water and returned to the office. I ambled over to the boarded-up door and repeated my "disturbing the peace" routine. BAM! BAM! BAM! "HEY, HOW YOU TWO DOIN'?"

This time, the suit came all the way out of his chair. He was yelling. "HEY, I TOLD YOU NOT TO DO THAT. NOW GET AWAY FROM THAT DOOR."

Campbell's voice came from the other side. I could hear him laughing. "HOW THE HELL ARE YOU DOIN'?"

The suit was still demanding attention. "DIDN'T YOU HEAR ME?"

He looked like he was going to stamp his foot.

"Not bad," I called back. "Any of the lawyers over there with you?"

"No. Did you see them yet?"

"Just Caplan." I responded. "He said he'd be right back. I'll give you a holler when he comes."

I heard him laugh. "I know you will."

As I sat back down, I could hear the suit jabbering to the cop. "I don't want him to get out of that chair again."

I just grinned at him. "Who gives a fuck what you want?"

He stood there glaring at me, with his hand on his hip. It was obvious from the pouty look on his face that he'd like nothing better than to punch me in the face, if he only knew how.

I opened up my book to see how Lazurus Long was doing. As I read, I was vaguely aware that Prescott had been in and out a few times. I didn't realize that he'd returned again until I heard my name. "Uh Steve, uh, are you interested in going in the cage next door?"

He'd taken me by surprise. "What?"

"Would you like to go next door, with Campbell and Keigney?" He repeated. His discomfort was so obvious. He was openly embarrassed.

I scooped up my belongings, biting back the nasty, sarcastic remark that was struggling to spring from behind my teeth. "Would I *like* to go in with them?"

I said, "Let's go."

A minute later, I was in the cage with Jackie and Arthur. Once we were through the initial greetings and amenities, Campbell said, "How the hell did you work this?"

"I'm not exactly sure," I answered. "Alan went to see the judge a little while ago about getting us together. I imagine that had something to do with it."

Arthur said, "Delahunt must be hot enough to fuck."

"I'm sure he is," I said. "Prescott couldn't even talk straight. He was legitimately stuttering. Ya know he had the balls to ask me if I *wanted* to come in here? He couldn't even look me in the face."

Keigney said, "You still in the RB?"

"Yeah," I said. "Why? You know somethin' I don't?"

"No," he laughed. "But who knows where *you're* gonna be, the way you move around."

We were gabbing and catching up, and I told them what Dick Falk had said after my d-board hearing, on the ride back to Bridgewater, about me not being able to be housed in Walpole and what I'd said to him.

They both looked at each other and busted out laughing.

Arthur was standing there, grinning at me.

Jackie said, "That's perfect, and you don't even have a clue. The mornin' after they took you to the grand jury, I came out to take my shower. The screws were just off the tier, right by the gate. As I get to the shower, one of them says, 'Hey Jack, check this out.' They gimme the paper an' it's open to the page with the story sayin' you were testifyin'. I read it. Then I bring it down to Arthur's cell. As soon as he read it, he went, 'Whew, better him than me.' Just what you said."

We talked for a few more minutes. I told them what we'd found out at Bridgewater from Tommy McInerney and at Norfolk from Joe Rego and Bobby Lee.

Then, Caplan came through the door and approached the screen. "Hello there. Christ, that was quick. Mazzone must've called as soon as I left. He didn't even know that they were keeping you separate. Look, I'll be back in a minute. I want to see if the other lawyers are here yet."

A few minute later, the three lawyers came in together.

Jackie's lawyer, Al Nugent, introduced me to Arthur's new lawyer, Usher Moren. We exchanged greetings. Then, the six of us closed in around the screen while they explained what was going to happen at the hearing.

Moren said, "We're going downstairs in front of Mazzone in a few minutes."

The one thing that always stuck in my mind about that hearing was Prescott's lying to Judge Mazzone, in response to our request for any other false accusations that had been made by Carden, specifically about Knothead. Prescott told him that there were none.

Based on that lie, Mazzone denied our motion.

eighteen

I n August, the autopsy report was finally released. To everyone's amazement, it showed that Bobby had died shortly after eating his noon-time meal. As Carden's story had him still being alive at 7 o'clock on the night of the murder, it was obvious that he was lying.

One of the lawyers was told that when Lt. Bergin saw the autopsy report he told the DA, "Drop the charges. You've got no case."

Instead, the DA offered all three of us a deal.

They brought us to the courthouse. When the three lawyers came in, the six of us huddled together at the screen.

Al Nugent said, "We've talked to Prescott, and he's going to let us have a room downstairs for a private conference. We'll meet you down there in a couple of minutes."

The lawyers left, and the court officers and the Walpole transportation guards came in to get us. Five minutes later, we were seated in a room on the first floor. The lawyers were waiting for us when we got there, and they arranged themselves around the table. After a short discussion of whether the room was bugged (Campbell, Keigney, and I were all sure that it was bugged; the lawyers weren't so sure.), we got down to business.

Nugent started it off. He said, "Well, they've offered us a deal. What it comes down to is this: they'll reduce the charge to 'Accessory After' if you'll cop out. The max is seven years. But I'm sure we can do better than that— probably two and a half to three, concurrent with the sentences that you're already serving."

Al Caplan said, "Delahunt doesn't give a shit how much time you get, just as long as he gets a conviction."

Then he said, "If Arthur and Jackie will plead in, they'll drop all charges on you."

That part was "unofficial." But Caplan had been "made to understand," in that surreptitious manner that lawyers have of communicating with each other without ever actually saying what it is that they're saying.

In a very similar situation, of which we were all aware, i.e., a Walpole prison murder, an inmate found murdered in his bed, one lying witness, another falsely accused inmate, Johnny Grey, was made the exact same offer. He took it. He pled in to accessory after, even though he did not commit the crime. He was given a one- to two-year sentence to be served concurrently with his original sentence, i.e., time served. Furthermore, it was done under an "*Alford*" plea. An Alford plea only occurs under unique circumstances, the most extreme of which being when you plead guilty even though you are actually innocent of the crime, because, at that point in time, it is in your best interest to plead guilty. Al Caplan represented Johnny Grey.

Nobody said anything for a minute. Then, Keigney shook his head. "No way. I don't care if they offer me a suspended sentence. They wouldn't be makin' an offer like that if they had any kind of a case. All they've got is that asshole Carden, and we've already caught him in a dozen lies."

Moren said, "You're right, of course. The case is weak. But at the same time, it's a good offer. I'm not telling you that I think you should take it. That's your decision. You're the one that's got to do the time. But what I am saying is this: Any time you go in front of a jury, you stand a chance of being found guilty. But, as I said, it's your decision."

Nugent said, "How do you feel about it, Jack?"

Campbell replied, "I don't want nothin' to do with it."

Nugent nodded and said, "Uh huh. Well, that's understandable. But, like Mr. Moren says, you've got to remember that any time you go to trial there's a chance you'll be found guilty. Admittedly, it doesn't look like much of a chance in this case, but the chance is always there. And, in your case, where you wrap up in about two years, it wouldn't cost you anything if you copped to a two-year concurrent bit."

"I know," Jackie replied. "But there's no case here. The fuckin' thing should be thrown out. I don't see how he can even take the stand without gettin' nailed for perjury."

Nugent said, "Again, I agree. But if I didn't point out the advantages of all of your options, I'd be derelict in the performance of my duties as your lawyer."

Al Caplan looked at me and said, "Stevie?"

I said, "Well, my case is different than theirs. I'll say this much. I'm not going to take it."

Moren said, "He's right. As little as they've got against you two, they've got even less on him. In fact, if you two accepted the offer, they'd probably drop the charges on him. That's how little they've got."

Nobody said anything for a minute. Then Keigney said, "I don't think they've got anything on any of us. I'm gonna fight it all the way."

Nugent turned to his client and said, "What about you, Jack? Are you sure?"

"Uh huh, I'm goin' all the way."

Nugent looked around the table for a few seconds. Nodding his head, said, "Okay then, that's settled. We're gonna pick twelve. Let's get to work."

I sat back feeling a combination of relief and disappointment. My instincts told me that the three of us would have no problem being found not guilty. Still, a small part of me was hoping that they'd take the offer. This case was the only thing standing between me and the street. If one of us were going to get a better offer, I was glad that it was me. While their decision had caused a momentary pang of disappointment, it was immediately replaced by a feeling of relief. Now we could get on with the trial, and I knew we'd win.

The bottom line was, Carden's story was the only evidence against any of us, and the state's own autopsy report clearly proved that he was lying. So, we each refused the offer.

Big mistake. Although Walpole in the 1970s reportedly had the highest murder rate of any prison in the country, it also had the lowest conviction rate, *none*! The Norfolk County DA's Office was being pilloried by the media for its inability to convict anyone. Between recently having been forced to throw in the towel on the highly publicized Walpole murder of the infamous "Boston Strangler," Albert DeSalvo, and the expectations created by the publicity that Delahunt had generated with the "Execution Squad" headlines and his midnight raid on Walpole, Delahunt just couldn't afford another loss. He needed a conviction.

nineteen

The trial began on November 14, 1977. Judge Francis Keating came out of the door to the right of the judge's bench and sat down. He had a round, red face. He looked like a malevolent pumpkin that had been placed on top of the long, flowing robes.

It started out with the disposal of certain motions that had not yet been addressed. (It quickly became apparent that, in this case, "addressed" was simply a synonym for denied.) Keating denied every significant defense motion.

Among the motions that Keating addressed, we requested a daily transcript of the testimony. Denied.

We asked for copies of any and all statements made by government witnesses. This motion was allowed, with the exception of withholding the testimony of Mr. Carden—*the only government witness who had made a statement.* Judge Keating said that we could see Carden's statements, *after the DA removed any material that he did not want us to see.*

We went through a few other motions. Keating denied most of the questions that we wanted asked of the jurors during voir dire. Voir dire is from the French, "to speak the truth." It is a procedure intended to eliminate jury bias, by asking questions of the prospective jurors. In most of the United States, a lawyer may conduct voir dire—not in Massachusetts. But you can request that the judge conduct the voir dire. We did. Keating wouldn't. We wanted him to question each of them individually as to their attitude(s) and possible bias toward prison inmates. We would have preferred not to be judged by jurors who hated prisoners. Understandably, many people do.

But the most important motion was a motion to allow the jury to view the scene of the murder. We wanted the jury to view the murder scene. The DA did not want the jury to view the murder scene. We knew that if the jury could view the murder scene, they would know that Carden was lying.

We pointed out that if this was a murder in a barroom, or in somebody's house, the jurors could identify with it, but this case had happened in a unique setting that none of the jurors had ever been in before and that the primary consideration as to whether or not a view ought to be allowed or denied should turn on one point: namely, whether or not it will substantially assist the jury in ways that could not be done by testimony from the witness stand.

Prescott made it clear that he did not want the jury to see the murder scene. Instead, he said that they would bring in Walpole deputy superintendent, Al Carr, with slides of the institution. He also expressed his concern that the jurors would be abused and intimidated by the inmates at Walpole.

Prescott's argument was so weak that Keating did not even want to discuss it. He said, "I will deny all three motions for view. I think whatever is necessary to be shown can be shown by slides and diagrams and by description from the stand."*

Al Caplan pointed out that a similar first-degree Walpole murder case had been tried in the same court just two months earlier, in which a view had been permitted, yet the Commonwealth had made no argument that would differentiate our case from that case, thereby denying me equal protection of the law and rendering Keating's denial of a jury view as a denial of my Constitutional rights.

Prescott had no comeback, so Keating responded, "I am denying the motions not so much for the reasons advanced by the district attorney about danger to the jurors, because I don't think that enters into it, or inconvenience to the jurors, because I think the only consideration here is that these men are on trial for first-degree murder and that they receive a fair trial."

Except, he then went on to say, "However, in my discretion, I deny the motions, because I feel that it can be depicted in other ways. I think an institution is particularly subject to diagrammatic drawing and descriptions."

That took Prescott off the hook.

Caplan took another shot. "May I make one more suggestion, Your Honor, which is that before denying the motion, the court first of all put Mr. Carr on the stand under oath and take a look at these pictures and give the defendants and counsel an opportunity to point out why these pictures that Mr. Prescott on his sole representation says are adequate may not be adequate, and then the Court could decide, rather than having to do it piecemeal at the time and arguing the matter each time it comes up."

Keating's reply was abrupt, in a voice laced with sarcasm. "The court thanks you for your suggestion, but I am not going to do it."

We asked if we could just view the pictures. Keating said that we could,

---

* All quotations in this trial are cited in the Trial Transcript (Tr.Tr.).

but that it would have to be done either on our lunch break or after four o'clock, but then said that I could not see them until Prescott presented them in the middle of the trial.

When Caplan introduced Judge Mazzone's order, that we were supposed to see the pictures in advance so we could have our objections prepared, Keating could not deal with it on a logical, legally responsible basis, i.e., he could not legalistically rationalize his unwillingness to honor Judge Mazzone's original order. So, he simply said, "I will deny whatever you are moving for and save your exception."

Attorney Moren pointed out that if a jury view was not allowed, we would have to rely on slides prepared by the Commonwealth. Therefore, the jury's only perception of the murder scene would be based on the Commonwealth's slides.

Al Nugent pointed out that where the DA's position is always "Save time, save time, save time," that a view of an hour and a half would be far less time-consuming than the time being taken in the preparation of photographs and all the time that would be taken in examining witnesses on the stand, with photographs and explanations, and that there was no way that photographs were going to show the real thing as well as a view.

He also pointed out that if this were a civil case, where just one side had a set of photographs, it clearly would not be allowed to be done that way and that it was patently unfair to do this in a criminal case.

Keating was obviously frustrated. The three lawyers had each made the point that the only fair and proper way to handle the situation was to allow the jury to view the murder scene. Everyone sitting in the courtroom knew it.

Keating had no proper response—only an improper one, the only one that counted.

He said, angrily, "If that is a motion, I am denying it. And that is the last time I am going to have that motion argued. I have denied it, and your rights are saved."

|||||||||||||||||||||||||||||||||||||||||||||||||||||||||||||||||||

ALAN REQUESTED THAT I be permitted to sit at the counsel table with him or that I at least be allowed to sit up closer to him than where they had me, so he might be able to consult with me.

Keating blew him off. "That is denied," which meant that there would be no one at the lawyer's table with any inside knowledge of what Walpole was really like. Whereas, the prosecutor was allowed to have Lieutenant Bergin, who was going to be a witness, and who was quite familiar with the settings in Walpole, sit with him.

Unintentionally, I'm sure, Keating had just peeked the prosecution's hole card. He had blatantly displayed his obvious bias. Before becoming a judge, Keating had been a prosecutor. Apparently, he still was.

twenty

We started off jury selection by asking that the jurors be brought in and questioned one at a time. Keating rejected our request. He said that he was going to bring them all in and question them together.

Al Nugent responded that if we proceeded in that manner, with the jurors responding to the court's questions in a group rather than individually, they would be responding with desired answers rather than truthful answers, and in the interest of justice, they should be brought in one at a time and in the absence of the other jurors.

Keating said, "That motion is denied."

Keating then proceeded to have one hundred potential jurors file into the courtroom. From the one hundred, he had sixteen of them take seats in the jury box. He asked the statutory questions and a few others, not the ones we wanted. He then declared the jury to be indifferent.

The prosecutor quickly agreed with him.

We spent the rest of the morning selecting and rejecting jurors. Al Caplan had to keep coming back and forth to discuss things with me.

After lunch, before the jurors were brought back in, Caplan made a request. "Your Honor, I don't mean to belabor the point, but when Mr. Doherty and the other defendants are placed physically where they are, the only way I can conceivably confer with them is to go outside the bar enclosure and all the way around, because I can't even lean over to confer with them privately."

"Again, I would ask if they could possibly be positioned at the bench in back of me here instead of inside the enclosure. I think it would then save the court's time and make things a little easier to confer with them. And I suggest this just to expedite things."

Keating said, "I am going to deny that request."

Keating was well aware that questions and issues were going to arise that would require inside knowledge of the prison, knowledge that we had, but that the lawyers did not have, knowledge that Bergin had, as he sat at the table with Prescott.

We continued with the jury selection.

At one point, Alan arose, saying, "May I have a moment Your Honor?"

As he turned and walked back to me, Keating said, "Yes. And let the record show that counsel for the defendant Doherty, Mr. Caplan, is discussing the selection of jurors with the defendant."

By the end of the day we had run out of potential jurors. Keating ordered that another fifty be brought in at nine am the next morning.

twenty-one

D ay two started with Al Caplan challenging the sixteen new potential jurors that had been called. The chief court officer, Mr. Lonergan, had come up with them by calling people who had been on past jury lists.

Alan found that nine of the sixteen were retired people and, of the remaining seven, six were either housewives or stay-at-home people. This was not a fair cross section of the population, which is required by law.

Alan suggested that Mr. Lonergan use a different, accepted method of recruiting jurors in order to have a better cross section.

Keating denied his motion.

Al Nugent attempted to call Mr. Lonergan and have him testify, under oath, as to where these new jurors were called from and the manner in which they were called.

Keating denied his request.

Al Caplan had had trials in Norfolk County in the previous couple of months. So, as the new jurors had been selected from old jury lists, he requested that Keating inquire of the jurors as to whether they had been on any cases in which he was involved. Two of them had already identified themselves as having sat on one of Alan's earlier cases—one of whom had been challenged by Alan, the other by Prescott.

Caplan finished his request by saying, "It seems only fair that I at least have that opportunity and knowledge that Mr. Prescott has and which may not be volunteered by people that were challenged."

Keating denied the request.

The jury selection continued. Keating would not allow us to challenge any of them for cause unless he absolutely had to do so. One woman admitted to knowing Lieutenant Bergin. Her husband had actually gone to high school with him.

Keating refused to discharge her.

After the jury was selected, Keating spoke to them. In the course of his monologue, he told them not to read any accounts of the trial in the newspapers, but if they should happen to hear something on the radio, or see something on the television, that they didn't have to leap up and shut it off.

Al Caplan made a motion to sequester the jury.

Keating denied it.

twenty-two

Prescott made his opening statement, outlining the impending testimony of his only witness, Carden. He also made it a point to tell them that Carden was scared of me. That he had always been scared of me. He also implied that I was much bigger than Carden. For the record, I've weighed about a hundred and forty-seven pounds since I was eighteen years old. Carden was actually bigger than me.

After Prescott was finished, Al Nugent made a motion for a mistrial.

Prior to the selection of the jury, a motion had been agreed upon by both sides and allowed by Keating that no potential witness, with the sole exception of Lieutenant Bergin, would be allowed into the courtroom until after they had testified. That way, their testimony could not be influenced by other witnesses' testimony or by Prescott's opening argument.

It turned out that four prosecution witnesses had been in the courtroom listening to Prescott's opening statement: Dennis Spicer, the medic who pronounced Perrotta dead; George Vose, the head of the internal investigation; CO Peter McGuire, who was the block officer on the night of the murder; and Captain Al Carr, who was going to be their resident expert on Walpole, interpreting the slides and thereby avoiding a jury view.

Keating immediately denied the motion. Then, after denying it, he "questioned" Prescott by saying, "I assume you didn't know they were there."

Prescott quickly agreed with Keating, saying, "I certainly did not know they were here. I still don't know that they were here, and I am still not assuming that they were here throughout the opening either. I didn't see them till I got up and turned around and saw my brothers."

When Al Nugent tried to go into it, Keating wouldn't let him. He cut him off, telling him that they'd deal with it the next day.

twenty-three

ay three began with a side-bar conference supposedly to deal with the matters left over from the day before.

The first item was Nugent's motion for a mistrial. Prescott admitted that the witnesses had been present in the courtroom when he gave his opening argument.

Keating's response was, "What else do you have?"

Caplan said that, in response to our discovery motions, the Commonwealth claimed that Mr. Carden made no false reports of criminal activity on the part of other people that the Commonwealth knew about. He asked that the Court further examine that portion of the transcript of Carden's statements that had to do with the death of James Aloise and, more particularly, whether Carden suggested that one Michael Donahue had anything to do with that death; because in a disciplinary hearing at Walpole whereby Mr. Donahue was charged with the murder of Mr. Aloise, after Carden started talking to the state police, it turned out that Donahue was exonerated, because he was on a visit at the time of Aloise's death.

Keating said he'd look it over and asked what else we had.

Caplan requested the tape of the disciplinary hearing inside Walpole whereby we were found guilty of the Perrotta murder, in which George Vose, a deputy superintendent at Walpole, who was the reporting officer in that hearing, said that he had either seen or received a report by the state police that said the medical examiner stated that the time of death of Mr. Perrotta was two hours after ingestion of food.

Prescott's response was that, "There is no such report."

So, Keating said, "Mr. Prescott says there is no such report. Let's get started."

That ended the bench conference.

There was nothing on the motion for a mistrial that had been pending since the day before, even though Prescott was forced to admit that his witnesses had been present during his opening argument.

There was nothing on the documentation that Carden had falsely accused Mickey Donahue of murder at the same time that he accused us, just Prescott lying in open court again.

There was nothing on the medical report that the investigating officer, Deputy Vose, had admitted seeing that proved that Carden was lying. All that Prescott had to say was, "There is no such report."

As far as Keating was concerned, that ended that.

|||||||||||||||||||||||||||||||||||||||||||||||||||||||||||||||||||||

DEPUTY SUPERINTENDENT AL Carr was the first prosecution witness. One of his functions was to be their Walpole resident expert by showing slides of Walpole to the jury and explain what they were seeing, as opposed to allowing the jury to go to Walpole and see for themselves.

As they were setting the slides up, we renewed our motion for a jury view. Keating denied the motion.

Carr described the first slide as "the entrance to MCI Walpole." Actually, it was the parking lot outside of Walpole.

The next slide was the outside door going from the parking lot into the administration building outside of the prison.

The third slide was an angled shot from outside into the visiting room.

Number four was a shot of "no-man's land," which is the area between the inside of the wall and a hurricane fence.

The next one was an outside picture of blocks A-1, A-2, and part of the hospital.

The sixth one was an outside picture of the tower over the entrance.

The next one was from the control room down the corridor aiming toward the A section.

The eighth shot was similar to the seventh; just a shot of the hallway, only a little closer.

The next one was also a shot of the corridor, just closer.

Those were the first nine slides. Not one of them had anything to do with the murder scene.

The next nine slides were of "A" section blocks. One of the "A" block slides was so dark that Carr admitted that it was not a familiar site.

Under cross-examination, Al Caplan went through the first nine, the irrelevant ones. Then, he started questioning Carr on the last nine.

On the first one, Carr admitted that he couldn't see it that good but that maybe it was A-1.

Next slide.
CAPLAN: "Which block is it?"
CARR: "That I cannot say."
Next slide.
CAPLAN: "And what block is that?"
CARR: "I can't identify the block."
Next slide.
CAPLAN: "What block is that Mr. Carr?"
CARR: "I can't identify it."
Next slide.
CAPLAN: "This is a view of which block, if you know, Mr. Carr?"
CARR: "I am not sure."
Next slide.
CAPLAN: "What is that a picture of?"
CARR: "That is a block in the A section."
CAPLAN: "Do you know which block it is?"
CARR: "I cannot identify it."
CAPLAN: "Do you know where the picture was taken from?"
CARR: "I have no knowledge, no."
CAPLAN: "By looking at it, Mr. Carr, could you give us any idea of where it was taken from?"
CARR: "I can't describe it. It is hard to describe."
CAPLAN: "Too dark?"
CARR: "It is too dark."
Next slide.
CAPLAN: "What cell block is that?"
CARR: "I am not sure. I don't know."
Next slide.
CAPLAN: "What cell block is that?"
CARR: "I can't identify that."
Next slide.
CAPLAN: "Again, this is an inside view of one of the minimum blocks, but you don't know which one?"
CARR: "I do not."

Al Carr—whose expertise regarding Walpole was the justification that Keating had used to deny us the right to have the jury view the murder scene—was unable to identify even one of the "A" block slides as to just which block it was.

During cross-examination, Caplan attempted to question Carr about door pegs. This was quite relevant, as Carden was claiming that Perrotta had had his door pegged on the night that he was murdered.

CAPLAN: "the cell doors in the A section are set up so they cannot be locked from the inside, is that correct? They are only locked from the outside, is that correct?"

CARR: "With a key, yes."

CAPLAN: "However, Mr. Carr, again based on your twenty years at Walpole, have you ever seen situations where inmates fashion devices for locking doors from the inside of the cells?"

CARR: "Yes."

CAPLAN: "They call them pegs?"

CARR: "Yes."

CAPLAN: "And this type of thing is called pegging the door, is that correct?"

CARR: "Yes."

CAPLAN: "And there are various kinds of pegs, is that correct?"

CARR: "Yes."

CAPLAN: "And can you describe for the jury the various kinds of pegs that are used?"

KEATING: "No, Mr. Caplan, I am not going to allow that."

CAPLAN: "May we approach the bench?"

KEATING: "No. You can take your exception to my ruling. We are not going into the various types of pegs. There may be 3,000. We are not going into it."

CAPLAN: "I believe that the Commonwealth—may we approach the bench?"

KEATING: "Not at this time. Let's go on. If it becomes important later on…"

CAPLAN: "May I reserve the right to have Mr. Carr available should it become necessary to go into this subject?"

KEATING: "I will not keep him available. Next question."

CAPLAN: "If a door is pegged, Mr. Carr, with a good peg, is it possible to open it from the outside?"

PRESCOTT: "Objection."

KEATING: "Excluded."

CAPLAN: "May I make an offer of proof as to the relevance of the question?"

KEATING: "Not at this time. You are asking him generally if a peg can keep a door locked."

CAPLAN: "If Your Honor please, Mr. Carr has been offered by the Commonwealth as an expert on the running of Walpole, the activities within the institution, and with his twenty years as a correction officer and as an administrator and supervisor at MCI Walpole, I would suggest that within the legitimate limits of cross-examination, we be allowed to inquire further into these areas."

KEATING: "I have excluded it. Next question."

And that ended that. Their expert was not only unable to identify even one single cell block, he was also protected from having to answer questions that would hurt the prosecution's case.

twenty-four

Their next witness was Peter McGuire. He had been the block officer on the night of the murder. McGuire testified that, when he took the five pm count, Perrotta was in his bed sleeping.

Countless times during the trial, there were instances where I wanted to clarify a prosecution witness's testimony to Alan. Unfortunately, because Keating would not allow me to sit anywhere near him, I was unable to do it. I was seated about ten to fifteen feet behind him on the other side of a railing, with guards and court officers lined up behind us so the jury would know how evil we were.

At one point, during McGuire's testimony, he was describing how Perrotta had been called for a visit on the night of the murder.

PRESCOTT: "Now, sometime during that evening, specifically, sometime after 7 o'clock and before 7:30, did you have occasion to receive a call with respect to a visitor for inmate Robert Perrotta?"

McGUIRE: "Yes. I did. At 7:20, I received a call notifying me that Robert Perrotta had a visit."

PRESCOTT: "And in consequence of this call, what if anything did you do?"

McGUIRE: "I notified Robert Perrotta in the regular manner that we notify inmates that they have a visit. The manner is actually just a loud shout. You shout for the person. You shout their name and, usually, but not always, they respond. They come out to the tier, and they ask you what you want and you tell them that they have a visit. I shouted several times, and then I yelled up that he had a visit."

PRESCOTT: "Well, sir, when you say you yelled up and yelled out that he had a visitor, can you tell us just where room 62 or cell 62 is with respect to your position?"

McGUIRE: "My position in the block was on the flats. His room is on the third tier, and it is down to the left on the left side. It is the second or third room on the third tier on the left side of the block."

PRESCOTT: "Approximately how far away from you would that be, Mr. McGuire, if you know?"

McGUIRE: "From where I was standing to the railing outside Mr. Perrotta's room is thirty-eight feet."

Alan, who was sitting sideways at the end of his table, turned his head toward me and raised an eyebrow in a questioning manner, as if to say, "Does that sound right?"

Judge Keating in a clearly acrimonious tone, cut in on the questioning. Loudly, he snapped at Alan, "*If you have any puzzlement, Mr. Caplan, I would appreciate it not being reflected on your face as you look at your client.*"

Alan, in a voice filled with incredulity at Keating's open animosity, responded, "If Your Honor please, I looked at my client, as I think I have a right to do, but I …"

Keating, physically leaning forward across his bench, his ill will plainly evident, interrupted Alan, "*I am interpreting your expression. I do not appreciate it.*"

Then, turning back to Prescott, with a wave of his hand, he said, "Go ahead."

I believe that that was the very first time that I came to the conclusion that Keating was a drunk. Up to that point, I had sensed that something was amiss. Long before the end of the trial, it was apparent to me, and to the others, that Keating was hung over (and cranky) every morning and half stiff (and sarcastically nasty) every afternoon.

McGuire, went on to testify that Perrotta did not respond to the 7:20 visit call, but that he didn't take it as being unusual. When he received a second visit call for Perrotta, at 7:30, McGuire went and called him again. When Perrotta still didn't answer, an inmate that was walking down the tier went into the room, came out of the room, and said that he wasn't in the room. McGuire said that he could not identify the inmate.

He testified that Carden returned to the block one to two minutes after 7:30 and that he was walking fast and appeared anxious.

Later on, during cross-examination, Keating's bias peeked through again.

As a result of the poor visibility of the slides being caused, at least in part, by the darkness in the cell block, McGuire testified that there were a number of lights on the top two tiers that had either been smashed or were just out and that they had been that way for some time before the night of the murder.

CAPLAN: "Now, Mr. McGuire, this is a photograph or a slide of cell block A-2?"

McGUIRE: "Yes."

CAPLAN: "And it is slide no. 19 in a series that has been shown?"

Keating cut in sarcastically, "Do you agree Mr. McGuire? Are you testifying Mr. Caplan? Do you agree? Is that A-2?"

CAPLAN: "Does this appear to be a minimum section block?"

McGUIRE: "This is a minimum section cell block."

CAPLAN: "And does it appear to show the second and third tiers of that minimum section cell block?"

McGUIRE: "Yes."

CAPLAN: "And does it show lights on the left-hand side underneath or at the top and lights underneath the top tier? Does that slide show that?"

McGUIRE: "Yes."

CAPLAN: "Were those the lights that had been largely smashed that night when you came on duty in A-2?"

KEATING: (Again, derisively) "Were those the lights that had been largely smashed? *Come on, Mr. Caplan.* You ask him what lights were on."

CAPLAN: "Which of those lights were on, Mr. McGuire, were on that night, if you recall?"

McGUIRE: "I couldn't point out the exact lights that were on that night."

CAPLAN: "Were there very few lights on that night?"

KEATING: "Change 'very few.'"

CAPLAN: "How many lights were on that night?"

McGUIRE: "I couldn't tell you. I didn't count them."

CAPLAN: "Was there more than one?"

McGUIRE: "Yes."

CAPLAN: "Were all of the lights on?"

McGUIRE: "No."

CAPLAN: "Could you estimate a percentage of the lights that were on?"

Keating immediately cut in. "No, I am not going to have the jury have evidence of estimates of percentages. I think we can be a little more exact than that."

CAPLAN: "Mr. McGuire, have you any estimate of how many lights were smashed on the second tier?"

And here came Keating, again. "Excluded. I am not allowing the jury to hear estimates."

CAPLAN: "Mr. McGuire, searching your recollection, do you know how many lights were on in the second tier that night?"

McGUIRE: "No."

CAPLAN: "Do you know how many lights were on in the third tier that night?

McGUIRE: "No."

CAPLAN: "Were lights out on the third tier?"

Keating immediately jumped in. "You had that. He said yes; there were lights out."

Shaking his head in obvious frustration, Caplan turned away and walked back to the table, saying, "My exception, please, to the court's failure to allow further questions as to how many lights were on or out."

This type of behavior went on throughout the entire trial. If one of the lawyers got into a good rhythm, Keating would throw him off of the track.

One time, when Caplan was questioning McGuire about the mechanics of taking a count, he asked him a legitimate question.

"And when you say you see flesh, you mean literally that, if you can see any part of the person's flesh, then you know that it is not a bundle of clothes or something under a blanket?"

Keating interrupted, asking him snidely, "Mr. Caplan, is that a question?"

Caplan replied, "Yes, Your Honor."

Keating would not be dissuaded. He said, "I am not going to take narrations from you or summaries. You will ask questions."

Under further cross-examination, it came out that when McGuire was making the five o'clock count, Perrotta was in the same position in which he was found dead at 7:30.

It also came out that, contrary to McGuire's initial testimony that he could not identify the inmate who had been walking along the tier at 7:30 and had gone into Perrotta's cell and come out to tell him that Perrotta was not there, McGuire had, in fact, already identified that person as inmate Joseph Yandle.

At the end of the day, we renewed our motion for a view in light of the district attorney's telling McGuire to go back and check distances in the cell block and to come back the next day.

We objected and Usher Moren got up saying, "I renew my motion for a view in light of the district attorney's statement. The jury should be able to see for themselves."

Keating ignored our request for a view. He simply said, "I will let the remark stand. You can go to work right now, officer."

twenty-five

D ay four started with Officer McGuire being called back to the stand
by Prescott who questioned him on the distance into the block
from the doorway to the front stairwell on the right-hand side of
the block and the length of the overhang above the doorway.

McGuire testified that the stairwell was approximately fourteen feet
from the doorway and that the overhang over the entrance into the block was
nine feet, seven inches.

Under cross-examination, it came that there was a second overhang,
along the right side of the block over the stairwell that was five feet, seven
inches wide and that for McGuire to see Perrotta's room from the stairwell,
he had to stand four feet out from the stairwell.

Caplan also attempted to clarify just how many other inmates were in
the block at the time that Carden claimed that Perrotta had been murdered.
The day before, McGuire had testified that besides Campbell, Keigney and I,
twenty-five other inmates had not left the block on the night of the murder.

After reviewing the block logs, it turned out that a number of the inmates who had left the block had returned before seven o'clock. Caplan
handed McGuire the block log and asked him to review it and tell the jury
how many of those inmates had returned to the block before seven. Before
McGuire could answer, Keating cut in and refused to allow him to answer
the question.

twenty-six

The next witness was Dennis Spicer, the medic who had been first called to the murder scene.

Spicer testified that he was called to the block at 7:40. He also testified that Perrotta was covered with either a sheet or a blanket.

Prescott wanted to show the jury the pictures of Perrotta lying dead with his penis sticking out of his mouth.

We objected on the grounds that the pictures were inflammatory and had no evidentiary value that would override the obvious prejudicial nature of the pictures.

Keating said that he was going to allow the jury to view the pictures, because Spicer had originally thought that it was his tongue.

Al Nugent responded that we would stipulate that it was his penis.

Nice try. There was no way that Keating wasn't going to make sure that the jury saw those pictures. Ironically, I never got to see them.

||||||||||||||||||||||||||||||||||||||||||||||||||||||||||||||||||||

AT THE MORNING recess, there was a conference held in the judge's lobby. The issue under discussion was the defense attorneys' wish to interview Carden alone.

During the recess, Prescott, Bergin, a court clerk named Mr. Sheehan, and the three attorneys had gone downstairs to the state police office where Carden was being held. It came out that either Prescott, Bergin, or one of the transportation officers had told Carden that he did not have to talk to the lawyers. So he chose not to.

Caplan made a motion that Carden be brought to the witness stand and placed under oath, outside of the presence of the jury, and informed by the court that defense counsel have a right to consult with him outside of the presence of any other people behind closed doors.

Keating denied the motion and turned to the court officer, Mr. Sheehan, asking him, "And what do you say, Mr. Sheehan. You were there."

Sheehan answered, "Initially, Your Honor, Mr. Prescott and the three attorneys and Detective Bergin and myself went into the room. At the request of counsel, Mr. Prescott, Detective Bergin, and myself left. They also requested the transportation officer to leave, but he explained he had to keep the fellow in his sight; so he left the room but stayed in the doorway where he had all parties under observation. The transportation officer was about twelve feet away from all parties."

Caplan asked, "And do you remember my also asking that the door be closed?"

Sheehan replied, "Yes, you did."

At which point, Keating said, "Mr. Caplan, are you psychologically able to let somebody else talk without an interruption or an addition?"

A remark that is almost grotesquely humorous in light of Keating's constant interruptions and badgering of the defense attorneys, throughout the trial, especially Caplan.

twenty-seven

Their next witness—really their only witness—was Carden.

Prescott started off by having Carden describe his relationship with Perrotta; that they were brothers-in-laws, as Perrotta had been married to Carden's sister. He then had him identify Campbell, Keigney, and me.

As soon as that was done, Prescott immediately guided Carden to the Thanksgiving Day meal on the day of the murder.

PRESCOTT: "Do you recall Mr. Carden, what the fare was, what the meal was on Thanksgiving Day of last year?"

CARDEN: "Yes."

PRESCOTT: "Will you tell us, please?"

CARDEN: "They had portions already made out."

PRESCOTT: "What was it?"

CARDEN: "Turkey with stuffing, peas, and mashed potatoes. As a matter of fact, one of the officers commented it was one of the worst Thanksgiving dinners he had seen in a few years."

PRESCOTT: "Did you have occasion to make observation as to whether Mr. Perrotta actually ate his meal?"

CARDEN: "Oh, yes, yes."

PRESCOTT: "And did you have—your answer is yes?"

CARDEN: "Oh, yes, sir."

PRESCOTT: "Did you have occasion to observe whether or not Mr. Perrotta ate the meals of any other inmates?"

CARDEN: "Mr. Perrotta had a very large appetite. He ate his meal, and since the Thanksgiving meal wasn't that good, somebody on the table—I don't recollect who it was—said they weren't going to eat it and gave it to him. And Bobby made a couple of sandwiches, very thick sandwiches, with the turkey and stuffing and mashed potatoes. And I think he threw some peas in too. I'm not exactly sure."

PRESCOTT: "Do you have a recollection as to whether or not you made observations as to what he did with this sandwich, if that is what you call it?"

CARDEN: "Well, we take napkins out of the officer's desk and..."

NUGENT: "I pray Your Honor's judgment."
KEATING: "What did he do?"
PRESCOTT: "What did you see him do if anything?"
CARDEN: "He wrapped the sandwich up and concealed it inside his bathrobe or his coat."
PRESCOTT: "And what did he do then?"
CARDEN: "Well, he put it in his coat when he finished eating and left."

This was the first time that we had heard anything about any sandwiches being brought back from the chow hall. The prosecution had just ambushed us by having Carden change his story. His new claim, that Perrotta had brought two sandwiches back from the noon meal, created the implication that Perrotta must have eaten the alleged sandwiches sometime later in the day, thereby moving the time of death back to conform with his otherwise patently false story.

It also explained why they went forward with the trial after we refused their offer to let us plead in to a lesser charge in exchange for no more time. At that point, the autopsy report had exposed Carden's story for the canard that it was. So, they came up with this "sandwich story." If they could convince the jury that Bobby had brought sandwiches back from the noon-time meal, it could change the time of death.

He went on to testify that he and Bobby had been in his room, cell forty on the second tier, between three-thirty and four o'clock on the afternoon of the murder. That somebody had called Bobby out of the room. That Bobby returned three or four minutes later to pick up some rolling papers and left again. That Bobby was very nervous and very scared. That he (Carden) left his room about two minutes after Bobby, proceeded to the back of the block, and went up the rear stairs to the third tier, which is where they brought me into the picture.

PRESCOTT: "And upon climbing these back stairs to the third tier, did you have occasion to meet anybody?"
CARDEN: "Yes. I did."
PRESCOTT: "And who did you meet?"
CARDEN: "Stephen Doherty."
PRESCOTT: "And did you know Stephen Doherty well at that time?"
CARDEN: "I knew of him."
PRESCOTT: "Was Stephen Doherty a friend of yours at that time?"
CARDEN: "No, sir."

PRESCOTT: "Had you had prior conversations with Stephen Doherty?"

NUGENT: "I object, because Mr. Prescott is leading, and he has been leading all day. I know it may save some time but I think…"

KEATING: "I disagree he has been leading all day, but he is leading now."

NUGENT: "I mean with this witness, judge."

KEATING: "You may have whether or not he had been friends with Doherty before this time."

PRESCOTT: "Thank you."

PRESCOTT: "Whether or not you were friends with Stephen Doherty at that time?"

CARDEN: "No, I was not friends with Stephen Doherty."

PRESCOTT: "Mr. Carden, can you tell us where you stood and where Mr. Doherty when you met him?"

CARDEN: "He stood right in front of me on the third tier landing."

PRESCOTT: "And would you otherwise describe this meeting with Mr. Doherty? Tell the court and jury just what happened."

CARDEN: "Well, I got to the third tier, and I was proceeding down to Bobby's room and Stephen Doherty stopped me by putting his hand on my shoulder. He started a conversation and wanted to know if I wanted to buy some grass or something like that. He sort of held me up for a while, and he was talking in a very loud voice. And then, approximately three or four minutes went by, and he seen me looking down towards Bobby's room."

MOREN: "I move what somebody else saw him do be stricken."

KEATING: "You can't tell us what he saw."

KEATING: "The jury will disregard 'he saw me.'"

PRESCOTT: "Mr. Carden, while you were so listening to Mr. Doherty, where if anywhere were you looking at that time?"

CARDEN: "I was looking at Bobby's room, Bobby Perrotta's room."

PRESCOTT: "And can you describe the position of Mr. Doherty with respect to you?"

CARDEN: "Yes sir. He was right in front of me."

PRESCOTT: "Right in front of you?"

CARDEN: "Yes."

PRESCOTT; "Did you make any effort to get by him?"

CARDEN: "Yes sir, I did."

PRESCOTT: "What effort did you make?"

CARDEN: "I tried to pass him, but he kept his hand on my shoulder."

PRESCOTT: "Did you have occasion to see Mr. Doherty turn away from you at any time?"

CARDEN: "Yes, I did."

PRESCOTT: "And what happened then?"

CARDEN: "That is when Bobby's door opened."

PRSCOTT: "And what did you observe?"

CARDEN: "I seen Arthur Keigney walk out, and then I seen Bobby Perrotta walk out, and then I seen Jackie Campbell walk out."

PRESCOTT: "And what about Doherty? Did he do anything at that point?"

CARDEN: "He immediately stopped the conversation and let me proceed."

He said that he went down to Bobby's room, but that they didn't talk; they just stood outside the cell, leaning on the railing.

PRESCOTT: "Do you recall and can you tell us just how Bobby appeared to you, this longtime friend of yours, at that time?"

NUGENT: "I object."

MOREN: "I object."

NUGENT: "May we approach the bench?"

KEATING: "I will let him have it and save everybody's exception."

Then, turning to Carden, Keating asked him, "How did he look to you?"

Carden replied, "Very scared, very nervous."

At which point, Moren asked that it be stricken.

So Keating told the jury, "You will disregard 'scared.'"

Keating pulled that maneuver numerous times throughout the trial. Prescott would ask a question that was obviously out of line. The defense lawyers would object. Keating would overrule their objections and allow Carden to answer. Carden would give an improper response. Then Keating would tell the jury to disregard the answer.

And we could all pretend that they didn't hear it.

By this point, it was obvious to anyone who knew what a Walpole cell block looked like, just how farfetched Carden's story was. For one thing, the thrust of his five o'clock story was that I was acting as a peek man to warn Campbell and Keigney that Carden was coming, by talking loudly.

The only problem with that is, the area where Carden claimed that I stopped him, and did this loud talking, was about eighty feet away from Perrotta's cell.

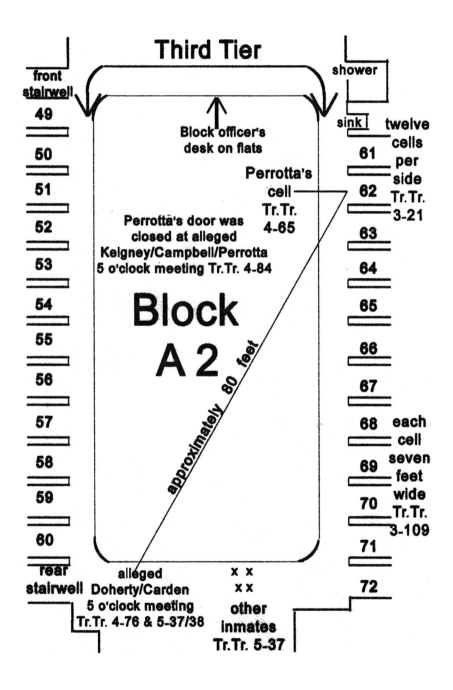

Third Tier

front
stairwell

49

50

51

52

53

54

55

56

57

58

59

60

rear
stairwell

Block officer's
desk on flats

Perrotta's door was
closed at alleged
Keigney/Campbell/Perrotta
5 o'clock meeting Tr.Tr. 4-84

Block
A 2

approximately 80 feet

alleged
Doherty/Carden
5 o'clock meeting
Tr.Tr. 4-76 & 5-37/38

Perrotta's
cell
Tr.Tr.
4-65

x x
x x
other
inmates
Tr.Tr. 5-37

shower

sink   twelve
cells
61   per
side
62   Tr.Tr.
3-21

63

64

65

66

67

68   each
cell
69   seven
feet
70   wide
Tr.Tr.
3-109
71

72

So, what Carden was actually saying was that I was giving this warning by offering to sell him marijuana, for three or four minutes, *in a voice loud enough to be heard by someone behind a closed solid steel door some eighty feet away with a guard sitting right there at his desk, in an open cell block.*

He also said that I had my back to Perrotta's cell while I was doing all this yelling. So that means that I had to be yelling in the opposite direction.

This would have been crystal clear to the jury if they'd been allowed to view the scene of the murder, and Prescott and Keating both knew that. (See diagram of Block A-2, page 103.)

Carden went on to testify that when the doors opened at six o'clock, after the count, he went straight to Bobby's room. That he looked into Bobby's room and saw him lying in bed wearing his headphones. That he then went out of the block, over to block A-3, for ten or fifteen minutes. That, upon returning to A-2, he went to his room. That he then went back up to Bobby's room.

PRESCOTT: "And can you tell us what you did if anything at Bobby's room?"

CARDEN: "Well, I rapped on his door."

PRESCOTT: "Keep your voice up."

CARDEN: "He had the headphones on, so I rapped quite a few times."

PRESCOTT: "Keep your voice up."

CARDEN: "He had his headphones on; so I rapped a few times, and he finally got up and opened the door and let me in."

PRESCOTT: "When you say he finally opened the door, did you try to open it yourself?"

CARDEN: "Yes."

PRESCOTT: "What was the result of that?"

CARDEN: "It was locked."

PRESCOTT: "When you say it was locked, do you know where it was locked from?"

CARDEN: "Yes. It is a homemade; they call them door pegs. It is a homemade thing that you can lock your door with."

PRESCOTT: "From the inside?"

CARDEN: "Yes, from the inside."

He said that he spent about ten or twelve minutes with Bobby and that Bobby gave him two bags of marijuana to bet on a football game He said that he left Bobby's room and went to Tom McInerney's room, that McInerney was a friend who lived on the third tier, and that he spent seven or eight minutes with McInerney. That he then went over to block A-3 to place a bet on a football game with the bookie, leaving McInerney standing out on the third tier.

That he was in A-3 between ten and fifteen minutes when he heard somebody yell, "Perrotta visit" about 7:20, 7:25. He said that when he heard the call again, he headed back to block A-2 and that, when he went into A-2, he looked up and saw me leaning over the tier in front of Bobby Perrotta's room. He said that he started up the stairs, and when he got to the second tier, he looked up and saw me walking down toward the back of the block and Arthur Keigney and Jackie Campbell walking out of Bobby's room.

He said he went up to Bobby's room and found his body and called the guard.

twenty-eight

Al Nugent started the cross-examination. It came out that during at least three of Carden's earlier interviews with Bergin and Prescott, there had been a stenographer present. At that point, Nugent requested a conference at the bench.

The conference went as follows:

NUGENT: "The witness has testified that while he was at Bridgewater, he was interviewed."

KEATING: "Yes."

NUGENT: "And that there was a stenographer there on that occasion. We are aware of the Salem Jail occasion and the Norfolk occasion. We do not have the transcript of any interview with this witness at Bridgewater. We have the one at the Salem Jail, where he is now, and I take it, the other one took place at Norfolk."

PRESCOTT: "Yes."

NUGENT: "I am now making a demand pursuant to the motion that was allowed that Mr. Prescott furnish us at this time with the transcript or the notes, if he made them himself, of that Bridgewater confrontation and interview. I would ask to suspend with this witness until that time."

KEATING: "What do you say, Mr. Prescott?"

PRESCOTT: "The witness is mistaken. There was no stenographer. A stenographer came down with us to Bridgewater, but we never used her."

"And very frankly, I have no recollection of seeing this kid down at Bridgewater. We saw other people down there."

KEATING: "Why would you bring a stenographer down and not use her?"

PRESCOTT: "We didn't get to talk to those people."

KEATING: "You didn't get to talk to him?"

PRESCOTT: "I don't even recall seeing him down there at all. I know there were other people down there that we intended to interview, but we got no conversation from them. It was a wasted trip."

KEATING: "I would assume on Mr. Prescott's representation that you are going to have to wait until Lieutenant Bergin gets on."

PRESCOTT: "I will be seeing him this afternoon, but I am sure he didn't take a transcribed statement."

MOREN: "I move we suspend and have a voir dire on this issue alone and determine it now."

KEATING: "I will do that."

|||||||||||||||||||||||||||||||||||||||||||||||||||||||||||||

WHEN BERGIN TOOK the witness stand, Al Nugent began by asking him just how many times he had interviewed Carden. We had just discovered that there was at least one more transcript of whose existence we had not been informed. Who knew how many others there were?

NUGENT: "Now, could you tell us, sir, from memory, first, how many different occasions did you interview Thomas Carden?"

BERGIN: "I wouldn't be able to give you an accurate account of that."

NUGENT: "Well, wouldn't there be some documentary statement or record somewhere that would show when you went to interview Carden and where?"

BERGIN: "Not in my records."

Bergin kept his responses vague. Moreover, Prescott and Keating immediately began disrupting the questioning. Where Bergin had not been in the courtroom when Carden had accidentally spilt the beans about there being at least one more transcript of his earliest statements, he was unaware of just what we were trying to find out. After one of Prescott's objection interruptions, Keating jumped in to help him.

KEATING: "Isn't there just one issue here?"

NUGENT: "We are getting to it if Mr. Prescott will let me continue."

KEATING: "You certainly are getting to it slowly."

Then, turning to Bergin, "Are you aware of any transcripts taken of Mr. Carden's testimony?"

BERGIN: "Transcripts?"

KEATING: "Yes, transcripts, which were transcribed of an interview when a stenographer was present."

Keating had just let him know what we were looking for.

At one point, Nugent asked him how many times he had interviewed Carden and, once again, Prescott objected and the following exchange took place.

NUGENT: "This is why we are here."

PRESCOTT: "We have a simple issue."

KEATING: "The issue is a simple one, and I assume Lieutenant Bergin is going to be subjected to cross-examination later. I suspended the trial of this case at the request of Mr. Moren for the purpose of finding out if there are more transcripts than were given to the defense. That is the issue. Let's get to it."

NUGENT: "If I just ask him the blanket question, he is just going to say, 'I don't remember,' and I am trying to refresh his memory at this point so ..."

KEATING: "It seems to me you can get to it much quicker."

"Now, when the district attorney makes a representation to counsel that he has two transcripts and is not aware of any other transcript, in the absence of you offering some proof of another transcript, I am ready to call the jury back at this time."

NUGENT: "For the record, I object and take exception to the court's comments, because now the witness knows exactly what the answer ought to be if he is in doubt."

And that was that. Keating had just told Bergin what he needed to know.

At most, he now only had to admit to knowing of two transcripts of interviews with Carden. Without him, we couldn't prove that there were any more, even though Carden had inadvertently released the information about there being a stenographer with them when they interviewed him at Bridge-water. Bergin was well aware of how important the transcripts were. We had already caught Carden in numerous contradictions of his earlier statements.

From that point on, Bergin blithely blew off all questions. No matter what Nugent asked him, the essence of his response would be as follows.

"To the best of my knowledge."

"I do not have a good memory of that."

"I don't recall."

Then he slipped up.

NUGENT: "When you were in the Foxboro State Police Barracks, was there a stenographer present at that time?"

BERGIN: "I don't think there was."

NUGENT: "And when you interviewed Carden at Walpole, was there a stenographer present at that time?"

BERGIN: "During the interview, no."

NUGENT: "Okay. Now, with respect to the interview at Walpole, did you make any notes of that?"

BERGIN: "Yes, I did."

Prescott leaped to his feet, shouting, "Objection."

Bergin had just opened the gate to another whole issue. Not only were they hiding the transcript of the Bridgewater interview, they were also hiding Bergin's written summary of Carden's statements.

In response to Prescott, Keating just looked at him and said, "He said yes."

NUGENT: "And you have preserved those notes?"

BERGIN: "I reduced them to a report."

NUGENT: "And have you furnished that report to Mr. Prescott or the district attorney's office?"

BERGIN: "Yes, I have."

NUGENT: "When did you do that?"

BERGIN: "Maybe a week after that. I don't know. I would have to look at the date on the report."

NUGENT: "Maybe a week after?"

BERGIN: "Maybe."

Keating stepped in. "That is the end of that."

Then, turning to Bergin, "Did you ever go to Bridgewater and interview Carden there?"

NUGENT: "That was my next question."

BERGIN: "I have been down to Bridgewater on many occasions Your Honor, and I don't recall whether it was to interview Carden or some other inmate."

KEATING: "Do you recall being there with either Gail Parrish, who took one transcript, or any other court reporter or stenographer?"

BERGIN: "I couldn't answer that."

NUGENT: "You say you couldn't answer, meaning you can't remember?"

BERGIN: "No. I have been with Miss Parrish on many occasions, and I can't recall if this was one of the times or not."

KEATING: "Well, was any court reporter present? I don't limit it to her. Do you recall being in Walpole and taking a court reporter with you?"

BERGIN: "I recall her at Walpole, but I do not recall her taking any statement."

KEATING: "I am going to let Lieutenant Bergin step down."

NUGENT: "I have one other question as to Norfolk. Do you recall interviewing Carden at Norfolk?"

BERGIN: "I don't recall."

||||||||||||||||||||||||||||||||||||||||||||||||||||||||||||||||||||||||

EVEN THOUGH HE stopped Al Nugent, he had to let Moren and Caplan ask their questions.

MOREN: "On occasions when there was no stenographer there, would you then take notes yourself?"

PRESCOTT: "Objection."

KEATING: "What is the point of that question, Mr. Moren? The issue here is whether or not there is a missing transcript. I can't see whether he took notes in the absence of a stenographer has any import in this case."

MOREN: "Thank you, Your Honor."

KEATING: "All right."

CAPLAN: "Just a minute, if I may."

KEATING: "It is going to be exactly one minute."

NUGENT: "Just a couple of questions." "Lieutenant, would your records of transportation going from point A to point B and keeping track of your mileage refresh your recollection as to where you may have been on a certain day?"

BERGIN: "No, sir."

NUGENT: "That would not?"

BERGIN: "I don't keep those kind of records."

NUGENT: "So from sometime in November of 1976 up to the present time while you were in charge of the investigation of a homicide that took place in Walpole at that time, you have absolutely no records of where you went and who you talked to, is that what you are telling us? You just have a vague memory of it, is that it?"

KEATING: "I won't allow him to answer that question. It is a pretty vague question."

NUGENT: "And you submitted a report, sir, to the district attorney's office?"

BERGIN: "Yes, I did."

Again, Prescott leaped to his feet, shouting, "Objection!"

His fear of Bergin's hitherto hidden report coming out was so obvious that Keating said, "Don't get excited, Mr. Prescott."

Moren said, "I have a motion to make, Your Honor. I move that we be furnished with a copy of the lieutenant's report. A motion for statements of Commonwealth witnesses was allowed as to written statements and as to oral statements, which were reduced to writing."

KEATING: "Do you have that, Mr. Prescott, the statement of Lieutenant Bergin?"

PRESCOTT: "I have Lieutenant Bergin's summary of his investigation to his superior officer."

KEATING: "Was that ordered to be furnished by any court?"

PRESCOTT: "No, Your Honor."

KEATING: "All right. Then let's get on with Mr. Carden."

"And you can make all the motions you want about his report at the end of the day, Mr. Moren."

NUGENT: "Is the lieutenant going to be a witness, Your Honor?"

KEATING: "I don't know. I understand he is."

"We are going to finish with Mr. Carden today, gentlemen, if we have to go until midnight so you may do all your conferring now while you have a chance."

MOREN: "May counsel approach the bench?"

At the side-bar conference at the bench, Prescott admitted that he had a copy of Bergin's report of Carden's statements. That brought on the following obvious attempt by Keating to justify not releasing the report.

KEATING: "What do you want to say now, Mr. Moren?"

MOREN: "In view of Lieutenant Bergin's testimony on voir dire, I respectfully move that counsel be furnished with a copy of Lieutenant Bergin's report."

KEATING: "Mr. Moren, just within the last few minutes, I told you that I would take those matters up at 4 o'clock."

MOREN: "Well, may I just point this out, Your Honor. His report includes what Carden said, which we may have to use in cross-examination of Carden. That is the only reason I bring it up now."

KEATING: (to Prescott) "Has some judge acted on a motion and refused to give them police reports?"

PRESCOTT: "Yes. The motion was allowed as to police reports under the statute. This is not a police report per se."

MOREN: "I am not arguing that, Your Honor. The judge allowed a motion for written statements of Commonwealth witnesses and oral statements, which had been reduced to writing."

KEATING: "Statements that they made."

MOREN: "Statements which had been reduced to writing under the Lewinski standards. We have a transcript of the hearing before the judge on motions. The Lewinski standards include the notes of a law enforcement officer reducing what a person is telling him to writing as part of his report. That is what was requested."

PRESCOTT: "I submit that the Lewinski…"

KEATING: "Just a minute."

Then, to the defense attorneys:

"Are you suggesting to me that you just now learned that this lieutenant filed a report, which was reduced to writing with the district attorney?"

NUGENT: "Yes, I am, Your Honor. I will take an oath on that. This is the first time I knew."

KEATING: "Have you at any time, Mr. Moren, or you Mr. Caplan, or you, Mr. Nugent, made any attempt to see Carden at Walpole State Prison?"

NUGENT: "No."

MOREN: "I wasn't in this case when he was at Walpole."

KEATING: "At any time since you have been in this case?"

MOREN: "I knew he wasn't there."

KEATING: "Well, wherever he was, have you made any effort to see him?"

MOREN: "I was told he was in protective custody, and we couldn't see him."

KEATING: "Have you made any effort to see him this week before he came here today?"

MOREN: "To see him at the prison?"

KEATING: "To see him here this week?"

MOREN: "No. In the transcript of the hearing on the motions, Mr. Prescott said he would make him available to us. We waited for a convenient time."

KEATING: "And the convenient time is when he is testifying. All right."

"For the record, I am going to deny the motion for Lieutenant Bergin's report."

It was such an unethical decision that Keating turned to Prescott and said, "You don't want to give it to them?"

PRESCOTT: "If Your Honor please, this is not a police report as such. It is simply a report from Lieutenant Bergin to his own superior officer. I submit that is only work product and not an item under the Lewinski principle or any other principle."

So, in essence, his only argument was that the report from the investigating policeman was not a police report. It was enough for Keating.

He said, "The motion is denied."

It was such an egregiously unscrupulous decision that Keating actually said, "If I were Mr. Prescott, my instinct would be to give you anything I had in my file. However, I can't try his case. And if there is anything in Lieutenant Bergin's report as you gentlemen expect there is, I would hate to be in his position in coming to this point and allowing these three fellows to be tried with the consequences, which may accrue."

PRESCOTT: "Really, judge, I am not concerned."

KEATING: "Why you don't want to give them the report, I don't know, Mr. Prescott, but I am not going to order that report be given to counsel. It will be a Pyrrhic victory if you are trying this case three years hence. I just don't understand your position."

PRESCOTT: "Judge, these fellows have everything they are entitled to under any theory I know and then some."

MOREN: "I must respectfully request that this report be marked for identification and impounded so it is part of the record. I have no choice, Your Honor."

KEATING: "I am not going to do that."

Once again, Keating had bailed them out.

Years later, when we finally got to see the five-page Bergin report, it clearly showed that there was information in there that they should have provided to us. Moreover, there was a blatant misrepresentation of a piece of information (i.e., a flat-out lie), which, if the jury had been aware of, would have almost certainly resulted in a not guilty.

twenty-nine

When Carden's cross-examination resumed, Al Nugent went right to the noon time Thanksgiving Day meal.

And Carden's guardian angel, Keating, was right there for him.

An integral part of Carden's rationale for Perrotta having an extra meal with which to make the alleged sandwiches was that the Thanksgiving Day meal was so bad that another inmate gave his meal to Bobby. Consequently, the following exchange took place.

NUGENT: "Was it the worst Thanksgiving meal you had seen in jail or..."

KEATING: "Aren't we being a little frivolous now? Is it terribly important whether it was good or bad?"

NUGENT: "Yes, Your Honor, I think it is very important. I wouldn't take the time if I didn't think so."

As questioning continued, it came out that Carden was unsure how many sandwiches that he'd claimed Perrotta had made.

NUGENT: "And how many do you say he made?"

CARDEN: "I think I said two. I am not exactly sure."

When Nugent tried to press him on the issue, Keating once again intervened.

KEATING: "The jury has a memory, too, Mr. Nugent."

NUGENT: "I am wondering if the witness has."

Then, turning back to Carden, whose vacillation on his sandwich story was obviously the reason that Keating had stepped in, Nugent pressed, "You think it was two?"

CARDEN: "I think he made two sandwiches."

NUGENT: "It could have been three or it could have been one?"

CARDEN: "It could have been three."

Despite Keating's repeated interruptions, Nugent's pressing cross-examination did yield some discrepancies in Carden's testimony, obviously, to Keating's displeasure.

Keating stopped Nugent from questioning Carden on how many times he claimed that he'd heard Perrotta called for a visit.

He finished his interruption by saying, "Let's get on with some questions that have some relevance."

NUGENT: "Those are the only ones I am trying to ask."

Then, to Carden:

"It wasn't once, and it wasn't three times, and of that you are sure?"

KEATING: "I will see counsel up here."

A CONFERENCE TOOK PLACE AT THE BENCH AS FOLLOWS:

KEATING: "I want this on the record."

"If you feel, Mr. Nugent, that continuing on, after my stopping you on a particular line of questioning, is showing either bravado or intelligence, let me warn you right now that if we have one further incident, I will hold you in contempt. I will send the jury out first."

"I recognize you have a duty, but I cannot allow counsel to flaunt an order of the court by a repetition of a question I have excluded."

"That's all. Let's go ahead with this case."

NUGENT: "Your Honor, may I say something for the record?"

KEATING: "No."

Nugent continued a little while longer and caught Carden in some more "inconsistencies" with his earlier testimony in front of the grand jury. And Keating kept trying to play it down.

NUGENT: "Do you recall testifying at [the grand jury] as to the size of John Campbell and the size of Robert Perrotta?"

CARDEN: "Yes, I do."

NUGENT: "Now, could you tell us today what is your estimate as to the height and weight of Robert Perrotta on November 25, 1976?"

CARDEN: "Robert Perrotta's height was five-six, five-seven, and he weighed about 140."

NUGENT: "About 140. Now, have you discussed the size of Robert Perrotta from the time you were in front of the grand jury until the time you testified today?"

CARDEN: "No, I haven't."

NUGENT: "Is there some reason why you have changed it?"

CARDEN: "Have I changed it?"

KEATING: "That is improper, Mr. Nugent."

NUGENT: "Will you read your testimony before the grand jury as to your description of the size of Robert Perrotta?"

KEATING: "Read it to yourself."

CARDEN: "Yes, I see it."

NUGENT: "What did you say in front of the grand jury?"

CARDEN: "I said 120 pounds."

NUGENT: "You said 120 pounds?"

CARDEN: "That's right."

NUGENT: "And now it's 140?"

CARDEN: "I estimated."

NUGENT: "Did you estimate before the grand jury?"

CARDEN: "It says 'about,' sir."

NUGENT: "Are you estimating today?"

CARDEN: "I said 'about.'"

NUGENT: "So you are changing your estimate twenty pounds, is that right?"

PRESCOTT: "I pray Your Honor's judgment."

KEATING: "Let's give the jury credit for being able to add and subtract, Mr. Nugent. Next question."

Nugent went on to bring out that, conversely, Carden had described Campbell as being larger than he really was, to the grand jury. He ended with the following:

NUGENT: "So is it fair to say you made [Campbell] a little bigger and Perrotta a little smaller? Did you do that on purpose?"

CARDEN: "Of course, I didn't."

NUGENT: "Of course you didn't?"

CARDEN: "Of course, I didn't."

NUGENT: "That's all."

thirty

Then, it was Al Caplan's turn.

He started off by asking Carden about his claim that he and I had never spoken. He denied ever having played ping-pong with me, but admitted that we had played monopoly together.

He then brought out that we had lived in the same block for nine or ten months and that we both worked in the computer room.

He then moved on to Carden's earlier admission that he and Perrotta had been smoking grass that day. He had also testified earlier that everyone on the block was drunk or high that day, except for him. He was the only sober person in the block on Thanksgiving Day.

CAPLAN: "And who brought the grass in? Was it Bobby's grass that you shared?"

CARDEN: "Yes, sir."

CAPLAN: "Did Bobby have any other kind of pills or narcotics?"

CARDEN: "That day?"

CAPLAN: "That day."

CARDEN: "No."

CAPLAN: "How about the day before?"

PRESCOTT: "Objection as to the day before."

KEATING: "A day before is pretty remote. Let's get to Thanksgiving Day and limit it to that."

CAPLAN: "If I may ..."

KEATING: "I am going to limit it to whatever he saw on Thanksgiving Day. You may have that."

CAPLAN: "Did Bobby supply you pills?"

PRESCOTT: "Objection."

KEATING: "When?"

CAPLAN: "Generally, as part of your partnership, did Bobby supply you with pills?"

PRESCOTT: "I beg the court's indulgence."

KEATING: "You are going far afield. I won't allow that."

CAPLAN: "May I approach the bench and tell the court the relevancy of this?"

KEATING: "Well, we are going to suspend now. We have reached the hour for adjournment."

And that was that.

So much for, "*We are going to finish with Mr. Carden today, gentlemen, if we have to go until midnight.*"

thirty-one

D ay five began with a conference at the bench.

We had issued subpoenas to the DOC and to Walpole for Carden's and Perrotta's institutional records. A representative of the DOC, named Robert Claridge, was in court claiming that the material was hearsay and not relevant to any issues at the trial. His argument was that the DOC was forbidden from releasing this material to members of the public, including counsel for inmates other than the inmates named in those files.

Al Caplan pointed out that information under that criminal record system procedure was obtainable by the Massachusetts Defender Committee but that other defense counsel needed a court order, which he submitted was a denial of equal protection under the constitution."

When questioned, Claridge admitted that he had not read the files.

So, Keating turned to Caplan "Well, the purpose of this summons is to accomplish what, Mr. Caplan?"

CAPLAN: "The purpose of this summons is to have these files examined for possible exculpatory evidence. For example, other persons having equal motive to ..."

KEATING: "Would you find information concerning other persons in Carden's file?"

CAPLAN: "I haven't seen his file."

KEATING: "You are telling me you are going to find other people with equal motive to commit this act?"

CAPLAN: "We have other information with respect to certain arguments taking place between Carden and Perrotta or certain illegal activities, which took place between Carden and Perrotta, and, which, resulted in arguments. We are aware of the fact that the Department of Correction keeps what they call so-called incident reports in these files. Incident reports are not disciplinary reports that go to the inmates, but they can be the result of informant information of one kind or another, casual observations by guards, or other corrections staff personnel. Every little detail of this kind is put into these files. It is for these reasons we want to see if there is such information that would be exculpatory to our clients."

Without one iota of justification, Keating simply denied the request.

Usher Moren responded by moving that the court examine all the materials, then make a ruling for the record, and that the materials be marked for identification and impounded for possible use as part of the record on appeal.

Keating denied that too.

A discussion began on a motion for some of Carden's records that we had summonsed from the Salem House of Correction, where he had been secretly held. After stating that he did not want us to see the records, Prescott changed the subject, saying, "Mr. Claridge would like to be heard further."

Claridge said that, in addition to the excuses he had already given, there were serious security reasons why the files shouldn't be handed over. First, he claimed that it was not a closed investigation and handing over such files would seriously impair the investigation.

Not a closed investigation? The case was in the middle of a trial!

He went on to say that the file contains the names of informants, including inmates and police officers, and that there was security risk if their names became known.

That is such a distortion of the truth. All that they have to do is redact any names that they don't want in there, cops or stool pigeons. They do it all the time.

With respect to the Salem Jail records, Keating denied our request.

Shortly after that, Prescott admitted that Carden had been given a furlough from Salem. Keating told him to give that part to us.

Usher Moren made one more motion. He requested that, if we were not going to be given all of the Salem material that had been summonsed, that Judge Keating himself should examine it and that it be made part of the record for any possible information that might tend to be exculpatory or tend to reflect promises, inducements, or rewards to Carden.

As usual, Keating denied the motion.

Throughout the trial, Keating consistently refused to review any of the withheld material that we requested that he examine before denying us access to it. That way, when it turned out that the material did contain exculpatory evidence, Keating could claim that he didn't know that the material contained exculpatory evidence.

thirty-two

A l Caplan resumed the cross-examination.
       Armed with the transcripts of two interviews that Carden had
given to Bergin and Prescott, in days immediately following the
murder, Alan immediately caught Carden in a number of lies—provable lies,
despite Keating's obvious irritation.

The interviews had been given on December 1, 1976, and December
10, 1976. Keating allowed Prescott to "edit" the December 1 transcript of
information that Prescott could decide was not relevant. Out of twenty-seven
pages, eleven were totally cut out; eight more were partially cut out. Years
later, when we finally saw the unedited transcript, it showed that Prescott had
"edited" highly relevant information—some of which he perjuriously denied
existed.

Carden's story was that the only time that he left the block that night
was after seven-fifteen to place the bet. But the block logs showed that he had
actually left the block earlier, from 6:10 to 6:25.

So Carden changed his story to say that he got the betting slip when
he left the block at 6:10, until Alan pointed out that he had told Bergin and
Prescott a different story. He'd told them that he'd gotten the betting slip at
five o'clock, before he went in for the count.

The lies went on and on.

He testified that he had made the bet with a bookie named Shotgun,
until Alan pointed out that he had originally told Bergin and Prescott that he
had placed the bet with a bookie named George Pinto.

This exchange set Keating off again.

CAPLAN: "And who did you place that bet with?"

CARDEN: "A fellow named Shotgun. I don't know his full name."

CAPLAN: "Shotgun?"

CARDEN: "Yes."

CAPLAN: "Do you recall describing this incident to Mr. Prescott and
Lieutenant Bergin on December 1?"

CARDEN: "Do I recall?"

CAPLAN: "Yes."

CARDEN: "I don't."

CAPLAN: "I ask you to look at line 21 on page 6, lines 21 through 24 of that transcript."

CARDEN: "Yes."

CAPLAN: "Who did you say you placed the bet with on December 1?"

CARDEN: "George Pinto."

CAPLAN: "That is not Shotgun, is it?"

CARDEN: "No, sir."

CAPLAN: "Now, do you recall what you said to Lieutenant Bergin on December 10 with respect to the bet?"

CARDEN: "If you refresh my memory again, maybe I will."

CAPLAN: "Read from line 1 on down through the page, if you would please."

CARDEN: "Okay."

KEATING: "Is this relative to whom he placed the bet with?"

CAPLAN: "Yes."

KEATING: "Can't you just point out one sentence? Must he read the entire page to find one name?"

CAPLAN: "This entire page contains not only names but other substantial discrepancies."

KEATING: (In unmistakable exasperation) "Go ahead."

Alan resumed cross-examination. He initially touched on a few other issues. Then, he went back to the sandwich story.

CAPLAN: "Now, in the course of these various interviews, Mr. Carden, that you had with Lieutenant Bergin and with Mr. Prescott, when was the first time that you told them about the Thanksgiving Day sandwiches?"

PRESCOTT: "I beg the court's indulgence. He is assuming a fact that is not at all in evidence."

Even Keating was puzzled.

KEATING: "What fact?"

PRESCOTT: "He is assuming as a fact that Lieutenant Bergin and Mr. Prescott were told about the Thanksgiving Day sandwiches. I am not saying it is so or not, but it is not in evidence at this point."

CAPLAN: "I will withdraw the question."

Then, to Carden:

"Did you ever tell Lieutenant Bergin and Mr. Prescott about the Thanksgiving Day sandwiches?"

CARDEN: "No, sir. I was never asked."

CAPLAN: "So that the first time that you ever told the story about the Thanksgiving Day sandwiches was in this courtroom yesterday?"

CARDEN "That is correct."

And there it was. Prescott was right. We had assumed a fact that was not in evidence. We had assumed that Prescott was aware of the sandwich story. So hadn't Keating. Otherwise, how could they have proceeded with the trial? If the district attorney's office did not know about the sandwiches before trial, what was their theory of the crime? What time did they think that Perrotta had been killed? After supper as Carden claimed or after the noon meal as the autopsy report showed? Without the sandwich story, Carden's claim that Perrotta was alive until seven o'clock that night was provably false. So how could they proceed if they had not known about the sandwich story?

I wanted to have Prescott called to the witness stand. Realistically, Keating never would have allowed it.

The cross-examination continued.

Carden admitted that Perrotta's door was pegged shut from the inside, with "one of the better types" of door pegs, when he left him to go place the bet. He then tried to downplay the effectiveness of the door peg by saying that the door still "could be opened from the outside."

He went on to admit that the only way that that could be done was that if somebody outside the cell reached their hand under the door with a pair of pliers or a hex wrench to open it.

Keating continued to intrude.

While questioning Carden on what happened after he had found the body and notified the guard, Caplan asked him a simple question that called for a yes or no answer.

CAPLAN: "Did you go back in the room?"

CARDEN: "When I walked into the room, after seeing what happened to him ..."

CAPLAN: "Strike it out. My question was ..."

PRESCOTT: "May he answer the question?"

CAPLAN: "May I get an answer to my question?"

KEATING: "Let him finish his answer. He was in the middle of the answer when you interrupted."

CAPLAN: "If Your Honor please, my question was ..."

KEATING: "He may finish his answer. You may save your exception."

Carden then went on to give an impassioned, well-rehearsed performance of the effect that finding Bobby's body had had on him.

CARDEN: "When I walked into the room and I saw the condition of Bobby, I was in a shock. I was nervous. I felt like I was in there three or four days, you know. The time was completely lost. I completely lost control of time. I felt like I was there for an hour, but then I went back out and called the guard. I was just completely shaken up."

A response that had nothing to do with the question that Alan had asked him. Alan had simply asked him if he had gone back into the room. It did, however, give Carden the opportunity to create a perfect excuse for a number of "discrepancies" that had come out in his testimony.

Then, when Alan tried to question him on it, Keating immediately put a stop to it. "That is at least the third time you have gone over that point, Mr. Caplan. He was shaken when he first walked in. Next question."

|||||||||||||||||||||||||||||||||||||||||||||||||||||||||||||||||||

ALAN THEN MOVED on to the issue of "promises, inducements, and rewards."

Anyone even remotely familiar with the "justice" system, especially as it applies to inmates, knew that Carden was going to be rewarded for his testimony. He had, in fact, actually told people that he was going to get out of prison for testifying.

However, when he was on the witness stand, he strongly denied ever telling that to anyone. And, as the people that he'd told were other prisoners, the prosecutor was able to seriously undermine their credibility in his closing argument to the jury, when he described the defense witnesses as a united front of inmate society against the jury and everybody else in this state.

However, there was one moment, right at the end of Alan's cross-examination, when the truth peeked through.

Before trial, I had found out that Carden was corresponding with a young girl, named Cheryl Stokes. (I think she was fifteen, at the time.) I was advised that he had told her in a letter that, after the case was over, he was going to get out of prison and go to Ireland.

Unfortunately, for reasons that had nothing to do with the trial, the girl's mother would not allow her to testify. Nor, would she turn over the letter.

When I told Caplan about it, he said that we couldn't bring it up unless we had the letter. He said that if he asked Carden if he'd written the letter, and Carden denied writing it, then by law Caplan would have to produce the letter. If he couldn't, Keating would eat him alive.

All during cross-examination, Carden steadfastly denied ever telling anyone that he was going to be released for testifying. However, right at the end of his cross-examination, the following exchange took place.

CAPLAN: "Now Mr. Carden, you stated yesterday, I believe, that no one had promised you anything to induce you to testify here?"

CARDEN: "That's correct."

CAPLAN: "Do you have any expectations of favored treatment for testifying here?"

CARDEN: "Of course not."

CAPLAN: "Well, you are not at Walpole anymore, are you?"

CARDEN: "That's correct."

CAPLAN: "And you have gone out on a furlough, haven't you?"

CARDEN: "An escorted furlough."

CAPLAN: "You didn't have any furloughs while you were at Walpole, did you?"

CARDEN: "No, I didn't, sir."

CAPLAN: "Have you ever told anyone that you expected after this was all over to be back in Ireland?"

CARDEN: "No, I haven't."

Alan, who was standing by the defense table, picked up an envelope and removed a sheet of paper from it as he asked, "You never told…"and, glancing down at the sheet of paper, he concluded, "…a Cheryl Stokes that?"

Carden responded weakly, "Who?"

Alan repeated, "Cheryl Stokes."

The response was electrifying. I really wish that they were televising trials back then. Carden looked to Prescott who, in turn, looked appealingly up at Keating who just as quickly interjected himself into the questioning by demanding of Caplan, "Is Cheryl Stokes going to testify?"

As Caplan nodded his head in response, Keating turned to Carden and, with obvious exasperation, asked, "Did you ever tell that to anybody?"

Carden muttered, in a barely audible voice, "I might have. I don't recall."

Usher Moren and Al Nugent both jumped up, saying, "What did he say?"

Keating asked Carden, "You say yes, you might have, but you don't recall?"

Carden replied, "That is what I said."

Moren said, "I didn't hear."

Keating then said to Usher Moren, "Mr. Caplan will repeat his answer Mr. Moren, if you don't hear it."

Mr. Caplan chose not to do this, as any further probing of the issue might have led to the discovery that he'd had been holding a blank piece of paper in his hand when he'd asked the question.

thirty-three

Usher Moren took over the cross-examination.

MOREN: "Now, you know before November 25, 1976, of course, that there were serious and substantial marital difficulties between your sister and Mr. Perrotta?"

CARDEN: "That is correct."

PRESCOTT: "If Your Honor please, I object."

KEATING: "I will let him have that."

MOREN: "As a matter of fact, you and Mr. Perrotta had a number of disagreements about that marital situation, didn't you?"

CARDEN: "I did not."

MOREN: "You certainly had a number of discussions about it in the presence of other inmates, didn't you?"

CARDEN: "I did not."

MOREN: "Never discussed it at all in anyone's presence?"

CARDEN: "I don't discuss family problems with other people."

MOREN: "Did you ever say to Mr. Perrotta, 'That's my sister. Why do you treat her like that? You don't care about your family.'"

CARDEN: "Of course not."

MOREN: "Did you ever say to Mr. Perrotta concerning his girlfriend who came up to see him, who was married to someone else, 'You've got a lot...'"

KEATING: "Are you going to have some evidence that this was said?"

MOREN: "Yes."

KEATING: "On that representation, I will allow it."

MOREN: "Did you ever say to him, 'You have got this other pig coming up to visit you'? Did you ever say that to Mr. Perrotta?"

CARDEN: "No, I didn't."

MOREN: "Did your sister ever visit you at Walpole with her children before Mr. Perrotta's death?"

CARDEN: "Yes."

MOREN: "Did you ever have an argument with Mr. Perrotta about him not seeing his kids on that visit?"

CARDEN: "No, I didn't."

(One night, at a function in the auditorium, Bobby and Carden were having a rather heated discussion as I was walking by them in the aisle. Bobby stopped me and said, "Hey, Stevie, lemme ask ya somethin'. When my ex-wife—his sister—comes up to see him, she brings my kids, but he won't tell me when she's comin'. So I never get t' see 'em. You think that's right?" I just held up my hand and said, "Not my business, Bobby." He immediately held up his hands and said, "You're right. I'm sorry. I shouldn't ask ya somethin' like that. It's just drivin' me nuts.")

MOREN: "Did you ever tell anyone that you were ripping off pills from Mr. Perrotta?"

CARDEN: "No, I did not."

Carden continued to deny that anyone had ever told him that it might help him to get out early if he would testify. Or, that he would receive any help in regard to some pending bank robbery cases on which he had yet to be tried.

At one point, Moren asked him, "Sir, you would do almost anything to get released early, wouldn't you?"

Even as Carden was denying it, Keating jumped in with, "I will exclude that question. The jury will disregard it."

Further on, Moren asked him, "Sir, have you ever stated to anyone that when this case is over, you are going to get your other charges knocked off and you are going to Arizona? Did you ever say that?"

CARDEN: "No, not in the …"

KEATING: "Do you have someone who will testify to that Mr. Moren?"

MOREN: "Yes, Your Honor."

On redirect examination, Prescott tried to mitigate the impact of some of Carden's unavoidable lies.

PRESCOTT: "Now, Mr. Carden is it true or is it not true that someday, if you live long enough, you would like to get back to Ireland?"

NUGENT: "I pray Your Honor's judgment."

CARDEN: "That is true."

CAPLAN: "I object."

NUGENT: "I object."

PRESCOTT: "And have you told somebody that?"

CARDEN: "Yes, I have."

KEATING: "Wait a minute. Let me in on this."

"Mr. Prescott that is clearly an improper question."

"The jury will disregard the question and the answer."

PRESCOTT: "It was opened by my brother."

KEATING: "No. I am striking it from the record. This is your witness."

Then, as Prescott said that he had no more questions, Keating casually dropped in, "We might all like to go there someday."

|||||||||||||||||||||||||||||||||||||||||||||||||||||||||||||||||

NUGENT WAS NEXT.

When Al tried to question him on certain discrepancies in his earlier testimony Carden fell back on his 'I was in shock' spiel. "I said when I went in; I completely lost all track of time."

Nugent then went on to a different issue.

NUGENT: "Mr. Carden, you knew John Stokes, didn't you?"

CARDEN: "Yes."

NUGENT: "Did you or Robert Perrotta or the two of you together discover his body when he was found dead in his cell?"

CARDEN: "There was about six people that discovered it."

NUGENT: "You were right there and you were one of the first people in the cell?"

CARDEN: "There were about six people there."

NUGENT: "And you were here too, when Robert Perrotta was found?"

CARDEN: "Yes."

KEATING: [To the rescue] "Did that happen in the same cell block?"

CARDEN: "Yes."

KEATING: "It would be hard for him to be not there."

NUGENT: "He was in the same cell, not merely the same block."

On further redirect examination, Prescott went immediately to the Stokes' killing.

PRESCOTT: "Was Johnny Stokes a friend of yours?"

CARDEN: "Yes, sir, me and Johnny..."

KEATING: "Wait a minute. I am going to end all questioning about Johnny Stokes or any other incident."

PRESCOTT: "I pray Your Honor's judgment. He opened it up. The inference is left he is involved in another killing. This was his best friend."

NUGENT: "I pray Your Honor's judgment."

KEATING: "He answered he was friendly. That is the end of it."

PRESCOTT: "What about Bobby Perrotta? Was he a close friend of Stokes?"

CARDEN: "Yes."

NUGENT: "I pray Your Honor's judgment."

CAPLAN: "I object."

But now, Keating liked where Prescott was going with it.

KEATING: "He can have that."

CARDEN: "Yes, he was."

PRESCOTT: "Do you know of your own knowledge whether Bobby Perrotta saw the killing of Stokes?"

CARDEN: "Yes, he did."

NUGENT: "I pray Your Honor's judgment."

CAPLAN: "I object."

KEATING: "The question is improper as far as loading goes, but if you people open it up, he has a right to develop it."

NUGENT: "If Your Honor pleases, I opened up the fact that he discovered with other people this other deceased."

KEATING: "You just can't have the part you like and say the other parts will be kept from the jury. But that is the end of it, anyway, Mr. Prescott."

Prescott agreed, quite satisfied. The inference now in front of the jury was that *we were involved in another killing.*

thirty-four

Day six began with Prescott calling a Dr. Shenker to the stand. Shenker was the doctor who had been called to Perrotta's cell on the night that he was murdered.

Shenker testified that it was his opinion that Perrotta had died within two hours of Shenker's having seen him. Shenker examined the body around nine o'clock on the night of the murder.

Dr. Shenker's opinion was based, somewhat, on the opinion of the Walpole medic, Dennis Spicer, that the body was still warm when he examined it, which is no surprise. When the heat is on in Walpole, the third tier is always excruciatingly hot.

Shenker had testified for Prescott that he had been a medical examiner for forty-one years and that he had examined at least a thousand bodies.

However, under cross-examination, Al Caplan got him to admit that his actual practice was internal medicine and cardiology and that he was neither a full-time medical examiner nor a board-certified forensic pathologist.

During further cross-examination, Dr. Shenker seemed to resist Usher Moren's attempt to get an objective view of how the time of death should be determined by body temperature.

MOREN: "Doctor, did you take the rectal temperature of the body in the cell?"

SHENKER: "I never do."

MOREN: "You would agree with me that a determination of the time of death is a relative thing, is it not?"

SHENKER: "To a point."

MOREN: "It is fair to say, is it not, that a rectal temperature is a more accurate indication of the temperature of the body than touching the body, isn't it, doctor?"

SHENKER: "Not necessarily."

MOREN: "Did you have a rectal thermometer with you when you went to Walpole that night?"

SHENKER: "I never use one."

MOREN: "Please answer my question."

SHENKER: "I did not."

MOREN: "Did you inquire of anyone as to whether they had a rectal thermometer at the institution?"

SHENKER: "No, sir."

Prescott's next witness was the doctor who performed the autopsy on Perrotta, Dr. Katsas.

Dr. Katsas testified that Perrotta had been alive when his penis had been torn from his body. This was determined by the fact that there were three sets of bite marks on Perrotta's penis, which were consistent with being the result of biting by the decedent when the organ was placed in his mouth.

He testified that Perrotta had two bruises, one on his lower chest/upper abdomen and the other on the left side of his head.

He testified that the five hundred grams of Thanksgiving food that were in Perrotta's stomach had been consumed within one hour, and certainly not more than two hours, before his death.

These were all straightforward, albeit gruesome, facts.

However, when Prescott asked him to give an opinion as to the time of death of Robert Perrotta, he prefaced his question by asking the doctor to base his opinion on a full page of assumptions.

PRESCOTT: "Doctor, *if you will assume* that this same body of Robert Perrotta, upon which you did this autopsy and made these observations, was seen by a paramedical person at approximately 7:40 pm. *Assume further*, if you will, doctor, that that paramedical person made these following observations:

"*Assume that* through the use of a stethoscope, that paramedical person found no heartbeat. *Assume that* by means of touching the right hand or arm, he determined that there was no pulse. *Assume that* he made observations of an appendage, which he did not identify but did describe, extending from a corner of the mouth. *Assume further* that this paramedical person said that the body was warm and, in particular, the hand and fingertips were still warm at that hour, 7:40.

"*Assume further*, if you will, doctor, that a medical doctor, one Dr. Shenker, examined the body, this same body, sometime after nine o'clock but before nine-thirty on the same evening, *and assume that* Dr. Shenker indicated that rigor mortis had not yet, at that time, between 9:00 and 9:30, set in.

"Now, doctor, assuming all those facts, would you have an opinion as to the time of death of Robert Perrotta?"

The lawyers immediately objected—to no avail.

KEATING: "I will let him have that."

KATSAS: "Yes, sir, I do have an opinion."

PRESCOTT: "And what is that opinion?"

Again, the lawyers objected.

KEATING: "Again, I will allow it."

KATSAS: "It is my opinion *on the basis of the assumptions you gave me*, sir that Robert Perrotta died shortly before he was examined by the paramedical person. And by 'shortly,' it is my opinion that he died within at least a couple of hours and within two to four hours at the most prior to the observations of the medical examiner."

He was the only real pathologist there, and he got to base his "expert" opinion on eight mingled assumptions—the majority of which came from a DOC employee!

When Prescott was finished, Keating stepped in for a quick assist.

KEATING: "Doctor, you referred to the penis being amputated. Were you able to determine in what manner or how, whether with an instrument or how?"

KATSAS: "I formed an opinion."

KEATING: "And what was that?" (As if he didn't know!)

KATSAS: "It is my opinion that the penis was pulled with force."

KEATING: "Thank you." (Once a prosecutor, always a prosecutor)

And every guy on the jury went "*OUCH*," and so did I. That was the first time that I'd heard that.

Usher Moren began the cross-examination. He went right to the body temperature as a means of determining the time of death.

MOREN: "Were you furnished by anyone with a rectal temperature of the deceased taken following discovery of the body?"

KATSAS: "No, sir, I was not and I inquired about it, and no such temperature was taken, sir."

MOREN: "You inquired about it, because it would have been significant, isn't that so?"

KATSAS: "It would have been helpful, sir."

MOREN: "Very helpful, as a matter of fact, as to the time of death, isn't that right?"

KATSAS: "It is one of the factors we consider for the time of death."

MOREN: "And a rectal temperature is a scientific factor as opposed to a personal observation isn't that so?"

KATSAS: "It is an objective determination of the temperature, sir."

MOREN: "Thank you. It is an objective determination?"

KATSAS: "That is correct."

MOREN: "Had you been on the scene shortly following death, doctor, you certainly would have taken a rectal temperature, isn't that so?"

Prescott quickly objected, so Keating wouldn't let him answer.

At one point, Katsas admitted that, if the only factor that he had before him to determine time of death was the stomach contents, then his opinion would be that death occurred approximately two hours after the ingestion of food.

Moren's final question was, "You said there were chunks of meat, turkey or chicken, and raisins, did you not, in the contents of the stomach?"

KATSAS: "Yes, sir."

MOREN: "Raisins?"

KATSAS: "Yes."

This alone proves that the Thanksgiving food in Perrotta's stomach was eaten in the chow hall at noon. The only raisins served with the Thanksgiving Day meal were in the mince pie. The sandwich story specifically did not include mince pie in the sandwich. Outside of that, raisins were not allowed in Walpole as they could be used to make home brew.

Katsas was the Commonwealth's last witness. After he finished testifying, the Commonwealth rested their case.

We then each filed a motion for a directed verdict of not guilty.

At this point, the court called for the morning recess. When we returned from the recess, Keating dismissed the jurors for the rest of the day.

thirty-five

The arguments for a directed verdict began.

KEATING: "All right Mr. Nugent, your motion is the last one. I will let you argue first."

NUGENT: "If it doesn't appear to be out of order, Your Honor, may Mr. Caplan go first, because we distinguish his particular case factually from ours?"

KEATING: "I had in mind you going first and Mr. Moren second, because those two cases are different than the case of Mr. Doherty."

NUGENT: "Then may I let Mr. Moren go first as to the defendant Keigney?"

KEATING: "Yes."

So Moren argued first for Keigney. He stuck strictly to the law, citing comparable cases. He finished with the following:

"In our case, may it please the court, all we have is bare—and I emphasize that word—bare presence and opportunity. And we do not have unusual opportunity. We have no motive. We have no possession of incriminating evidence. We have no bloodstains. We have no consciousness of guilt. We have nothing but bare opportunity."

"I suggest to the court that bare opportunity as we have in this case is equally consistent with innocence as with guilt and, if that is the case, then the law requires that we have a directed verdict."

"And I quote from the Fancy case, *Commonwealth v. Fancy*, 349 Mass. 196 at page 200: 'When the evidence tends equally to sustain either or two inconsistent propositions, neither of them can be said to have been established by legitimate proof.'"

"There is no evidence that Mr. Keigney killed anybody or put a hand on anybody. The Commonwealth's case, if believed, is that he was seen coming out of the room. That is equally consistent with his not having done anything. On that basis, I suggest to the court, the Commonwealth's case must fall."

Al Nugent went next. Basically, he adopted Moren's argument for Keigney as the case against each of them was the same.

Then it was Al Caplan's turn.

He started off by citing a Massachusetts Appeals Court case, where the witness observed one of the defendants, Murphy, throw something into a house and then get into a car in which the second defendant, Tilley, was seen driving the car later. They held that Tilley could not be found guilty even if he were present at the scene and even if he failed to take affirmative steps to prevent the crime. To be found guilty, one must associate himself with the venture, participate in it, and seek by his actions to make it succeed. Mere knowledge that a crime is going to be committed is not enough.

KEATING: "That is the Murphy case?"

CAPLAN: "Yes. And in that case, there was no showing of an agreement to stand by and tender aid or in any other way to participate."

"Now, the Fancy case has already been alluded to by my brothers, and I won't repeat it, but the same proposition would lie there."

KEATING: "What about Doherty stopping Carden, if he is to be believed, an hour or two earlier or whatever time it was? Could the jury consider that, considering that he had never spoken to him before and he now stops him this day? Carden testified he tried to look around him and Doherty held him up."

CAPLAN: "First of all, on cross-examination, Carden admits he has had a little more contact than his original story."

"However, even when you examine the facts of the situation as he testified, there was no testimony that after Carden sees Keigney and Campbell leave Perrotta's room that Campbell and Keigney and Doherty huddle together. As a matter of fact, he said very specifically that Campbell and Keigney stopped a few cells down and Doherty was with a completely different group of inmates until lock up time."

"I suggest there is not one shred or scintilla of evidence that in any way identifies Mr. Doherty with Messrs. Campbell and Keigney. There is not one piece of evidence to show that they even spoke to each other in their entire lives prior to becoming codefendants here. In fact, well, I will leave it just at that, that there is no evidence that they had any kind of communication whatsoever."

"In order to find Doherty guilty of what went on in that room, you would have to show some common purpose of association. There is nothing to show that, not one drop of evidence to that effect."

KEATING: "There is the association earlier that day of the three of them in the same cell area."

CAPLAN: "There is no such evidence."

KEATING: "There is evidence Carden saw Doherty and Keigney and Campbell at Perrotta's cell when he came up at 5 o'clock."

CAPLAN: "No, no, Your Honor. The testimony is that Campbell and Keigney came out of the cell, but Doherty stayed down the end of the tier, and there is no evidence the three of them got together then."

Keating did not repeat his challenge to the fact that, not only was there no evidence that I had been with Campbell, Keigney, or Perrotta, but their own witness's testimony specifically placed me about eighty feet away from them at the far end of the block. (See diagram of Block A-2, page 103.)

Prescott's argument began with the type of insidious, underhanded ploy that was so characteristic of this case from start to finish.

PRESCOTT: "My brothers have been mercifully brief, Your Honor, and I will try to be as brief as any one of the three."

KEATING: "I don't care how brief you are. I would like you to address yourself to what they had to say. Take Doherty's participation first."

PRESCOTT: "I will do that.

"First of all, the Commonwealth's position is that this matter is not only three inferences of consciousness of guilt. *I submit, as Your Honor briefly alluded to it, the coming out of the room of Perrotta after this murder and turning abruptly and going down the block...*" [emphasis added]

Mind you, per Keating's direction, Prescott was specifically talking about me *"coming out of the room of Perrotta after this murder and turning abruptly and going down the block."* [emphasis added]

He had just taken testimony that was applicable only to Campbell and Keigney and applied it to me. Worse, he had surreptitiously twisted Keating's argument with Caplan, as to what the testimony had been, in reference to the five o'clock incident, to make it sound as if Keating had been right, but that he had been talking about the 7:30 incident—'as your Honor briefly alluded to it.'"

After getting that in, Prescott spent most of the rest of his closing argument citing cases.

When he finished, Al Caplan said, "There is one other item, if I may, one other fact that was left out. That is that Mr. Carden testified that when he left the cell, the door was closed and pegged behind him, locked, and he had checked that."

KEATING: "All right."

"Gentlemen, I am going to look these over, and I will look the cases over."

"However, I don't expect, in the event of an adverse ruling, for you to be devastated to the extent that you are not prepared to go forward. So come in prepared for good news or bad and, in the event of bad news, from your point of view, at least, be ready to go forward."

So ended day six.

thirty-six

Day seven began with one sentence by Keating. "Gentlemen, I am going to deny all three motions for directed verdict."

Actually, the day began earlier, before we went into the courtroom. My codefendants and I were in the holding pen across the hall from the courtroom when the lawyers arrived.

The focal point of the conversation was whether or not we were going to take the witness stand There was a brief bit of speculation regarding Keating's impending decision regarding the motion for a directed verdict. I say brief, because we all realized that it was merely wishful thinking.

As to testifying, Jackie and Arthur were definitely not going to get on the stand. I, on the other hand, intended to testify. The problem was that none of the lawyers wanted me to testify. Their argument was that the prosecution had not made anywhere near a strong enough case to require a rebuttal, especially against me.

Al Nugent said, "Listen Stevie, any other judge would give you guys a directed verdict, especially you. Hell, this guy might even give it to *you*. They have nothing on you."

I said, "Swell. If he gives it to me, I won't have to testify. But if he doesn't, I want to. I think somebody should get up and say we didn't do it."

He nodded his head in agreement, saying, "I know. And ordinarily I'd agree with you, but not in this case, especially against you. There is no case. Caplan made that clear yesterday in the arguments for a directed verdict. Like he said, there's no evidence that you even know Jackie and Arthur."

I looked at Al Caplan. He just smiled and with a half a shrug said, "Look, you know it's your decision. But, for what it's worth, I don't think you should take the stand. I think you'd make an excellent witness. But then they get to bring up your record. Stevie, if they had any kind of a case against you, I'd tell you to take the stand. But they don't."

Then, nodding toward Nugent, he said, "Like Al said, there's no evidence that connects you in any way, shape, or form to Arthur or Jackie, or Perrotta either, for that matter."

139

I was truly torn. I really wanted to get on the stand. I really wanted to get up and say, "I did not do it," and some other things. The problem was, while I objectively believed that it would be good for the case, I also realized that, subjectively, at least in part, I wanted to do it for the personal satisfaction of having done it. I was legitimately innocent, and I wanted to say so. I also knew that I'd almost surely be held in contempt of court if I said some of the things that I really wanted to say. There was no way that I would be able to take the stand without telling the jurors that we wanted them to view the murder scene, but that Keating and the DA wouldn't let them.

The other problem was that I had never taken the witness stand before. I had only had one other trial. It was a bank robbery trial in federal court. Same kind of a situation: One witness, a guy who was looking to get out for testifying.

The thing was that I had wanted to testify then too. The lawyers, one of whom was Al Caplan (mine), convinced me that we would be better off if I didn't.

I went along with them, and it worked out. The jury went out at noon, ate lunch, and was back with a not guilty by 2:20 pm.

As Al Caplan reminded me, in that case, they had a guy that claimed to have robbed a bank with me. In this case, they had no evidence that I even knew anyone else that was involved.

So, I accepted their advice. I did not testify.

The lawyers then extended their theory to our other witnesses. They decided not to call any of them. Their argument being that, where the Commonwealth had not made even a weak case against us, all the other inmate witnesses could do was to hurt us.

By law, though, they did have to call three witnesses as offers of proof that they had had a valid reason to ask certain questions regarding incidents that Carden had denied had ever happened.

thirty-seven

The first witness was Thomas McInerney.

McInerney described his relationship with Perrotta as friendly and said that he routinely sat at the same table in the chow hall with Perrotta and Carden. He said that when he got to the table with his tray of food, on Thanksgiving Day, Bobby was getting up to leave, and his tray was still half full. He said Bobby was wearing a T-shirt and dungarees, and he didn't see any sandwiches or bulges under his T-shirt.

He testified that, on the day after Perrotta was murdered, he had a conversation with Carden in the counseling area at Walpole. He asked Carden if he had any idea as to what happened on Thanksgiving Day and that Carden told him that he did not know.

On the same day, he was involuntarily transferred to Bridgewater. At one point, in his first week at Bridgewater, he was told that he was being taken to the superintendent's office. Instead, he was taken to a small, bare room past the superintendent's office on another floor. Carden came into the room and asked him if I had seen anything on the day of the murder. McInerney told him that he really hadn't seen anything. Carden asked him if could do him a favor and say that he saw something, that he needed him for a corroborating witness. Carden told him that they would take good care of him and put him in an easy place like Framingham or someplace like that and change his name. He told him if he played it right, he could even hit the street if he backed him up.

McInerney told him that he wouldn't do it.

When they put him back in his cell at Bridgewater that night, they put Carden in the cell right next to him.

Carden kept talking to him, trying to convince McInerney to back him up and lie. He kept saying things like, "Think about what I said." "You are never going to get out of prison." "Do you want to live like this the rest of your life?" "Do something for yourself." "Think about what I told you."

The next witness was Ronald MacDonald.

He testified that he and Bobby were next-door neighbors, that they were very friendly, and that he was on a speaking basis with Carden.

McDonald swore that, a few days before the murder, he went over to Bobby's room to borrow some coffee. When he knocked on the door and went in, Carden and Perrotta were arguing. Carden was yelling at Bobby about his sister and his kids, stuff like, 'You won't let my sister and the kids come up to see you, but you let that pig girl friend that was visiting you.' Carden also called Bobby "a fucking asshole."

McDonald testified that that was just one of several occasions in which he heard similar arguments on the same subject matter between the two of them.

During cross-examination, Prescott didn't even try to challenge Mac-Donald's testimony. He basically tried to imply that we were all friends.

He did get in one shot. In reference to the three of us, he asked, "They are all Charlestown boys, are they not?"

Seemingly a meaningless question, unless you view it in its proper context. From day one, on page one of the *Boston Globe's* "execution squad" duplicity, everyone was led to believe that Perrotta was killed for being an informant. If you're from anywhere around Boston, you know that Charlestown was known for having such an aversion to informants, that it was analogous to the "code of silence."

So, on the first day of trial, within the first minute of his opening remarks to the jury, Keating let them know that we were from Charlestown. Then, in Prescott's opening argument, he reminded them that "You are already aware that these three defendants are from Charlestown."

This led him smoothly to ask Ronnie MacDonald, "They are all Charlestown boys, are they not?"

I wonder if he would have asked the same question if we were all Newton boys or Brookline boys?

The next witness was a guy none of us had ever met, or even heard of, before that day. He was the reason that Usher Moren had asked Carden if he ever told anyone that he was going to go to Arizona when this case was over. His name was Robert Guzowski. Moren had been appointed to represent him more than a year before our trial on a case that was now disposed.

He swore that he did not know, and had never even seen, Keigney, Campbell, or me before this day; that he had never met Moren before he was appointed by the court to represent him; and had never talked to Caplan or Nugent about this case.

He testified that he had been lodged in the Salem Jail, awaiting trial on the disposed of case and, when he was bailed on about April 3, 1977, Attorney Moren gave him a ride home. Prior to that, he had met Carden in the Salem Jail. They lived about six cells apart. Then somebody moved out, and they were about three cells apart.

MOREN: "Now, before you got bailed, did you ever hear Tommy Carden say something about going somewhere?"

GUZOWSKI: "Yes."

MOREN: "What did he say?"

GUZOWSKI: "He said when he got through with his trials and his cases, he was going to get away from here and go to Arizona."

MOREN: "Thank you."

Under cross-examination, Prescott made an effort to twist Guzowski's simple and uncomplicated testimony.

PRESCOTT: "Tommy Carden mentioned Arizona to you?"

GUZOWSKI: "Yes."

PRESCOTT: "Did he say Arizona State Prison?"

GUZOWSKI: "No, he didn't."

PRESCOTT: "He didn't say that?"

GUZOWSKI: "No."

PRESCOTT: "You are sure of that?"

GUZOWSKI: "He said the state of Arizona."

PRESCOTT: "That was the end of the conversation?"

GUZOWSKI: "Right."

PRESCOTT: "Did you ask him where he was going..."

GUZOWSKI: "No, I didn't."

PRESCOTT: "...after this trial?"

GUZOWSKI: "No."

PRESCOTT: "He just brought it up?"

GUZOWSKI: "We were in our cells at the time talking, because, like I say, we were locked up twenty-three hours a day, and the only conversation we could have would be through the wall, wall to wall."

PRESCOTT: "He didn't tell you he wanted to go to Ireland, too, did he?"

GUZOWSKI: "He told me..."

PRESCOTT: "He told you that, too, didn't he?"

GUZOWSKI: "No, he didn't, sir. He told me that his family, you know, so and so, was from Ireland originally, that he was Irish."

At that point, Prescott quit. It was obvious that this kid Guzowski was telling the truth.

thirty-eight

Closing arguments began.

Moren went first for Keigney.

Basically, he described the lack of consistency in Carden's testimony. He also pointed out that Carden was the only one to have claimed to have seen Perrotta up and alive and doing anything after the five o'clock count.

He also pointed out that Carden had never told anyone, including Prescott and Bergin, that "sandwich story" before the trial.

He then summarized the testimony of McInerney, MacDonald, and Guzowski.

"You heard the first one, Mr. McInerney. What axe does he have to grind in this case? You heard him say that the day after this happened, he said to Carden, 'I'm sorry. What happened?' And Tommy Carden said, 'I don't know.' The day after it happened, he didn't know."

"Now let's tie this up with the facts that Mr. Carden tells you here. He tells you the first time he told this story—I will call it a story—the first time he told the story that he told here in court was on December 1. Well, if he saw it at the time and if he was in custody there on the 25th and he was taken out of Walpole, why wasn't he shouting at the top of his lungs, 'These three bastards killed my friend and did that to him?' Why didn't he shout it on the 25th, the 26th, the 27th, the 28th, the 29th, and the 30th? Was it somehow more convenient to shout it on December 1? Why? Why? Why? Why didn't he say something about it on all those days?

"Isn't that consistent with what McInerney says happened on the 26th: 'Tommy, I'm sorry. What happened?'"

"'I don't know.'"

"And then we come to the following Tuesday, still before December 1—alone in a room at Bridgewater. He says to McInerney, 'What did you see?' and McInerney says, 'I didn't see anything.' He says, 'You've got to get behind me on this. We can ride this to the street. We can get out of here. Do you want to spend the rest of your life here?'"

"And he still hasn't told his story, because December 1 is Wednesday, and it is undisputed that this meeting took place on Tuesday. You have heard no evidence to the contrary."

"Can you find somebody guilty of first-degree murder on that kind of testimony and that kind of evidence? And we haven't even come to the rest of it."

"Mr. MacDonald comes in. What does he know? Within the week, they had had an argument about the way he was treating his sister and the kids."

"And Mr. Guzowski comes in. He doesn't know these people from a hole in the wall. He knows me, because I was appointed to represent him in another case. He is waiting for trial in Salem and he gets bailed. Tommy Carden is in there a couple of cells down: 'When I get my case over with, I am going to Arizona.'"

"That's the kind of person Tommy Carden is. Is there any question in your mind that he would say anything that he could invent, anything that he could think of, anything that he could conjure up to help himself?"

"You saw him on the stand. He is a coward. He is a crybaby. He would walk over anybody to get himself out of jail. It is quite that simple."

"It took him six days to come up with that fantastic story. And if he had sixty days or six months, he still couldn't tell a story without all these inconsistencies that popped up and which my brothers will refer to in their arguments."

"But the question here is this. Are you willing to believe that witness beyond a reasonable doubt to a moral certainty and say that based on that testimony, Arthur Keigney is guilty of first-degree murder and Arthur Keigney did this horrible thing to this guy? Are you willing to believe that beyond a reasonable doubt to a moral certainty? I don't see how you can."

Al Caplan went next.

Alan started off by pointing out that, except for Carden's testimony, the only evidence connecting us to the crime was that we were in the block when it happened. Or, to be more accurate, when Carden *said* it happened—as were at least twenty-five other guys. Nothing else. We were in the block.

Then Alan started listing all of the numerous inconsistencies in Carden's testimony.

He reminded the jury that, without the last-minute invention of the sandwich story, a strict interpretation of the forensic evidence, based on the amount of undigested food in Perrotta's stomach, would have placed the time of death at no later than sometime in the afternoon.

Then, getting to the heart of the matter he reminded them that I had had no discussion with Campbell and Keigney.

"And, indeed, ladies and gentlemen, there is no evidence whatsoever, not one shred of testimony that other than the fact that they all lived in the same block that Campbell, Keigney, and Doherty knew each other before coming to court."

He then went on to list more inconsistencies, i.e., lies, in Carden's testimony.

He went into Carden's alibi story, where Carden supposedly was at the time that he says that Perrotta was killed. He discussed how he went across the hall to block A-3 to place a bet. The first time he told the story, on December 1, he said that he made the bet with a guy named Pinto. The next time he told it, he said that he had made the bet with a guy named Shotgun.

Then he dissected Carden's story of how he returned to the block and supposedly saw me outside of Perrotta's room.

"Anyway [Carden] says he is in the corridor, he hears the second call for the Perrotta visit, and he comes rushing into the block. He is concerned. He wants to get to Bobby's room."

"Now, we have been shown that there is—and this is by Officer McGuire's testimony—a nine-and-a-half-foot overhang coming right into the block. In addition, there is a four-foot overhang or more than that on either side. The distance diagonally from the center of the doorway to the stairwell is fourteen feet. That is not fourteen feet straight in under the overhang. It is a diagonal distance."

"Carden comes into the block, and he is walking very fast going right for the stairway, but, of course, he claims that he instinctively looks up and happens to see Doherty on the rail. Now, let's look and see at whether he could see Doherty on the rail."

"You have heard virtually uncontradicted testimony as to the degree of darkness, how very dark it was in that cell block that evening. You have seen pictures of it. You have seen the difference in the pictures as between day and night and the effect of the lighting conditions. And at this time, you don't even have the normal lighting conditions existing. You have a large number of those lights being out. All right."

"You have Officer McGuire's earlier testimony that he sees someone just a few minutes earlier go into Perrotta's room and his best guess, if he had to say it was someone, is that was an inmate named Joseph Yandle. That is his best guess."

"Why couldn't he see that well? It was dark."

"Yet, in a quick look, an instinctive look for things being thrown down, according to Carden, he says, 'Yes, it is Doherty.' He sees that as he is rushing in with a concern to go in exactly the opposite direction to that stairwell to get upstairs. And he says that he sees them not running, but walking away."

"Well, I leave it to you, ladies and gentlemen, as to whether or not he in fact could have seen what he said he saw."

"And with respect to Mr. Doherty, even if you were to cut through all of that and somehow believe Carden, believe these inconsistent, preposterous stories, there is not one shred, not one scintilla of evidence before you today that Mr. Doherty, even if you could believe that, had any knowledge of what happened in that room or, indeed, that either of the other defendants had any knowledge of what happened in that room or whether they, like Mr. Yandle, went in and out of the room, too."

"And with respect to that timing, you have the testimony of Officer McGuire saying that Yandle or somebody he thinks is Yandle going in there and saying, 'He is not there', and walking down the corridor. Then Officer McGuire starts calling the other blocks for a Perrotta visit a second time. Can you believe that if in fact Doherty were out there on the rail or keeping the peek, he is going to hang out where Officer McGuire is looking up, looking around for Perrotta, where calls are being made all over the place for Perrotta, but he is going to hang out right there to be seen?"

"Ladies and gentlemen of the jury, I would submit to you that it could not have happened the way Carden says it happened."

Al Nugent went next.

Al pretty much recapitulated the evidence or lack thereof.

Then, to erase any doubts as to whether or not Carden was a liar, he interspersed this with even more discrepancies in Carden's tale.

Then it was Prescott's turn to give his closing argument.

I have never understood the rationale behind forcing defendants to make their closing arguments first, thereby allowing the prosecutor to have the last word. The whole concept of a jury trial is to have the state present all of the evidence that it has to a jury in order to substantiate the charges that they have brought against the defendant. Then the defendant is allowed to respond to those charges, which makes sense, right up to the closing arguments. Then it suddenly becomes topsy-turvy. Because defendants have to make their closing argument first, it is, in essence, redundant and superfluous—nothing more than a subjective summary of the response that they have already made to the prosecution's original presentation of the evidence. Then the prosecution gets to make their closing argument. They get to summarize the evidence from their point of view. This time, however, at one of the most crucial points in the trial, when the prosecution has free rein to present *their* interpretation of the evidence, the defendant is not allowed to give a response, even when the prosecutor misstates the facts.

Prescott immediately went to the issue of whether or not Carden was going to receive any reward for his testimony.

"I would like to point out, immediately, if I may, and just ask you this question—I ask you to ask yourselves this one vital question. Has there been any credible evidence, any evidence whatsoever, that Tommy Carden has any arrangement whereby he goes to Ireland or Arizona or wherever it may be? Is there anything concerning that before you other than some conversation he allegedly had with a couple of people who were brought in here this morning?"

You can bet that Al Caplan would love to have been able to respond by reminding the jury of Carden's unhappy confession that he *had* said that he expected to get out after the trial and go back to Ireland—*when he thought that Alan had the letter in his hand that he'd written saying it.*

He then went to the issue of Carden's lies, which he described as inconsistencies. He was forced to own up to several of them, in an attempt to downplay their significance. In the end though, even Prescott had to characterize segments of Carden's story as ridiculous.

Then, shamelessly, he went on to state, "The Commonwealth is not adopting his position any more than we have to, really. I put Tommy Carden on the stand so up to a point, I am responsible for what he says; but what does that really have to do with the guilt or innocence of these three defendants?"

Excuse me? What does what Carden says have to do with our guilt or innocence? Everything! It was the *only* thing that had anything to do with our guilt or innocence. Or, to be more accurate, the *state's* version of our guilt or innocence! Unfortunately, because the defense has to make their closing argument first, we had no opportunity make that response.

Any defense lawyer would love to be able to respond to a prosecutor who has just admitted that his only witness's testimony was ridiculous, filled with inconsistencies, and that they were only espousing his testimony because they had to (i.e., his lies were all that they had).

Sort of verification of the old cliché, "A bad story is better than no story at all."

As he went on, trying to put a truthful spin on Carden's testimony, there were so many contradictions that he had to keep on apologizing for them.

"And so, if you don't want to believe some of the things that Tommy Carden said, that is up to you. Some of them are incredible."

"And I ask you folks to discount whatever you wish of some of Carden's exaggerations."

Invariably, he would segue his admissions of Carden's misstatements into a downgrading of their significance.

He introduced the issue of the pictures of Perrotta early on in his narration. Then, he used them cutely. He first brought them up to detract attention from the issue of Joseph Yandle's presence at Perrotta's cell at the supposed time of the murder. Later on, he dropped them in, out of the blue, to get away from the subject of how Carden could have known what Perrotta looked like underneath the blanket if he never touched the blanket. Out of nowhere: "And wait until you see those pictures ladies and gentlemen. I submit that no human being's attention could be anywhere but on that horrible head."

In a classic example of twisting what was actually said, he went on to the block officer, Peter McGuire's testimony.

"And how about the other Commonwealth witnesses? How about that young McGuire? They talk about darkness and different degrees of darkness. Obviously there was some degree of darkness. There was a lot of testimony about that. But can you imagine a cell block in a state prison being so dark that you can't see who is who?"

Well, seeing as McGuire, and their "expert" witness, Deputy Superintendent Al Carr, testified to exactly that, they should be able to imagine it.

He finished with two sleazy twists. The first, regarding the witnesses that had to be called as an offer of proof, to justify certain questions that we had asked Carden.

"And you saw the witnesses who came in here today. 'No. I didn't talk to anybody out here.'"

"'We came up in a van.'"

"'No, we didn't talk about the case.'"

"Aw, come on. What do you think of that? Do you believe that?"

"And isn't the bringing in of these witnesses today another thing you want to consider in this whole picture?"

"Well those guys simply represent something that I asked you folks to make observations about at the outset as to why you think we have one prime witness and why we are so doggone fortunate to have even that one. Wasn't that a united inmate front, a united front of inmate society against you and you and everybody else in this state?"

What Prescott carefully avoided mentioning was that McInerney and MacDonald had not seen each other—had not even been in the same prison—since the day after the murder, and that neither one of them had ever met Guzowski before that day. There was nothing "united" about them, and Prescott knew that.

The truth is, the Commonwealth placed the witnesses in the same van and then implied that that was the witnesses' way of getting together to discuss the case.

The last issue that he mentioned wasn't even an issue.

"And remember one other thing, ladies and gentlemen. Carden was asked a question right at the end of his examination. He was asked about another murder. Bobby Perrotta saw that murder. Do you remember the answer? And Bobby Perrotta is dead. Who's next?"

"Folks, if you want a motive for Tommy Carden, you heard it. Parole eligibility, 1988. Never mind Ireland. Never mind Arizona. He is twenty-three and a half hours a day in lock up now—you heard that—in a county jail. If you want a motive, I suggest it is right there."

It was a perfectly sleazy finish for a perfectly sleazy case.

They had started off this case by claiming, for the news, that Bobby Perrotta, in fear of his life, had written a letter to the DOC identifying who his killers were going to be. Then, when we asked that the letter be introduced as evidence, as it would have cleared us, they said that there was no such letter.

Now, that the question was being raised as to what Carden was going to get in exchange for testifying, Prescott's response, actually his multiresponse, left the jury with the unchallenged assertions and implications that Carden was in fear of his life; that he wasn't going to get out of prison for another eleven years; and that we were somehow involved in a second murder.

As soon as he finished, Alan Caplan requested that they be allowed to approach the bench.

CONFERENCE AT THE BENCH AS FOLLOWS:

CAPLAN: "If Your Honor please, I believe Mr. Prescott's statement about a united inmate front united against society, against us, against everyone in the state was highly prejudicial and improper and that that should be stricken and the jury ordered to disregard it and the jury also informed it was highly improper. There was no evidence of any such thing, and I think it is highly and grossly prejudicial."

KEATING: "I will deny that motion."

thirty-nine

The only thing left was the judge's instructions to the jury.

Keating started off his charge by continuously defining being guilty beyond a reasonable doubt as being guilty to a moral certainty, or to a reasonable moral certainty.

He went on to describing the significance of a witness making inconsistent statements.

"If someone at a prior time said something different than what he testified to before you and if you find such statements were made, then any conscientious juror would, of course, pause and look twice at the credibility of the person who is attacked by having been confronted with something he said, which was different at a different time at a different place. But in considering that you also determine whether it is an inconsistency, which is major or which is minor. Is it a deliberate attempt to mislead you?"

In the course of his instructions, I lost track of how many times he used the words "atrocious," "heinous," "barbaric," "horrible," and "wickedness"—until he moved to the next step, where they became, "*extreme* atrocity or cruelty," "*extreme* heinousness."

Then, further on, on the issues of motive, and intent, the judge said:

"Now, it is not the burden of the Commonwealth to show motive... That is not their obligation."

"But at the same time, if motive is established, you may consider that in determining the facts and where ultimate justice lies. But don't put upon the Commonwealth the burden of proving as an essential element of the crime the fact of motive. It is not an essential element of the crime."

"But while motive is not essential, intent is. And this crime requires a specific intent. No crime can be committed without an intent."

"So how do you determine what is in someone's mind? Naturally, that is extremely difficult, and so the law allows you to work backwards by taking the effect or killing, if you will; determining the killing; and inferring from

153

that killing and from the acts of the participants what their intent was. *We are presumed to intend to do what we do do. Otherwise, we wouldn't have done it."*

"Now, if you do come to a point where you are convinced in your discussions and deliberations beyond a reasonable doubt that one of these defendants did in fact kill Robert Perrotta and another or others were present, you will then consider a principle of law known as joint enterprise or acting in concert. It has been said that a definition of what is meant by acting in concert comes to mind if one considers a musical concert, two or more musicians playing together, making somewhat different contributions, with the common purpose of intending to produce a single result, a melody."

"And so, in the law, acting in concert or joint enterprise means this. If two or more persons confederate, act together with a joint purpose to carry out an illegal design, and one aids and abets the other in carrying out that illegal design—and in this case, it would be to do bodily harm to Robert Perrotta—and *if the intent of* all of them or *any two of them* is to do grievous harm to the victim and as a result of their joint effort, their joint enterprise, their acting in concert the victim, Perrotta in this case, was killed, then it doesn't matter at all which one did the killing or which two did the killing; because if you are convinced of the existence of a joint enterprise, as I have defined it, if you are convinced beyond a reasonable doubt of its existence and convinced beyond a reasonable doubt that this joint enterprise resulted in Perrotta's death, *then they are all equally guilty."*

"It doesn't matter whether one is a lookout or whether one is standing by encouraging."

"How do you determine whether there is intent? Take the fact of the killing and take all of the surrounding circumstances and work backwards. And *if the inference is there* that there was an intent in a common purpose, then you draw that inference. If you cannot find it, if you cannot draw it, then you don't draw it. It's as simple as that."

As one-sided as Keating's instructions to the jury were, by far, the most egregious remark that he made, came out when he was ostensibly explaining the definition of premeditated murder. Keating paid Caplan back for proving him wrong, during the argument for a directed verdict of not guilty, on the issue of just who was present at the earlier meeting with Perrotta on the day of the murder.

He told the jury, "Now, premeditated murder is murder thought out beforehand, no matter how briefly or how instantly. Premeditated would be making up your mind beforehand to kill."

"And in that regard, *you may consider*—and again, the facts are yours to decide—*whether or not there was a meeting earlier between the three defendants and the victim. It is for you to decide.* If you disregard that, of course, then you would disregard that as relates to deliberate premeditation. If you find it to be a fact that there was an incident earlier, you may give that some applicability to the question of whether or not there was a deliberate planning of this killing. It is for you to decide."

||||||||||||||||||||||||||||||||||||||||||||||||||||||||||||||||||

At the close of Keating's charge to the jury, the lawyers vehemently objected to Keating telling them that it was up to them to decide whether there had been a meeting between the three defendants and the victim earlier on the day of the murder. Usher Moren described it as "an unwarranted and prejudicial comment by the Court." Attorney Caplan even pointed out that the matter had already been "discussed [the day before] in the motion for a directed verdict—that there was no evidence whatsoever of any meeting between the *three* defendants at any time."

All to no avail, Keating adamantly refused to either change, or correct, what he knew to be a factually inaccurate, and quite damning, instruction. At the worst possible time, just before the case went to the jury.

For the first and only time in the entire trial, the jury had just heard me placed in the company of the other two defendants—and with the victim. Not by any legitimate evidence, but by the judge, even though the evidence clearly and irrefutably placed me at the other end of the block when the meeting took place. Still, it was now in their minds: "Why would the judge tell us that, if there wasn't evidence that Doherty was with the others?"

And it was not a mistake. Keating knew what he was doing. When the subject had been gone into, in detail, the day before, without the jury being present, he had no response. He purposefully introduced false, devastating evidence against me. Something he would not have been able to get away with if the jury had been allowed to view the murder scene. (See diagram of Block A-2, page 103.)

||||||||||||||||||||||||||||||||||||||||||||||||||||||||||||||||||

That morning, after the lawyers and the prosecutor had finished their closing arguments, we had broken for lunch. As we were returning to the holding cage across the hall from the courtroom, one of the court officers had said to me jokingly, "I wish someone was takin' action on this case. I'd put the house on it. You guys are outta here." In the afternoon, when we were returned to the cage, after Keating gave his closing instructions to the jury, the same court officer would not even look at me. And I understood why. Keating had just killed us.

forty

The jury was out for two days. They returned late in the afternoon, on the day before Thanksgiving. As they filed back into the courtroom, any lingering hopes of a not guilty disappeared at the sight of two of the jurors openly crying. I guess they had to get home to buy their turkeys.

On the trip back to Norfolk, I wasn't in a very sociable frame of mind. The two transportation officers sitting in the front seat, while not bothering me with conversation, were discussing the case.

I heard one of them say. "I heard the DA talkin' to some people after the verdict came in. He said that they weren't even gonna indict Doherty except they was afraid of him as a witness."

I thought, "Swell, and I was so sharp I didn't even testify—sharp as a bowling ball."

forty-one

O n Monday, after the long weekend, I called Alan Caplan at his office. When he accepted the call, I said, "Hi. Spend the weekend feeling sorry for yourself?"

He said, "As a matter of fact, I did."

I said, "Me too. Ready to get back to work?"

He laughed and said, "Your goddamn right I am."

"Okay," I said. "C'mon down an' let's get started on the appeal."

Alan was so upset that, about a month or so after the trial ended, on his own, out of his own pocket, he retained the NATIONAL JURY PROJECT to interview the jurors, in an attempt to find out why they had voted guilty.

Unfortunately, after only two of them were interviewed, one of them must have notified the court, or told someone who did, because Keating called Alan and ordered him, in no uncertain terms, to immediately cease and desist the interviews.

Still, we got the results of those two interviews. They were quite illuminating, albeit aggravating.

The first interview was with the foreperson, a woman named Doris Riley. The following are some of Ms. Riley's comments, as quoted in the report.

"Mostly it narrowed down to the fact that they were all present ... None of them came forward to testify ... They never have a witness to any murders in jail ... *There had been a previous murder* (???) "Felt that the prosecution's witness had more to lose than to gain ... it was perfectly obvious to us that his life would be in jeopardy ... he seemed frightened and there was some confusion in his testimony ... (but) he didn't seem very bright and the errors could be from nervousness."

"It was pretty obvious to us that he (Perrotta) was in the cell when somebody walked by."

"It seemed likely to us that it could have happened ... the fact that someone said he was not in the cell."

"The final issue was that *it was most likely that they did it.*"

158

"I was one who was in doubt to the end. I was confused about this man who said he ([P]errotta) wasn't there. He had to be in the cell ... *probability that they were there.*"

Ms. Riley also disclosed "that the three defendants were always considered in a group: that [the jury] didn't analyze the evidence in relation to each one of them separately nor did they try to track each one's movements separately."

She also divulged that, on the first vote, only four of the jurors voted for guilty. The next morning, however, after about one hour's discussion, nine of the jurors voted for guilty.

In evaluating Ms. Riley, one of the interviewer's observations was that Ms. Riley was not a strong foreperson and that it was the interviewer's "feeling that one or more of the people who were for conviction in the first place ran the show from the get go."

The interviewer went on to state that: "This is critical, because it is pretty unusual that a minority prevails as apparently happened in this case."

One of the interviewer's conclusions was that "the decision to convict was hardly based on belief *beyond a reasonable doubt*. She used words like probably and likely too often. So I conclude that she did ultimately give in to the pressure of the group but probably felt that these were prisoners anyhow, so it didn't make much difference."

The second interviewee was a man named Stanley Miller. Right off the bat, Miller's bias against prisoners was as plain as day. In his opening comments he stated:

"The defendants were and witnesses were inmates. From what I learned during and after the trial about what goes on in the institution—in my mind, anyone who is in there is capable of doing almost anything ... the capability is there. I don't think these kinds of peoples' mental processes, consciouses, [*sic*] or whatever work the same way ... To say that these 3 defendants were the only ones (wouldn't be so) ... anyone in there was capable of it ... probably the majority of people there were capable of doing it."

When the interviewer probed Miller on this issue, "Miller talked about the availability of drugs and alcohol, the fact that everyone was high all the time could mean that even the most rational person might do things they wouldn't normally do."

Among Miller's other comments, he stated that, in regard to the defendants, he was:

"Kind of disappointed by the fact that none of them said anything… Couldn't understand, why doesn't somebody say something?… In other cases, the defendant testified, you could hear both sides of the story."

Miller stated that during the deliberations he switched back and forth many times. Not in terms of actual votes but in tending one way or the other. He couldn't remember exactly how many votes were taken or what the numbers were. His best recollection was that there were two or three closed ballots and two open ballots.

He said that, at one point late in the afternoon on the first day of deliberations, one of the jurors expressed frustration that they could not reach a verdict and that maybe they were hung. He said that he argued strenuously with that person that people were still changing their opinions, that it was too soon to say that they were hung.

However, he then went on to say that "I was very surprised when we reached a unanimous opinion… I was under the impression that some of the people who had some doubts still were not convinced."

In response to a question as to whether the jury had considered the charges against each of the defendants separately, he responded, "I think it was separately."

Nonetheless, he then went on to admit that "There was never an attempt to establish that they (the defendants) were individually or collectively anywhere else during the day."

He then went on to describe the issue of food digestion as the only humorous issue in the case and that jurors referred to "peas" during their own meals in order to break the tension.

He went on to say that, during deliberations, the jury "[c]ouldn't figure out why someone was trying to put so much emphasis on the sandwich."

They couldn't figure out that the sandwich story changed the time of death from afternoon to evening?

In summarizing the two interviews, the interviewer's general thoughts on our convictions were as follows:

1. "It was a result of the jurors being convinced that these defendants were probably guilty."

2. "General prejudice against prisoners and an assumption that prison inmates are more capable of committing violent crimes than other people was a determining factor in the verdict."

3. "The jurors couldn't cope with the fact that the defendants didn't testify and no clear alternative theories of the crime were presented."

4. "The only alternative theories they constructed seemed to assume that these defendants had to have been involved."

forty-two

I n February, in the middle of the Blizzard of '78, I was returned from the RB to Ten Block.

I was finally allowed access to the law library, not a great deal of time, once or twice a week for one or two hours. Still, I had to start somewhere. I had not appealed my bank robbery charge. So up to that point, I had never really gotten involved in the law library. Quite literally, I was legally illiterate. That had to change.

Despite the inadequate amount of time that I was allowed to spend there, I was fortunate in one aspect. The law library was run by a civilian law librarian. His name was Richard Adamo.

Richard Adamo turned out to be one of the most decent people that I have ever encountered, which might explain why he was not well liked by the guard's union. For the most part, their goal was to keep people in prison, whether they were guilty or not. Mr. Adamo had a slightly different perspective. He felt that his role was to conduct the law library in such a manner that it would truly familiarize legally unlettered inmates with the law, and, more importantly, with the legal procedures by which it is obfuscated—in other words, to truly do his job.

When he realized that I was sincerely interested in learning how to do legal work, he began to teach me. No question that I asked was too complicated or too dumb, as I'm sure that many of them were. He took his time and made sure that I understood the things that I needed to know. Within a reasonably short amount of time, I was able to look up case law. Then he showed me how to Shepardize case law. That opened the door.

To Shepardize is to look up a case in a series of books known as the *Shepard's Citation Service*. You look up a case and *Shepard's* lists every other case that has cited the case that you are looking up. This leads you to case law on the issue that you are researching. Legal research is impossible without *Shepard's*.

Many people that I know believe that the reason that I eventually reversed my conviction was through sheer persistence. To a degree they are right, but only to a degree. I certainly did not do it alone. Throughout the years, there have been certain people who have made a difference. Richard Adamo was one of the first.

Thank you, Richard.

‖‖

WHEN I WAS returned to Ten Block, I was placed in a real cell as opposed to a strip cell. Actually, I was right next door to it, in cell 13.

One day, it was noon time and I was sitting on the side of my bed eating my lunch and watching the news on TV. The news had just ended, and they were showing a "public service" editorial. It was being done by a spokesman for the DOC. The subject was strip cells. He was in the process of assuring the public that the DOC was as sorry as everybody else that, in the past, they had found it necessary to place men in strip cells. But that now the strip cells no longer existed. They had been abolished. He immediately went on to resurrect them (at least by implication). He said that, in the future, no one would be placed in a strip cell if they had not been seen by two psychiatrists.

As he was in the process of saying this, I heard a thumping, scuffling-type sound, punctuated by assorted familiar noises, screams of pain, and angry curses. I went to my door and stuck my hand mirror out to investigate. There were about a half a dozen guards carrying (rather rudely, I thought) a black inmate down the tier. He was doing a considerable amount of squirming and thrashing about and, as they were passing my cell, a sudden lurch to the side brought them up right against my bars.

As the only cells past mine were the blue rooms, it was obvious where he was headed. I couldn't resist. My face was already up against the bars and, for a brief moment, with our faces no more than a foot apart, we made eye contact.

I said, "Have you seen your psychiatrist today?"

If he replied, I couldn't quite make it out, as there was a rather large elbow pressed firmly into the bottom part of his face.

As he passed from view, head first, about five feet off of the ground, into the blue room, I heard the guy on the TV say something about "continued progress in prison reform."

A couple of days later, when they let him come out for a shower, I called him over to my door. He was a little leery, but he came over. I told him what had been on the TV when he went by my door. He stared at me for a moment while it sunk in. Then he got a big grin on his face.

He said, "Man, I heard exactly what ya said, when ya said it. After they threw me inna room an' slammed the do', all I could think of was 'Oh shit. They got me on a tier fulla nuts.' Then when y'all started sendin' me in smokes an' shit to read an' stuff, I thought, 'Okay, maybe it's just one nut.' But man, I thought *you* was a fuckin' bug. *Have I seen my psychiatrist today? Sheeit.*"

Welcome to Ten Block.

forty-three

POST-TRIAL SWINDLES

I n December 1978, we filed our appeals with the Massachusetts Supreme Judicial Court (SJC). Between the obvious constitutional errors, and the absolute paucity of evidence, a number of lawyers—plus others who were even more intimately familiar with the appellate process from an inmate's point of view, *jailhouse lawyers*—assured me that the SJC would have a difficult time in not reversing the conviction.

One lawyer stated flatly, "Any other judge but Keating would have given you a Directed Verdict of Not Guilty."

But, shortly after we filed the appeal, things got worse. The appeal was argued in February 1979 and, in March, they indicted Campbell and me for another Walpole murder—Johnny Stokes. Stokes' murder was very similar to the Perrotta murder. It had taken place just a few months before the Perrotta killing. It happened in the same cell block. Like Perrotta, Johnny Stokes was found dead in his bed. Finally, as with Bobby, the Commonwealth inferred that Johnny was killed, because someone was afraid that he was going to rat on them.

The only problem was both Campbell and I were out in the visiting room when Stokes was killed. Campbell worked there, and I was on a visit. To go from the visiting room to block A-2, where the murder occurred, you have to pass through two solid steel doors and three steel gates. It was physically impossible for either one of us to have done it. The log books in both the visiting room and the cell block would clear both of us.

So, why the indictments?

As in the Perrotta case, the only evidence against us was a lone inmate informant (named John Hines) who was being rewarded for his testimony. However, shortly after, we were indicted, Hines wrote to the assistant district attorney who was handling the case, ADA (now Judge) Robert Banks, and told him as clearly as possible that he was not going to testify. He also told him that he had already had the deputy warden, at the jail where he was then being held, call the investigating officer, State Police Lieutenant Jack Nasuti, and tell him that he could not go through with it. However, Nasuti would not let up on him. He admitted that the only reason that he had even said what he had said was to get out of Walpole, because he was afraid that he was going to die there. He finished the letter by stating that he could not testify *"... no matter what promises Mr. Nazzutti [sic] has made to me. I can't go through with it. Because only 60 percent is the truth on what I told."*

Apparently, Lt. Nasuti was performing the same tasks for the Norfolk County DA's office in 1979 that Lt. Bergin had performed in 1976.

As in the Perrotta case, the informant's letter was hidden from the defense.

Although the DA's office had this letter in March 1979, they kept us charged for Johnny Stokes' murder for another five months—until a few weeks after the SJC turned down our appeal and upheld the Perrotta conviction, in August 1979. Then, the DA quietly dropped the Stokes' charges and turned the letter over to us. It had served its purpose.

The SJC had a rule then called the "120 day rule." They had to decide a case in 120 days. On the 120th day, I received a notice from the SJC stating that, "In your case, we are waiving the 120 day rule."

Now, while it's highly unlikely that any of the SJC judges that upheld the Perrotta conviction would ever admit that they were influenced by, or even aware of the second murder indictment. The fact is, while they were deciding the Perrotta case, it was public knowledge that Campbell and I had been charged with another prison murder that had occurred under similar circumstances just a few months before Bobby Perrotta had been killed.

Judges are only human, and they don't live in a vacuum.

||||||||||||||||||||||||||||||||||||||||||||||||||||||||||||||||||||||

The following is a quick postscript to the Stokes' story that will give you a little insight into the way that some cops handled cases in Walpole.

The day that Johnny got killed, the state police who were investigating the murder interviewed all of the inmates who were living in A-2, where the murder happened. When my turn came, I told them that I had nothing to say.

It was none of my business. Plus, you learn very quickly that the MIRANDA warning is quite literally true: "Whatever you say, can, and will, be used against you ..." Even if they have to twist your words to make them sound as if they mean something that you really didn't say, so be it. That is what they do.

Anyway, when I told the investigator that I had nothing to say, he responded, "Why not? Are you afraid of someone?"

I said, "Yeah. You."

"Just tell us where you were," he said.

"That easy. Just check the log books."

He called me a rather disparaging name and told me to get out.

I did and that ended the interview.

However, a few years later, after they came down with the bogus Stokes' indictment, in response to our discovery motion, the court ordered them to give us a copy of the inmate interviews—which they did, as it was standard procedure, except, of course, in the Perrotta case.

The investigator's version of my statement was that I claimed to have been sleeping and that I said that I heard nothing. Not only did they flat out lie, and make up a story to put in my mouth, they obviously never looked in the log books either.

One other quick Stokes' postscript is as follows.

Shortly after I got out of Ten Block, in 1980, the block I was living in, B-3, and one other block, B-2, went down to the gym together; that's 90 guys.

Two guys got in a beef, and one of them died. One guy had a hockey stick. The other guy had a knife. The guy with the hockey stick died.

Nothing to me, I didn't know either one of them. They both lived in B-2. But, as was customary, they called out each inmate who had been present to be interviewed individually.

When my turn came, I went out to the interviewing room. I walked in, and there were two guys sitting there doing the interviews. I know one of them. He was a Walpole screw, named Frank, who'd worked his way up the ladder, not a bad guy.

We exchanged greetings and he said, "Stevie, I don't know if you know Lieutenant Nasuti. He's the investigating officer on the case."

Nasuti just nodded his head at me.

Now, while I had never actually met Lt. Nasuti, I was well aware of just who he was from John Hines' letter.

So I said to Frank, "Sure I know him."

Then, looking at Nasuti, I said, "You're the guy that tried to frame me for the Stokes' murder."

He immediately denied all knowledge and involvement. He was also stammering and garbling his words. I don't think he'd expected me to open up that can of worms.

He finished on an indignant note that he would never do anything like that, *yadayadayada.*

I said, "Gee, I must have you confused with someone else. Why don't I go back to my cell and get a copy of the letter that Hines wrote naming the cop that was trying to get him to frame me."

At that point, Frank interceded and said, "Listen Stevie, we're all done here. We know you had nothing to do with this thing down the gym. You can just go back to your cell."

I said to him, "OK"

But, as I was getting up, I said to Nasuti, "Unless you'd like to see that letter, lieutenant. See who I confused you with? I got no problem bringing it right back down here if you wanna check it out."

Nasuti just continued to look at the papers on the desk in front of him. He never looked up, and Frank just waved me out the door with a half a grin on his face.

By the way, a few years later, another inmate confessed to the Stokes' murder, one who was not a part of their imaginary "Execution Squad" publicity stunt.

forty-four

t's worth noting that, while the SJC did uphold the Perrotta conviction, in their decision,[6] they were forced to acknowledge that the evidence against Campbell and Keigney was "somewhat thin." They then went on to concede that the evidence against me was "a somewhat closer question" than the "somewhat thin" case against the other two.

It has to make you stop and think. Words have a specific meaning. If the evidence in a first-degree murder case is admittedly somewhat thin, then that puts it just barely over the line, which determines whether or not the evidence was sufficient to warrant a conviction.

Therefore, if you have a companion case where the evidence is *a somewhat closer question* than evidence that was barely adequate, how can it still be sufficient?

The SJC said that it was.

|||||||||||||||||||||||||||||||||||||||||||||||||||||||||||||||||

SOME OF THE other issues that the SJC ruled on were as follows:

They denied the issue of voir dire.

As I said above, the purpose of voir dire is to eliminate jury bias by asking questions of the prospective jurors. We truly would have preferred not to be judged by jurors who hated prisoners.

The SJC denied the issue.

Their rationale was that, where the only evidence against us came from another inmate, "the prejudice, if any, by jurors against inmates as a class, would be as likely to favor the defendants as to harm them."

Sounds good. It might even be valid and make sense if the jury had to decide between convicting us or convicting Carden. But they didn't have that option. We were the only ones liable for punishment. Any juror who had a bias against convicts had only one target for their antipathy, us.

|||||||||||||||||||||||||||||||||||||||||||||||||||||||||||||||||

THEY DENIED THE issue of our being allowed to see the results of the forced inmate interviews. In an obvious attempt to downplay the significance of the issue, they slid it in at the end of the decision, categorizing it under:

"*Miscellaneous alleged errors*. We have considered all the other alleged errors argued by the defendants and conclude that they are not sufficiently meritorious to warrant extended discussion."

They then limited their "finding," on the issue of our not being allowed to see the results of the forced inmate interviews, to four sentences.

"The mere showing that the Commonwealth interviewed a number of prison inmates does not, without more, create an obligation to tell the defense the results of the interviews or the names of inmates interviewed. See *Weatherford v. Bursey* [cite]. There is no showing on this record that defense counsel attempted to learn from any other source the names of inmates present in MCI Walpole on the day of the killing or to interview any of them. The prosecutor had no obligation to act as an investigator for the defendants. These facts do not implicate the rule of Brady v Maryland, [cite], requiring the prosecution to disclose evidence favorable to the defense on request. [cite]." It sounds precise and judicious, and it is. It is a very precise and judicious way of glossing over and getting around the issue.

First of all, the Weatherford decision that they cited to justify their finding was about a different issue. It was about an undercover agent, who testified, *after being present at supposedly confidential lawyer/client meetings*. In *Weatherford v. Bursey*, the United States Supreme Court ruled that "Brady [v. Maryland] is not implicated here *where the only claim is that the State should have revealed that it would present the eyewitness testimony of a particular agent against the defendant at trial*." Not our issue.

Now, let's take it one point at a time.

"The mere showing that the Commonwealth interviewed a number of prison inmates does not, *without more*, create an obligation to tell the defense the results of the interviews or the names of inmates interviewed."

Right, but there was more. Delahunt's comments, when he was grandstanding for the media on the day after they forced the interviews would certainly qualify as "*more*." He made it quite clear that they had uncovered, "*A lot of new … very productive … worthwhile … information*." Is that not "more?"

Then, to compound the above, on the day after we were convicted, Delahunt told the *Boston Globe* that he "credited the successful prosecution in large part to Corrections Commissioner Frank Hall, who, he said, allowed dozens of state troopers into the prison after Perrotta's murder to question every inmate in block A." Is that not "more?"

Well, let's see:

a. The specific purpose of the forced interviews was to gain information regarding the murder of Bobby Perrotta, which could be used at our trial.

b. Delahunt specifically stated, for the headlines, just hours after the interviews took place that new, very productive, and worthwhile information was discovered during these interviews.

c. Delahunt attributed our conviction in large part to the forced interviews.

d. However, none of this newly discovered, very productive, and worthwhile evidence was ever used at our trial.

e. If this information had been inculpatory, Delahunt certainly would have used it at trial.

f. But he didn't; so the information could not have been inculpatory.

g. Therefore, it had to have been exculpatory.

(Unless there is a third class of "new, very productive, worthwhile information" that I am unaware of, that is neither inculpatory nor exculpatory. Something like, "*maybeculpatory?*" Or "*wedonthavetotellyouifitsculpatory?*"

A purely objective evaluation of the facts, in our case, would seem to mandate that the information that Delahunt said was discovered during the forced inmate interviews had to be "favorable to the defense."

Next: "There is no showing on this record that defense counsel attempted to learn from any other source the names of inmates present in MCI Walpole on the day of the killing or to interview any of them. The prosecutor had no obligation to act as an investigator for the defendants."

From what "other source" do you request the information, "Who were the inmates in the 'A' Section of Walpole?", except from the Commonwealth? They are the only ones that know!

That's what we did. They wouldn't tell us. That was part of the issue!

And, no, the prosecution does not have an obligation to act as an investigator for the defense. However, when they are conducting an investigation for themselves and they discover evidence that is favorable to the defense, then they do have an obligation to disclose that information. It's not like our lawyers could walk into Walpole with twenty investigators and force every inmate in the minimum section to talk to them! As Al Nugent said to Keating at one point, "Judge, I have to wait an hour to get in, but Mr. Prescott goes there, and the doors open and carpets roll out. Not so for us."

They ended with: "These facts do not reach the point of implicating the rule of *Brady v. Maryla*nd [cite], requiring the prosecution to disclose evidence favorable to the defense on request [cite]." Well, in regard to the SJC's misciting of the *Brady* decision, there actually is a case quite similar to this case that specifically addresses the issue at hand. In *Schlup v. Delo* (cite) a prison murder case in which an inmate was wrongfully convicted, a federal court, in a decision that was upheld by the United States Supreme Court, used some rather edifying language regarding the issue of inmate interviews. To wit: "*I assume that transcripts of the prisoner interviews were available to trial counsel. Were they unavailable, Schlup is entitled to relief under Brady v. Maryland, (cite), due to the prosecution's failure to turn over such exculpatory evidence in violation of due process.*" (cite) [emphasis added]

|||||||||||||||||||||||||||||||||||||||||||||||||||||||||||||||||||

ANOTHER ISSUE THAT they tried to denigrate by burying it under "*Miscellaneous alleged errors*" was the issue of Judge Keating's instructions to the jury that contained numerous egregious errors and was clearly indicative of his bias.

The entirety of their ruling was as follows:

"The claims of alleged errors in the judge's charge are based on the lifting of certain phrases and fragments of phrases from their context in the charge as a whole. We have repeatedly said that a charge must be construed as a whole and that, in consequence, isolated misstatements or omissions do not necessarily constitute reversible error. [cite] None of the portions of the charge isolated by the defendants violates this test."

That was all well and good, all three sentences. But how about when he flat out lies?

Their "finding" avoids the issue of Keating blatantly introducing a falsely incriminating scenario by telling the jury that they could consider whether or not I had been present at the earlier meeting with the other defendants and the victim. Especially when it had already been made clear to him that the only testimony regarding the earlier meeting clearly showed that the meeting was between Campbell and Keigney, with Perrotta, and that Carden's testimony had placed me some eighty feet away from them at the time of the meeting.

It would seem likely to me that at least one of the five members of the venerable SJC who ruled against me should have been aware of the fact that the law of the land on that very issue, for well over a hundred years, was that:

"It is clearly error in a court to charge a jury upon a supposed or conjectural state of facts, of which no evidence has been offered. The instruction presupposes that there is some evidence before the jury which they may think sufficient to establish the facts hypothetically assumed in the opinion of the court; and if there is no evidence which they have a right to consider, then the charge does not aid them in coming to correct conclusions, but its tendency is to embarrass and mislead them. It may induce them to indulge in conjectures, instead of weighing the testimony." (cite)

At least that's what the United States Supreme Court said in a case called *United States v. Breitling*, back in the 1850s.

||||||||||||||||||||||||||||||||||||||||||||||||||||||||||||||||||||||||||

THEY DENIED THE issue of the prosecutor's summation.

The SJC justified Prescott telling the jury that the three inmates who testified were "a united front of inmate society against them and everybody else in the state," by saying that, "It was a reasonable inference from the evidence that the three inmates who testified for the defense had coordinated their testimony."

Not so. In fact, the evidence shows just the opposite. At no time, after the murder, were these three inmates ever located in the same institution. MacDonald was isolated in Ten Block. McInerney was housed at Bridgewater. Guzowski was at Norfolk, and he had never even met any of the defendants or their lawyers, let alone the other two witnesses.

The SJC's awareness of the weakness of their justification of Prescott's remark was obvious in their following statement:

"In another aspect, the prosecutor's remark can be understood as an explanation and apology for the weakness of the Commonwealth's case."

It was truly amazing. In essence, what they said was that the Commonwealth had such a weak case that they were allowed to make statements that were not only unsupported by the evidence but were flat-out provable lies.

||||||||||||||||||||||||||||||||||||||||||||||||||||||||||||||||||||||||||

ANOTHER ISSUE THAT they reduced to the category of "*Miscellaneous alleged errors*" was the issue of the restriction of the cross-examination of the Commonwealth's "prison expert." Deputy Warden Al Carr. This "finding" was down to two sentences.

They said that the issue of "Perrotta's use of a door peg...w[as] already before the jury with sufficient clarity."

Not hardly. In fact, all that the jury knew about Perrotta's door peg was that Carden described it as "one of the better types." The jury had no way of knowing what that entailed.

Without Keating's protection, Deputy Carr would have had to testify that some pegs worked so well that correction officers have had to tear solid steel doors off of their hinges to get inside the cell. This requires a lot of time and makes a lot of noise. It would have been impossible for anyone to have removed "one of the better types" of pegs from Perrotta's door in the amount of time that Carden claimed that it happened and/or so quietly that the block officer, sitting right downstairs, wouldn't have heard it.

Without the jury being allowed to view the scene, an in-depth description of a door peg was essential to the jury's understanding of the case.

||||||||||||||||||||||||||||||||||||||||||||||||||||||||||||||||||

THEY DENIED THE issue of the jury not being allowed to view the scene of the murder.

They said, "Our view of the transcript persuades us that the jury were able to understand distances, angles, and physical layout from oral testimony given in conjunction with prison slides."

I wonder where, in their "view of the transcript" they saw that?

This reasoning is totally refuted by the complete inadequacy of both the "oral testimony" and the quality, or lack thereof, of the "prison slides."

Prescott's argument against a jury view was that he had an expert bringing in slides of the murder scene, block A-2. Yet the expert was unable to identify even one of them as being A-2. One of the slides was so dark that he couldn't even give any idea of where in the block the picture had been taken.

It wasn't just Al Carr. Carden, while attempting to point out his own cell, had to admit that, "This picture is a little blurry. I don't even know if this is two cells or one."

If the slides were so bad that Carden was unable to pick out his own cell and a prison expert with twenty years experience couldn't identify even one out of nine slides of cell blocks that he was in charge of, how could you expect a panel of jurors, who had never seen the inside of a prison, to have any comprehension of what the murder scene even looked like?

Bottom line: This was the first time that a jury view had ever been denied in a Walpole murder trial. It was also the first time that they were able to get a conviction in a Walpole murder trial. It was no coincidence.

I wonder how many judges have denied a prosecutor's request for a jury view in a first-degree murder trial? Especially in a prison, a setting with which your average juror is totally unfamiliar.

forty-five

number of other issues came to light after the trial. After your first appeal to the SJC, all other appeals have to be initially filed with the trial judge. As expected, Keating's rulings were just more of the same.

In regard to the "sandwich story," which resurrected Carden's credibility after the autopsy report had showed him to be lying, we made a startling discovery after the trial.

One night, after we had been found guilty and I had been returned to Ten Block, I was lying in my cell, reading. Arthur Keigney was having a cell-to-cell conversation with a guy that we knew, named Freddie Allen.

Freddie had just come into the hole from population and, as we had been locked up for a couple of years, we hadn't seen him, and they were catching up on things. Naturally, he wanted to know everything about the case. Like everyone else, he had one question: "How the hell did you guys get found guilty?"

I wasn't really listening to them as I was reading. However, after you've been in the hole for a while, you develop an unconscious knack, a sort of subconscious awareness of what is going on around you. With fifteen guys living next door to each other on an enclosed tier, between conversations, televisions, and radios, there is always a certain noise level. You learn to adjust to it, and it becomes susurrus—white noise. However, if something is said that does concern you, it pierces the blanket of sound that encompasses you.

Although I really didn't hear what Arthur had said, he was obviously in the process of describing to Freddie how Carden had made up the story about Perrotta bringing two sandwiches back from the noon-time meal on Thanksgiving.

What I did hear, quite clearly, was Freddie's response. "Of course he lied. They don't serve bread on Thanksgiving. They serve those little rolls."

It was like an electric shock. I was off of the bed in a flash and up to the bars. I said, "What did you say?"

Freddie responded, "I said they don't serve bread on Thanksgiving. They got those little rolls. You ain't gonna make much of a fuckin' sandwich on one a' them."

I was speechless. I've never been much of a bread eater, especially on a day like Thanksgiving. You've only got so much stomach space, and I never liked the idea of wasting it on bread—especially when there's plenty of turkey and potatoes and cranberry sauce to put in there. Consequently, I was totally unaware that bread was not served with the Thanksgiving Day meal. I would never even have considered taking up any of the space on my tray with bread.

I went back over the autopsy report. It stated that Carden had approximately 500 grams of essentially undigested Thanksgiving food in his stomach, e.g., potatoes, turkey, peas, and raisins. There was no mention of bread.

When I told Alan Caplan about it, he immediately filed a request with the Department of Correction, asking that we be allowed to see the menu for Thanksgiving Day.

They denied the request, even though the document in question was a public document and should have been available on request. We were subsequently forced to file a discovery motion with the court. We filed it and asked that we be allowed to see the weekly Walpole dining room menus for the entire years of 1974, 1975, 1976, and 1977.

At the court's order, the DOC reluctantly turned them over—almost. It seems that out of the four years of menus that we requested—a total of some two hundred and eight menus—they claimed that two were missing, the week of Thanksgiving 1975 and the week of Thanksgiving 1976.

Hmm, that was probably a coincidence.

In an attempt to justify their withholding of the menus, the DOC sent the following letter to the Clerk of Court.

December 3, 1979
NORFOLK SUPERIOR COURT
HIGH STREET
DEDHAM, MASSACHUSETTS, 02026

Dear Sir,

I have examined all available records pertaining to food menus at M. C. I. Walpole, and have been unable to locate menus for Thanksgiving in both the following years, 1975 and 1976.

The information requested was for the Stephen Doherty case. To my recollection the actual Thanksgiving menus for 1975 and 1976 were submitted to the Attorney General's Office for evidence based on the Perrotta murder that took place at this facility in 1976.

Photo copies could not be obtained due to the type of paper that the menu was typed on. Because of this we had no other alternative but to submit the original ones.

I hope that this letter will be sufficient, however should additional correspondence be required due [sic] not hesitate to contact my office.

Sincerely yours,
Robert J. Allain
Steward

When we protested, the DOC finally conceded that bread had not been served.

To get around this glaring discrepancy, Keating ruled that "Carden never used the word 'bread' in his testimony."

Which, in fact, was a lie, albeit, a cute lie.

Attorney Caplan had used the word "bread" in his cross-examination when he specifically asked Carden, "[Y]ou do recall the *bread?*"

To which Carden replied, "That's correct."

Keating conveniently overlooked that. Based on that misleading "finding," Keating then went on to "find" that the alleged sandwiches could have been made on two of the small dinner rolls—sandwiches that would have had to contain over a pound of undigested Thanksgiving Day food! He stated that even if the rolls were very small, they still could have been used to make sandwiches.

I suppose, theoretically, that they could have. However, in the real world, you have to remember that these two rolls were two square inches and that there was at least a pound of Thanksgiving food found in Perrotta's stomach, not counting the alleged bread. Do the math. Maybe Julia Childs could have made sandwiches with that much food on those little rolls, but I couldn't. And believe me, I tried.

The following Thanksgiving Day (1978), when they brought the noon meal around, sure enough, there were the rolls, no bread, just rolls. I tried and tried, fruitlessly, to put the meal on the two rolls. You also have to take into account that the meals that were served in Ten Block were a lot smaller than the meals that were served in population. I still couldn't do it.

I got two more rolls from one of the other guys and very carefully wrapped them up in toilet paper. On my next visit with Alan Caplan, I brought them with me. I considered them to be evidence. I gave them to Alan and asked that he keep them safe. My feeling was that not only would they be necessary to our appeal, they would also be quite useful if we were tried again. If our original jury had known that bread had not been served, and had been allowed to see the diminutive dinner rolls, they would have known immediately that Carden's story was preposterous.

Also, to get around the fact that raisins were found in Perrotta's stomach, which even the sandwich story could not explain, Keating's justification was that Carden may have confused raisins with peas! This finding was based on absolutely no evidence and was about as likely as fitting over a pound of food on two, two-inch dinner rolls.

forty-six

When it came out after trial that it *was* Carden who had falsely accused Mickey Donahue of the murder of Jimmy Aloise, Keating dismissed that issue by saying that Carden had only been passing on second-hand information. He completely ignored the fact that Carden had told Prescott that he had actually seen part of the murder—which, by definition, took it out of the realm of second-hand information.

Carden had made this accusation in the very same interview in which he first accused us of having killed Perrotta. Unfortunately, when we requested a copy of the interview, Prescott didn't want to give it to us. (Understandable, seeing as he had already told a different judge [Judge Mazzone] before trial, that Carden had made no false accusations!) So, Keating told him that he could edit the interview.

Needless to say, when we received our "edited" copy, there was no mention of Carden's accusation that Donahue had killed Aloise.

Despite Keating's downplaying of its significance, the fact is, the DOC considered the allegation serious enough to officially charge Donahue with Aloise's murder. That is, until they found out that Carden had to be lying, because Donahue had been on a visit at the time of the murder. That's when they immediately dropped the charges.

My original plan to catch Carden in a lie regarding Knothead had gone awry. A couple of months after Knothead had agreed not to use his alibi at the d-board hearing (after I'd been taken in front of the grand jury and stashed in Bridgewater), the DOC dropped the charges against Knothead. When I heard about it, I assumed that he had told them that he was on a visit. Once he did that, they dropped the charges and buried Carden's statement.

That was in 1976. I didn't see Knothead again until sometime in 1980 or 1981, after I got out of the hole. The first thing that he said when he saw me was, "I didn't do it. I swear to God, I didn't tell them. Lemme tell ya what happened."

"Go ahead," I said.

"It wasn't me. It was my lawyer, Richard Vita. I told him not to say anything, but when we were in front of the d-board, he told them," he said.

I thought about it, and I believed him. Or, at least, I gave him the benefit of the doubt. I was familiar with the lawyer that he mentioned. He was young at the time and a publicity hound looking to make a name for himself.

Back when we had first been placed in Ten Block and had filed a civil action asking that we be placed back into population, things had reached the point where Al Caplan had pulled Arthur, Jackie, and me out of the suit. He said that, the way that things were going, not only were we going to lose the suit, but, far more importantly, we were giving the court an opportunity to make a ruling that would create bad law. He said that the problem was that Richard Vita, who was representing Knothead and a couple of the others, was going to go ahead with it.

Well, Alan was right on the money. The court issued a decision titled "FOUR CERTAIN UNNAMED INMATES v. [Commissioner of Correction] *Frank A. HALL*." The decision, in essence, "refined" the law regarding the procedure whereby the DOC could lock inmates in the hole, stating that it could now be done at the "whim of [the] commissioner."

||||||||||||||||||||||||||||||||||||||||||||||||||||||||||||||||||||||||||

IN THE INTERIM, between our meetings, Knothead had gotten out. While he was out, the cops framed him for a bank robbery and gave him a life sentence.

He told me all about it when he came back. He said that the cops were looking for two other guys for the bank. They thought that Knothead knew where they were. They told him that he had two choices. Either give up the other two guys or they would charge him with the bank. He told them he didn't know where they were. So, they indicted, tried, and convicted him.

After convicting him, they came back with their second offer, life or probation. If he would give them the other two guys, he'd get probation; if he didn't, he'd get life.

He got life and came back to Walpole.

Right around the same time, they were in the process of trying to frame Myles Connor for the murder of two girls. Myles had just received a couple of thousand pages of discovery. Included were a large number of statements that had been made by the informant in the case, Thomas Sperrazza, who happened to be the real killer.

As luck would have it, when Sperrazza rolled over, they took his wife into protective custody with him. When the cops turned over Sperrazza's statements to Myles' lawyer, Earle Cooley, they inadvertently included a statement that Sperrazza's wife had given them regarding Knothead.

It seems that, on the morning that the bank that they framed Knothead for was robbed, Knothead had been with Sperrazza's wife washing a car in the driveway of a motel.

Better yet, the cops had known this. They had had this statement in their possession *at the time that they were framing Knothead.*

I was sitting in the chow hall eating and in walked Knothead. He came over to my table and handed me a piece of paper.

He said, "Myles just gave me this. What's it mean?"

I looked at it and started to laugh. I said, "It means you're goin' home."

Still, they stalled him for a while, even shipped him to the federal system in early 1982, to stretch it out. But, in the end, the courts reversed Knothead's conviction, and they had to let him go home.

forty-seven

We filed an appeal of Keating's denial of our motion for a new trial, based on newly discovered evidence, with the SJC.

Massachusetts has a rather bizarre procedure, applicable only in first-degree murder cases, whereby the appellant must be granted leave to appeal to the full bench of the SJC, by a single justice of the SJC, i.e., the gatekeeper.

We drew Justice Wilkins as the gatekeeper. Wilkins was one of the judges who denied our original appeal.

Wilkins denied us leave to appeal to the full bench. Basically, he simply adopted Keating's findings.

One of the things he wrote was, "[Keating] heard Carden's testimony as well as the medical testimony concerning the time of Perrotta's death, and he was in a better position than I to pass on the effect the menu evidence might have had on the jury." (citation) I agree with the judge that the fact that dinner rolls may have been served instead of sliced bread is not necessarily inconsistent with Carden's testimony which, *as the judge noted, did not speak of "bread."*

Apparently, Justice Wilkins did not really read the transcript.

forty-eight

At one point, not long before I was released from Ten Block, I was given a d-report as a result of a minor scuffle with a few guards in Ten Block. I was, of course, found guilty. They gave me some time on the boards (isolation) and a sanction of three hundred days loss of good time.

When I wrote the appeal to the warden, one of the things that I mentioned was the three hundred days good-time hit. I pointed out that when they said that I had killed an inmate, they took a hundred and fifty days, but when they said that I punched a screw they took three hundred.

When Fred Butterworth responded, he upheld the guilty finding. However, he did reduce the good time sanction to a hundred and fifty days.

A couple of days later, I ran into him on my way back from a visit.

I said, "Hey Fred, I got your response to my appeal. Thanks for the hundred and fifty days back."

Then, smiling, I said, "But what's up with that? When ya said I killed a con, ya took a hundred an' fifty days, and now when ya say I punched a cop, ya take a hundred an' fifty. What's that mean, killin' a con an' punchin' a cop are about the same thing?"

He looked at me for a moment and then nodded his head. "Yeah," he said. "That's about right."

We both laughed.

forty-nine

When I was finally released from Ten Block, back into general population, in 1980, I began my own investigation.

Eventually, I discovered that, in complete contradiction of what John Prescott had told the jury—that Carden was not going to be rewarded for his testimony, that he couldn't even see the parole board for another eleven years—just one month after our trial ended (two days before Christmas on the last day of the court session), Prescott surreptitiously had Carden brought back in front of his original sentencing judge. He told the judge that Carden had done such a courageous job testifying against us—embellishing his unfounded claim that Carden's life had been threatened numerous times by falsely telling the Court that "Carden was the first inmate in the history of the institution, which goes back some twenty-three years, to have the courage to testify against other inmates on a murder case within MCI Walpole"that he deserved to have his twenty- to thirty-year sentence reduced.[7]

Prescott had a lawyer friend of his, (now Judge) Geoffrey Packard, come in and represent Carden.

The hearing was concise and to the point. It only took a few minutes. It also erased any questions as to whether or not Carden was being rewarded for his testimony. The judge reduced his sentence to nine to ten years.

When I first found out that Carden had gotten his sentenced reduced, I called Al Caplan. Alan was out in California at the time. He was defending one of the Hell's Angels in a RICO case.

When he got on the line he said, "Boy, have I got a story for you."

"Yeah. Well, I got one for you, too," I said.

"Okay, you go first. I'll hold mine, 'cause you're gonna love it," he said.

"Tommy Carden got his sentence reduced. He's either out or he's on the verge of getting out," I said.

There was a moment of silence. Then Alan said loudly, "WHAT?"

"I tracked down a guy that knows his people. He said that he's either on the street or on his way out the door," I said.

185

Alan, laughed and said, "Son of a bitch. We just found out today that the government paid the witness in my case seventy thousand dollars and dropped four murder charges. Now you tell me this. Listen can you call me back in a half hour? I want to make a phone call."

I said, "Sure."

When I called him back, he said, "You're not gonna believe this. I just called John Prescott. When I told him what you said, he never denied it. All he wanted to know was how I found out."

Carden also had a number of other Massachusetts sentences and (bank robbery) charges. Prescott arranged for these to simply go away.

It turned out that one of these bank robbery charges had actually been disposed of *before our trial.*

A few weeks after Carden testified against us at the grand jury, causing us to be indicted, he was brought into Suffolk Superior Court on bank robbery charges and received a seven- to eight-year sentence *that was to be served concurrently with the twenty- to thirty-year sentence that he was already serving.*

They never specifically stated in open court that Carden was testifying for the Commonwealth.

This allowed them to hide this information from us at trial. Furthermore, years later, when we uncovered this information, it allowed them to deny that Carden's getting a small concurrent sentence (i.e., no time) was in exchange for his testimony.

There was, however, a brief exchange between the sentencing judge (Judge Travers) and Carden's lawyer (Bernard Bradley), which makes it quite clear to anyone who wants to face the truth, that Judge Travers was well aware that Carden's twenty- to thirty-year sentence was going to be reduced somewhere down the road.

MR. BRADLEY. "I would ask your Honor to impose some kind of short concurrent sentence on both of these things just so the papers can be closed out and he can serve his time."

THE COURT: "What kind of concurrent?"

MR. BRADLEY: "Four to six, seven to eight."

THE COURT: "Seven to eight would not interfere?"

MR. BRADLEY: "No, Your Honor."

THE COURT: "All right, seven to eight concurrent."[8]

Interfere with what? A twenty- to thirty-year sentence? The last thing that Judge Travers did, before Bradley made his pitch, was to read Carden's record. So, he had Carden's record in front of him and thereby knew that Carden only had two to three years in on the twenty- to thirty-year sentence. Does anybody honestly believe that Judge Travers was so naive that he wouldn't know off the top of his head that a seven- to eight-year concurrent sentence could in no way interfere with Carden's twenty to thirty? So why did he ask? Why else? He had to know that Carden was going to have his sentence reduced at some point to a number small enough that a seven to eight might interfere with his getting out.

Judge Travers also disposed of a prison escape charge on that same day. He placed it on file.

After disposing of all of Carden's Massachusetts cases, Prescott then called the feds and arranged for Carden to receive an early parole from 3 twenty-year federal sentences that he was also serving.

The earliest that Carden could be released from the federal sentence was 1981. So, they arranged for him to be kept in a county house of correction in Massachusetts. Coincidentally, the seven- to eight- and the nine- to ten-year state sentences both happened to wrap up just when Carden became eligible for an early federal parole in 1981.

When it came time for him to be released, it turned out that, for all of the sentences that they had fixed for him, they had missed one. Even though they had fixed his escape charge, they had forgotten to wipe out the Concord sentence from which he had escaped. So, they quickly brought him in front of another judge, Judge Donahue, to take care of it. No problem. Carden was back on the street.

fifty

Even more startling, I found out, from a Walpole staff member, that a few days before Perrotta was murdered, he had been given a black eye *by Tommy Carden.*

In a conversation with Walpole Social Worker, David Powers, we were discussing my case.

"Yeah, I remember it. That case always stunk. Bobby Perrotta was on my case load. I ran into him in the corridor a day or two before he got killed. He had a black eye. So I asked him what happened. He told me that Tommy Carden had done it," he said.

I was completely stunned. I said, "Tommy Carden gave Bobby Perrotta a black eye just before he got killed? I never knew that. Did you tell anyone? Did you report it?"

"Well, not right away. I mean, this was Walpole in the mid-seventies. A black eye was no big deal, but I did report it the day after he was killed. I told my boss. I also put a memo in his file detailing the conversation that I had with Bobby about him having a fight with Carden over his ex-wife, Carden's sister, and Carden giving him the black eye," he said.

I could barely control myself.

I asked, "Could you get me a copy of that memo?"

He thought about it for a minute. Then he said, "Yeah, I could do that."

The next time that I saw him, I asked, "Did you get that memo?" "You know, it's strange. I can't find it. I went through his file, but it's not in there," he said.

I was crushed. I asked, "Are you sure? Could you have missed it? Could it be somewhere else?"

"No, I went through the whole file a couple of times. It's not there, and I can't think of any place else it might be," he said.

I asked, "Could you give me an affidavit?"

He drew back. He said, "I'm not gonna lie for you."

"Jesus Christ, please don't. I don't want you to lie. I want you to give me an affidavit stating exactly what you told me—that Carden gave Perrotta a black eye," I said.

He thought about it for a minute. I could see that he was uncomfortable with the idea.

Finally, he nodded his head, "All right. I'll do it."

He might not have been comfortable with doing it, but he knew it was the right thing to do. Fortunately for me, he was a person with integrity. It took a while, but he finally gave it to me.

COMMONWEALTH OF MASSACHUSETTS)

) **SS.**   **AFFIDAVIT**

COUNTY OF NORFOLK   )

       I, David Powers, under the pains and penalties of perjury, depose and say:

1. That, in November, 1976, I was employed as a social worker at MCI Walpole.
2. That, Robert Perrotta, an inmate who was assigned to my caseload, was murdered on November 25, 1976.
3. That, a few days before he was murdered, Perrotta told me that he'd had a fight with his co-defendant, and former brother-in-law, Thomas Carden.
4. That, Perrotta had a 'black eye' as a result of the fight.
5. That, Perrotta told me that the cause of the fight was an argument over Perrotta's ex-wife, (Carden's sister).
6. That, I subsequently wrote a memo describing the incident, and placed it in Perrotta's file.

David Powers

       Signed under the pains and penalties of perjury this **16th** day of **April**, 1981

If we had had this information at trial, it would have exposed the darker side of Carden's relationship with Perrotta. It would have shown that he was the one with the motive to harm Perrotta. Neither I nor Campbell or Keigney were ever shown to have had any motive to hurt Bobby Perrotta. Furthermore, it would have proved that Carden had lied on the witness stand.

More importantly, it would have corroborated Ronnie MacDonald's testimony at trial that Carden had been extremely hostile toward Perrotta shortly before the murder due to the fact that Perrotta and Carden's sister were going through a particularly bitter divorce.

But Carden had denied that there was any animosity between him and Perrotta, and Prescott had quickly disparaged Ronnie MacDonald's testimony by labeling him as part of a "united inmate front" who were united against the jurors.

He couldn't have gotten away with that if the jurors had been allowed to hear an impartial Walpole staff member testify that Carden had given Perrotta a beating shortly before he was murdered.

Ironically, Perrotta was waiting for a visit from his new girl friend when he was murdered. One can only speculate what the jury would have read into that, if they'd been aware of the fact that Carden had just given Bobby a beating, because he had dumped Carden sister for this new girl friend.

fifty-one

Shortly after filing a motion for a new trial, and making the Commonwealth aware of this newly uncovered evidence, Campbell, Keigney, and I were illegally transferred out of state to federal prisons around the country.

Actually, they shipped out, or locked up, fifty-two guys—twenty-two of us out of state. The purported reason for the transfer was that they had information that we were going to take hostages; kill twenty people, including the warden; and take over the prison. They started out saying that we were going to take hostages, then they upgraded it to, 'we weren't going to take hostages, we were going to kill everyone'. Using phony figures, they attributed the so-called problem to overcrowding. I wouldn't be surprised if DOC funding was coming up. The fact is I was never charged with anything, except in the media. Amongst other of their propaganda outlets, they justified shipping us out of state in the *Boston Globe* with a rather eye-catching headline that said that scheming inmates were going to take over Walpole and kill twenty people.* The article was written by Timothy Dwyer, a Globe Staff Member, who inflated the initial hostage-taking lie by saying that the evil inmates weren't going to take any hostages, that we were going to kill at least twenty prison officials and stool pigeons who were in protective custody. That allowed them to compare it to a riot that took place in a state prison in New Mexico a couple of years earlier, where thirty-three inmates were killed, most of whom, according to Dwyer, were allegedly stool pigeons in PC. They then went on to say that we were either going to kill the warden or take him hostage. Dwyer attributed this crock of bull____ to a source that he claimed was close to the investigation, but who asked not want to be identified. He said that there were fifty-two of us involved, that we had been planning it for months, and that we were going to use handguns, knives, and axes, but once we took over the prison we had no demands or further

---

* I'd love to print their red herring ploy verbatim, but, as I said above … (See footnote on page 19.)

plans! All nonsense. Unfortunately, as nonsensical as it was, for the people who bought it, it had to be pretty gruesome. At least it would have been if it had had even a semblance of truth. But then, if it had had even a semblance of truth, they would have filed charges in court. They didn't. Or, at the very least, given me a couple of disciplinary reports. I mean, come on, in a prison where they give you a d-report, and lock you up, for dropping a piece of paper on the floor, they're not going to give you a d-report for plotting to take the warden hostage, take over the prison, and commit twenty murders with guns and axes? They didn't.

I wonder why. They said that it was up to Delahunt to press charges.

You also have to realize that, if there had been any truth to it, the courts never would have ordered us to be returned.

||||||||||||||||||||||||||||||||||||||||||||||||||||||||||||||||||||||||

Although I was not charged with anything, I was sent to what was acknowledged to be the worst prison in the federal system, Marion, Illinois. I quickly realized that it was certainly the most difficult from which to do any legal work, especially on a state case.

When I first got there, I was kept in a lock down block, "I" Block, along with two other transferees from Walpole, Jean and Louis.

I requested on a daily basis that I be allowed to make an attorney call and. that I be allowed to call my family to inform them of my whereabouts. All requests were denied with the proviso that I must speak to Mr. Kendall (a pseudonym). Mr. Kendall handled all telephone calls. After four or five days of this, I was called downstairs to see some sort of a board. When I walked into the room, there were three suits sitting behind a desk. Before they could start, I spotted a telephone on the side of the desk.

I said, "Excuse me, before we start, I'd like to request that I be allowed to make a telephone call. I've been gone from Massachusetts for over a week now, an' I know that my family has to be worried sick about where I am."

One of them responded, "You'll have to talk to Mr. Kendall about that. He handles all phone calls."

I said, "I understand that. But I've requested to see him every day since I got here, an' he's never responded."

They did not respond. So, nodding at the phone, I said, "Listen, how about if you just let me make an attorney call? I've got a first-degree murder appeal coming up, and it's imperative that I speak to my attorney, as soon as possible."

"Sorry," the suit responded, "Mr. Kendall's the only one who can make phone calls."

"Okay," I said, pointing at the telephone on the desk, "How about this? I'll make you a deal. You let *me* make the call. I'll dial the number, an' you can all watch. That way, when I'm done, you'll all know how to make a phone call too. Then you won't have to depend on this Kendall bird."

That ended that hearing.

|||||||||||||||||||||||||||||||||||||||||||||||||||||||||||||||||||||

"I" BLOCK WAS similar in design to Ten Block. Four separated tiers, except that the tiers at Marion held eighteen cells as compared to Ten Block's fifteen cells. The particular tier, upon which we were kept, the upper left, was mostly populated by guys from Washington D.C. As none of them initiated any conversation, neither did we.

Jean, Louis, and I were in three cells in a row. After about a week, one of them stopped one of the D.C. guys on his way to the shower. We got to talking, and he was telling us about Marion. In the course of the conversation, something that he said struck me wrong.

I asked him, "Excuse me. Is this a PC tier?"

"No way, man. This ain't no PC tier," he said.

"Okay, sorry. I misunderstood something that you said," I said.

We continued talking. One of the things that was becoming more and more clear to me was that, somewhere else in this joint, there was a general population. Up to that point, I had never realized that Marion had a general population. Marion had been built to replace Alcatraz. I had always been under the impression that the whole place was a lock down joint, and, as "I" Block was a lock down block, it just confirmed my assumption.

Finally, I asked him, "So there is a general population here?"

"Yeah," he said.

I asked him, "Can the guys that are on this tier go out to this population?"

"Well, yeah," he said.

All control disappeared. At the top of my lungs, I started yelling, "Hey guardhouse ... *guardhouse.*"

No response.

"*Hey you fucking assholes. You get me offa this fuckin' PC tier!*"

That got a response. One of the guards came upstairs and yelled down the tier, "Hey, what's the problem. Who's doin' that yellin'?"

I responded, "This is Doherty in cell 7. You better get me off of this fucking PC tier, *now*."

Within a minute, they put the guy who was out on the tier into the shower. Then they were at my door. They immediately cuffed me and took me downstairs. At first, they started to threaten me with a disciplinary report for my behavior.

I cut them off. "Fine. Gimme a ticket. Then get me off this fuckin' PC tier, an' put me in the hole."

One of the guards looked at me rather askance, "You *wanna* go to the hole?"

I said, "No. I wanna go to pop', but I'll go to the hole before I'll stay on a PC tier."

One of them said, "You'll go where we put ya."

I said, "That's right. I will. An' if you put me back on the PC tier, I'll go."

He nodded at me with a tough guy look. "That's right."

Nodding back, I said, "An' as soon as I get there, the sink an' toilet are comin' out, an' the next time you walk by, you'll be wearin' 'em—you an' anybody else that walks by, cop or PC. You're all the same to me."

Just then, a large senior officer walked into the room. Looking around at all of us, he said, "What's the problem here? What's goin' on?"

They told him.

He looked at me for a minute. Then he asked, "Where you from?"

I said, "Boston ... Walpole."

He just nodded his head, "Mmm hm. Come into my office."

Turning away, he walked into an office. I followed him.

He said, "You sayin' you wanna go out inta population?"

"You're goddamned right I do," I said.

He held up his hand. "Okay, okay. Don't start. Ya know, there's lotsa guys *don't* wanna go out inta pop' here."

"Yeah. Well, I ain't one a' them. I been sittin' up on a PC tier for a week an' didn't even know it," I said.

He had picked up the phone while we were speaking. Now he said something into the phone. He listened for a minute and then hung up. "Go pack up your stuff. You're goin' to "D" Block."

When I went back upstairs to get my property, I told Jean and Louis what the cop had said. That all they had to do was request to be placed in population, and they would be. While we were talking, I could hear some of the other inmates talking. They did not sound happy.

One of them said, "Man, who's this mothafucka' sayin' we's PCs?"

I said, "My name's Stevie Doherty. If someone's got a problem with me, I'll be in "D" Block."

When I went back downstairs, the senior guard who had arranged my move to population was going through my property before I went out.

I asked him, "What's up with that tier you had me on? Are those guys PCs or not?"

"Well, some of 'em are, an' some of 'em ain't. Some of 'em are just layin' down,'" he said.

Totally perplexed, I asked, "What's *layin' down?*"

Eyebrow raised, he gave me a rather dubious look. "You don't know what 'laying down' is?"

"No. I never heard of it. What is it?"

"If an inmate puts himself into segregation an' stays there for a year without getting a disciplinary report, we'll transfer him to another prison," he said.

"He's gotta check *himself* into the hole?"

He nodded, "Uh huh, that's right."

"An' he ain't a PC?"

He nodded at me with half a smile, "That's right."

"That's the weirdest thing I ever heard," I said.

Months later, this tall, lanky fellow approached me in "D" Block. He asked, "You Stevie Doherty?"

I said. "Yeah. Who are you?"

He said, "My name's _____. I was on the tier in "I" Block the day you left."

I asked, "What were you doin' there?"

He grinned and shook his head. "Man, I was locked up. They had me on AA [awaiting action]. I just wanted you t' know that everyone on that tier wasn't a PC."

I said, "Yeah. I found out afterwards. I still don't get that 'layin' down' shit."

He laughed and said, "I know whatcha mean. I come from a state joint too. I never heard of it till I come to the feds either."

fifty-two

Federal prisons and federal prisoners are measured for security and dangerousness by a rating system of one through six (one being the least secure or dangerous and six being the most). Marion was a six, the *only* six.

I was a four. After giving me the maximum amount of points in every category that they could, the most that they could make me was a four. Consequently, I was constantly asking them what I was doing in Marion. If Marion was for sixes and I was only a four, what was I doing there?

Finally, I was told, by a case worker, that someone from Massachusetts had specifically requested that I be sent there, as opposed to another federal prison.

Because of my circumstances, I wound up having to retain a new lawyer. Alan Caplan had decided to move his practice to San Francisco. Between his being there, my being in Illinois, and the case being in Massachusetts, it was just too complicated.

I got Attorney Joseph Flak to handle the appeal. Joe was a nice fellow, but he couldn't handle Keating.

One of the excuses that the Commonwealth had been using to stall was that it would be too much of a problem to bring all three of us back for a hearing. Keating kept letting them stall.

So, Jackie (who was in the penitentiary in Lompoc, California) and Arthur (who was in the penitentiary in Lewisburg, Pennsylvania) both sent affidavits to the lawyer, who submitted them to the court, that they would waive their requests to be present if I could be there.

I finally received a notice that I was being returned for a scheduled hearing. Keating quickly put a stop to that. He had the hearing canceled.

It was over two years before we were returned, and then only at the order of the courts, which ruled that all of our transfers were illegal and gave the DOC a deadline by which to return all state prisoners to Massachusetts. The ruling came down in October 1983. The DOC had until April 1, 1984, to bring all of us back. I was returned on March 30, 1984. I was the last one to be returned.

Up until then, Judge Keating had simply ignored my new trial motion. At one point, when it was beyond avoiding the obvious—that Keating was just going to continue to stall and let the case lie dormant, ad infinitum—I told Joe Flak to just go ahead and request that he rule on the filings without a hearing. I knew that he was going to deny it anyway, so why not move on to the next level?

Keating ignored the request and continued to sit on it.

Then, when I was actually en route back, after his having sat on the motion for over a year and a half, he denied it without a hearing. They removed me from Marion on March 14, 1984. I was in transit from then until the day I arrived at Walpole on March 30. That was when I discovered that Keating had quietly denied my motion on March 20 while I was on the road.

Joe Flak tried to see him, but Keating ignored him. When Joe asked the clerk if Keating had said anything regarding his decision, the clerk said, "Yeah, he said, 'Fuck those guys. Let the SJC tip it.'"

fifty-three

In October 1983, two guards were killed, in two separate incidents, on the same day, in the control unit at Marion. The reprisal from the Bureau of Prisons was immediate and quite vicious. One thing that they did was to bring in screws from federal prisons all around the country to harass guys and give out beatings, a crew of them from one joint for a week or two and then a crew from another place—sort of rotating them.

I was in 'B' Block at the time, the only block where they weren't giving out beatings. They had to keep one block seemingly normal for the outside inspectors who they knew would be coming in to investigate the allegations of brutality. For once, I was in the right place at the right time.

One day, we were standing down by the grill. There were a bunch of guards from some other joint, wearing their Darth Vader outfits, milling around on the other side of the grill. The Move Team (otherwise known as the Goon Squad) when preparing to forcibly move an inmate, give out beatings, or attempting to intimidate wore these outfits that were reminiscent of Darth Vader's costume.

All of a sudden, one of them said, "Hey, is Stevie Doherty here?"

The last thing that you want to hear is your name from some cop from another joint who's wearing a Darth Vader outfit.

I said, "Yeah, I'm Stevie Doherty."

He said, "Mickey Donahue asked me t' tell ya 'Hi.'"

"Knothead? Where the hell's he at?"

"Reno," he said.

Then he laughed, and said, "What'd you call him? Knothead? Yeah, that fits. But I'll give 'em this, he's a stand-up guy. There probably ain't a half a dozen real convicts in that joint. But he's one of 'em."

Reno was a medium-security facility in Oklahoma.

He went on. "One day there's a couple a guys sittin' on the floor up against the wall playin' cards, and one of them's an informant. Here comes Donahue walkin' by. He stops and just stands there for a minute, like he's watchin' them play. Then a couple of other guys come walkin' by, and Donahue says, 'Hey, hey, watch out. Don't step on the rat's tail.'"

"The guys walkin' by just look around. One of them says, 'What are ya talkin' about? What rat?'"

"Donahue points to the guy sittin' up against the wall an' says, 'That rat right there. Ya don't wanna step on his tail.'"

"Now, the rat starts to get up. He's a real big guy, and Donahue's about as big as a minute. An' the big guy's sayin', 'Who the fuck you think your talkin' to? I'll kick your little fuckin' Yankee ass.'"

"And Donahue says, 'Yeah, c'mon, let's do it. Bring your knife. We'll go in the closet an' do it for real.'"

"Now the guy, all of a sudden, don't want nothin' to do with him. He says, 'I ain't got no knife.'"

"Donahue says, 'That's okay, I got two of 'em. C'mon, I'll give you one, an' we'll go in the closet.'"

I couldn't help laughing. I could picture Knothead doing just that. I asked him, "What happened?"

He just grinned. "Whatta ya think happened? The big guy shit the bed. I told ya, there ain't a half a dozen real convicts in that joint," he said.

fifty-four

Upon returning to Walpole, I was placed in the hole in Nine Block.

Once again, I changed lawyers. This time, I retained Attorney Steven Rappaport.

We appealed Keating's denial to the SJC, i.e., the gatekeeper. Once again, we drew Justice Wilkins. This time, the issues that I had raised were so egregious that Wilkins was forced to vacate the denial. Still, he wouldn't grant us leave to appeal to the full bench. Instead, he ordered Keating to grant us an evidentiary hearing.

In November 1984, Keating finally gave us a hearing. Among the witnesses called to testify were Alan Caplan, David Powers, John Prescott, and William Bergin.

Keating issued his ruling the following May. As expected, he ruled against us on all issues. Although, to do so, he had to blatantly lie and twist facts.

As to Carden having given Perrotta the beating; because the memo that Walpole staff member David Powers had placed in Perrotta's file was missing, Keating found that Powers was "not credible."

He based this finding solely on the fact that, on the day that Powers finally testified (some eight years after the incident occurred)—although Powers still clearly remembered Perrotta having the black eye and still clearly remembered Perrotta telling him that Carden had given it to him in a fight over Perrotta getting visits from his girl friend—Powers could no longer specifically remember the actual physical act of his placing the memo in Perrotta's file.

Even though Powers swore that that is what he would have done.

Even though, some three and a half years earlier, he had remembered doing it clearly enough to swear to it in the affidavit that he'd given to me. This was back before they'd illegally shipped me out of state, to Marion, causing the delay that resulted in Powers' memory loss.

As to Carden's being rewarded for his testimony by being released from prison, Keating ruled that the DA hadn't promised Carden anything.

He based this finding on a rather bizarre set of circumstances, replete with lies, blatant distortions, and perjury by John Prescott.

At the evidentiary hearing, Prescott admitted that even though he had told our jury that Carden was not going to be rewarded for his testimony, just one month after the trial ended, Prescott did, in fact, get Carden's twenty- to thirty-year sentence reduced as a reward for testifying.

He said that he was able to do this, because Carden had already had a motion pending for a sentence reduction—but that he hadn't misled the jury, because neither he nor Carden knew anything about the motion until after our trial had ended (even though the motion had been sitting in Prescott's office all during the trial).

Prescott explained this obviously dubious scenario by claiming that, shortly after our trial, he had received a telephone call from Carden's former attorney (now Judge) Thomas Sullivan. He said that Sullivan told him that if he wanted to do something for Carden, he should check Carden's file, where he would find a pending motion for a sentence reduction, i.e., a motion to revoke and revise the sentence.

As this was the first time that we'd heard this particular story (which we didn't believe for a minute), we'd had no way of knowing to call Judge Sullivan as a witness at the hearing. The prosecution certainly didn't call him.

So, a few weeks after the hearing, Rappaport and ADA (now Judge) Charles Hely sat down with Judge Sullivan and drew up a STIPULATION as to what Sullivan would have testified to if he had been called as a witness at the hearing.

The STIPULATION contained nine separate statements. The first eight being straightforward assertions to the effect that:

In April 1975, Carden received a twenty- to thirty-year sentence;

In April 1975, Sullivan filed a motion to revoke and revise the sentence.

Sullivan provided Carden with a copy of the motion;

Sullivan never spoke to Prescott about either Carden, or this case, prior to the conclusion of our trial;

Sullivan never informed Prescott about the motion to revoke and revise prior to the conclusion of the trial;

Sometime after our trial, Sullivan met Prescott at a social function and *Prescott said to him,* "Carden is a lucky man that I found out about the motion to revoke and revise that you filed;"

It was Sullivan's best memory that *It was Prescott who first raised the topic of Carden's sentence reduction* sometime after our trial;

Sullivan had no memory of ever having placed a telephone call to Prescott regarding Carden's motion to revoke and revise the sentence.

All straightforward statements of fact as Judge Sullivan remembered them. However, the ninth, and final, stipulation was somewhat different. It was obviously a response to a hypothetical question, or suggestion, from ADA Hely and had absolutely no validity whatsoever. In fact, it completely contradicted what Judge Sullivan had already attested to, i.e.:

"9. Sullivan would state that Prescott *may* have mentioned Carden to him after trial and that Sullivan *may* have mentioned the motion to Prescott, *but Sullivan has no memory of this.* [emphasis added]

This would be totally meaningless to an honest judge, but it was enough for Keating.

In his ruling, Keating completely ignored Judge Sullivan's first eight statements of fact. Statements that unequivocally repudiated Prescott's sworn testimony when Sullivan confirmed that Carden *did* know about the motion before he testified and that, when the subject was raised between Sullivan and Prescott after our trial, it was Prescott, not Sullivan who raised it, when he told Sullivan that he already knew about the motion.

Instead, by taking a segment of the hypothetical number nine and quoting it out of context, Keating was able to rule that Prescott really did not know about the sentence reduction motion till after trial, because "Sullivan…states 'he may have mentioned the filing of the motion to Prescott'…after the trial."

This was a total distortion of Judge Sullivan's testimony, yet completely in keeping with the manner in which Judge Keating handled this case from the very beginning.

They were able to get away with this by not making us aware of the Sullivan story *before* the evidentiary hearing and then springing it on us at the hearing.

It was similar to the way in which they ambushed us with the sandwich story at trial.

They knew that, if they had told us, we would have called Judge Sullivan to testify. His testimony would have totally discredited the lies to which John Prescott testified in order to defend his hiding from us, at trial, the fact that Carden had had a motion for a sentence reduction pending—thereby allowing him to cloak Carden with a facade of credibility by deluding the jury into believing that Carden was not going to get out of prison for at least another eleven years and that Carden was not going to be rewarded for his testimony.

If Judge Sullivan had been present at the hearing, there was no way that John Prescott could have attributed his discovery of the revise and revoke motion to Judge Sullivan—not with Sullivan waiting in the wings to tell the truth.

There was also no way that Prescott would have been able to claim that Carden did not know that he had a motion for a sentence reduction pending at the time of my trial.

We also found out after trial that Perrotta had testified at a federal grand jury regarding crimes that he and Carden had committed, information that certainly should have been given to us before trial. Then, when it came out at the 1984 evidentiary hearing that, at Perrotta's initial sentencing for his guilty pleas on his bank robbery and escape charges, his attorney's main disposition argument was Perrotta's cooperation with federal authorities and with State Police Lt. Bergin, Prescott admitted that he'd "heard" that Perrotta had testified before the grand jury. He said that Carden told him that him and Perrotta had both been called to testify but that they hadn't testified. (He couldn't have checked the records?)

So, as with the sandwich story, the black eye, and the revise and revoke motion, Keating ruled that Prescott just did not know.

fifty-five

The above are just a few examples of the evidence that was hidden by the Commonwealth and discovered piecemeal over the years. Consequently, there have been a number of appeals.

Unfortunately a number of these discoveries were never heard by the Massachusetts Supreme Judicial Court. The appellant in these cases is almost invariably the defendant. Rarely, is it the Commonwealth. Therefore, the standard for the gatekeeper to grant leave to appeal is extremely high. By law, the issue must be "new" and "substantial."

Throughout the eighties, I would invariably draw Justice Wilkins as the gatekeeper. He would invariably agree with Judge Keating and deny me leave to appeal to the full bench. This effectively ends the appeal in Massachusetts, as state law specifically states that there is no appeal from the denial of a gatekeeper.

This time was no different. We drew Justice Wilkins and, as usual, he denied us leave to appeal to the full bench—on my birthday.

Wilkins' decision was so outrageous that I sat down and wrote him a letter. The letter went as follows:

10-3-85

Dear Sir,

My name is Stephen Doherty and you recently denied my motion for leave to appeal my first degree murder conviction. (*Com v. Doherty.* No. 84-167)

I've never written to a judge before but in this case I feel compelled to, as I am totally befuddled by the rationale upon which you base your decision. I might add that everyone else that has read it, including attorneys, has the same reaction. I am utterly frustrated in my attempts to reconcile your conclusions with the facts in evidence. So, if you would, could you please clarify one issue for me, namely, the issue of "promises, inducements and rewards".

On page 2 you conclude that the issue of the lack of disclosure, by the prosecutor, of the fact that the prosecution's main witness (Carden) had received a 7 to 8 concurrent sentence, (Fn.1) does not pass the "newness test".

Your reason for this finding is that the defense should've known about it at trial because it was either:

a. "Apparent on the face of the record":
b. Subject to disclosure on cross-examination by defense counsel: or
c. Available "by independent investigation".

This is completely at variance with the facts in evidence.

In response to:

A.) It was clearly not "apparent on the face of the record". All three defense attorneys testified that they did not know that Carden's Suffolk County charges had been disposed of. But, more importantly, the prosecutor himself admits that the probation records that were made available to the defense attorneys, at our trial showed that Carden's Suffolk County cases were still pending. (Fn.2) Therefore, not only was the disposition of the Suffolk County cases not "apparent on the face of the record" it was, in fact, concealed by the record.

In response to:

B.) It would have been "subject to disclosure on cross-examination" if the prosecution's witness had not lied. Carden falsely testified, under cross-examination, that his armed robbery charge was still pending. (T.T. Vol. 5 pp 60-61). Between the erroneous probation record, and Carden's lie, we were effectively foreclosed from discovering the actual disposition of the Suffolk County charges.

Therefore, it was not "subject to disclosure on cross-examination. We tried. He lied.

In response to:

C.) We did attempt an "independent investigation" but were thwarted by the prosecutor when he opposed our request to review Carden's Salem Jail records for the purpose of determining Carden's various destinations (when he was taken out of the jail prior to our trial) for any possible information that might tend to be exculpatory or tend to reflect promises, inducements or rewards to Carden. (Please see Defendant's Memorandum in support of Motion for Leave to Appeal; Footnote 12).

Also, on pages 3 and 4 you state that, "There was no showing of an obligation on the prosecutor to disclose more than was disclosed to defense counsel concerning the Suffolk County charges".

I don't understand why not. At the motion hearing the prosecutor admitted that, (although the record showed otherwise and Carden testified otherwise), he personally found out, before our trial that the Suffolk County cases had, in fact, been disposed of, and what those dispositions were. (See M. Tr. 124–125) Nevertheless, he concedes that he *never disclosed that information to the defense.* (See M. Tr. 125)

This lie of omission was compounded, and became particularly egregious, when the prosecutor allowed Carden's false testimony to go uncorrected.

It seems obvious that there was "an obligation on the prosecution to disclose more than was disclosed to defense counsel concerning the Suffolk County charges". Particularly in light of such cases as , u.s. v oxman, 740 F2d1298, and the combined 'brady', 'napue', 'giglio', 'agurs' decisions. If the prosecutor had chosen to disclose the information that Carden's Suffolk County charges had already been disposed of, then Carden's lie could have been exposed to the jury, and the defense could have shown that Carden had received an extremely lenient sentence, for a very serious charge, just two weeks after testifying against us at the grand jury.

The salient point here is that you never mentioned Carden's lie in your findings on the *"Suffolk County Sentences"* issue. A careful reading of both the Trial Transcript and the Motion Hearing Transcript shows that *this is the issue which was improperly influenced by Carden's false statement.*

Unfortunately, you have misconstrued its actual significance by misapplying it to the Revise and Revoke issue. An issue on which it had no bearing whatsoever.

The <u>facts in evidence</u> in the Revise & Revoke issue are as follows:

1.) Carden knew before trial that he had a pending motion to revoke and revise 20 to 30 year Norfolk County sentence,

2.) The prosecutor's office knew before trial that the motion was pending,

3.) Carden stated before trial that he would get out of prison because of this case,

4.) At trial Carden denied he was expecting anything for testifying,

5.) At trial the prosecutor denied that Carden was going to get anything for testifying,

6.) One month after trial the same prosecutor arranged for Carden to have his Norfolk County sentence revised and revoked from twenty to thirty years down to nine to ten years as a *reward for his testimony*,

7.) This allowed Carden to complete his Norfolk County sentence at the same time that he completed his Suffolk County sentence and just in time for him to be eligible for an early parole from his federal sentence,

8.) The prosecutor told Attorney Alan Caplan that he was going to help Carden receive an early federal parole,

9.) Carden received an early federal parole.

Despite all of this you ruled that "the issue lacks substance . . . because at the trial Carden conceded that he had an armed robbery charge pending against him." And that, "The opportunity to argue to the jury that Carden had good reason to testify in favor of the Commonwealth was there (although for the wrong reason.)". And that, "any misinformation disclosed was wholly favorable to the defendants, opening up an area of possible bias not otherwise available".

This is simply not true! The only benefit the defendants received was the dubious, (and unsought), opportunity to question Carden on whether he expected to receive lenient treatment on a charge *which Carden knew did not exist*. Thereby allowing him to respond, quite truthfully, that he expected no favorable treatment on his pending cases.

Of course he didn't. There were no pending case(s). By definition, if there were no charges extant, then there could have been no future reward for the defendants to have uncovered.

Carden's lie not only allowed him to hide the concurrent Suffolk County sentence, it also enabled him to send the defense attorneys on a wild goose chase.

Therefore, for you to conclude, despite the facts in evidence, that the revise and revoke issue "lacks substance" simply because "Carden conceded that he had an armed robbery charge pending against him" is, in effect, saying that, although the prosecutor's main witness lied, the defendants are to be held responsible, and bear the onus, for that lie.

Why should the defendants have to forfeit their right to have made the jury aware of Carden's, then pending, revise and revoke motion, (and the benefits he was to derive from that motion), simply because Carden chose to lie about having a non-existent pending charge.

Particularly where the lie was in no way relevant to the revise and revoke motion but was originally intended to hide the fact that Carden had already received favorable treatment on an entirely separate and unrelated charge.

That the lie was successful in its original intent is singularly onerous. But, far worse, to now allow this lie to serve double duty, is to perpetrate a travesty of justice, and a blatant corruption of the truth finding process.

Your Honor, I honestly don't know what I hope this letter might accomplish. In all reality, probably nothing. But I couldn't live with myself if I didn't write it.

If I'm out of line in writing to you directly I apologize but I'm serving a life sentence for a crime I did not commit on a conviction that was obtained by the repeated use of lies and deception on the part of the state and now I'm told that I don't even have the right to appeal to the full bench all because the prosecution cheated.

And make no mistake about it Sir they did cheat.

They cheated and we caught them.

I can only hope that I've made it clear to you just how it was done. At least I've tried.

Thank you for your time and your consideration.

Fn.1 On Suffolk County Charges

Fn.2 (M.Tr. 108-109)

Respectfully yours,
Stephen J. Doherty

||||||||||||||||||||||||||||||||||||||||||||||||||||||||||||||||||||||

THAT WAS THE letter—grammatical errors, misspellings, and all. Written in the heat of the moment and, as expected, accomplishing nothing. Of course, Wilkins never responded.

There had been a number of other points that I had wanted to raise in the letter that I just could not fit in. One such issue was Wilkins' comment on Judge Travers' comment as to whether the seven- to eight-year concurrent sentence that he gave Carden before our trial would "interfere." We had, however, mentioned it in our brief to Wilkins as evidence that it was part of Carden's reward for testifying against us. After disposing of the issue itself, Wilkins added the following commentary, putting his spin on Travers remark.

"As an aside on the question whether there was a deal, I comment that I have no sense that in February of 1977, when Carden was sentenced on the Suffolk charges by Judge Travers, the judge believed that there was a "deal" between Carden and the prosecution concerning his testimony. It was then known that Carden had decided to cooperate in the case against the defendants. Carden's counsel argued for sentences concurrent with the one he was then serving. The judge suggested seven to eight years and asked whether that would interfere. I think that reference is clearly to the question whether defense counsel agreed that such a sentence would not interfere with the sentence being concurrent."

What the hell kind of double-talk was that? I don't even know what it means. How could the *sentence* interfere with the sentence being concurrent? It is a judge's discretion whether to give a sentence concurrent or consecutive. Moreover, the prosecution had already made it clear that they had no problem with it.

The only way that a seven- to eight-year concurrent sentence could interfere with the twenty- to thirty-year sentence that Carden was already serving, and only had two or three years in on, would be if the twenty- to thirty-year sentence ended before the seven- to eight-year sentence ended. Do the math. I'm sure that Judge Travers could add and subtract—unless Carden was *somehow* going to get his twenty- to thirty-year sentence reduced to a sentence that ended before the seven to eight.

But, that was Wilkins' rationalization for his finding that he didn't think that Judge Travers thought that there was any deal between Carden and the prosecution, just because he was testifying.

I was so naive in those days that I actually believed that being on the Massachusetts Supreme Judicial Court automatically guaranteed integrity. Silly me. Wilkins was just Keating with a longer robe.

When I tried to appeal Judge Wilkins' denial, Supreme Court Justice Ruth Abrams ruled that there was no appeal from the denial of the gatekeeper. She said that it wasn't allowed.

fifty-six

At the same time that all of this was going on, the DOC was trying to have me sent back to Marion, even though it had been years since I had received a disciplinary report.

Less than a month after I was returned from Marion, I was brought in front of a classification board for "Reclass following return from Federal Bureau of Prisons upon court order."

It is inherent in the concept of a classification hearing that an inmate has a right to an impartial decision-making board. Unfortunately, this particular "impartial" classification board was being chaired by a DOC hatchet man named Paul DiPaulo. The other two board members—Mike Maloney, who later became the commissioner of corrections, and a guy named Walonis whom I'd had a run-in with years earlier at MCI Norfolk—were equally "nonpartisan."

When I first arrived at Marion, one of the responses that I had received to my numerous questions as to just what I was doing there was a memo from the case manager, C. A. Craig. In the memo, Mr. Craig stated that there was a letter in my file, addressed to the Federal Bureau of Prison from the director of classification at Walpole, *Paul DiPaulo.*

I was represented at the reclass hearing by a young lady named Lynn Aaby. Ms. Aaby was a law student from the Prisoners' Assistance Project at Northeastern University School of Law.

At one of our meetings in preparation for the hearing, I told her about DiPaulo being the one who had had me shipped out to Marion in the first place. She called DiPaulo's office to apprise him that we were aware of his past involvement in the case and to ask him to recuse himself from sitting on the board. The call was taken by DiPaulo's assistant. When Lynn explained the situation to her, she promised to relay the information to DiPaulo. When she called Lynn back, she said that DiPaulo denied all knowledge of any letter to the federal authorities and that he would not recuse himself.

In response, Lynn wrote DiPaulo a letter repeating her request that he recuse himself. In a magnanimous attempt to help regenerate his obviously impaired memory, she also enclosed a copy of the memo that I had gotten at Marion. He did not respond.

On the day of the hearing, Lynn presented each board member with a copy of the Marion memo, along with a formal request that DiPaulo recuse himself from the hearing.

In true DOC style, they simply ignored the request, and he proceeded to chair the hearing.

The notice of the reclass hearing had specifically stated that it would be based upon:

"Any recent disciplinary action, adjustment reports, evaluative and factual data will be examined in determining your need for structure, security controls, and subsequent placement. Your adjustment since being returned to MCI-Walpole will also be considered."

Despite the fact that I had had no recent disciplinary actions, neither in my more than two years at Marion nor since being returned to MCI Walpole, and that my adjustment reports from Marion were excellent, all that DiPaulo and company would discuss was the Perrotta murder, the Stokes' murder, and the equally bogus hostage-taking story.

The board immediately recommended that I be returned to Marion. As follows:

"Based upon this man's history of institutional violence, conviction for the murder of an inmate and direct and central role and a planned takeover of MCI Walpole according to investigating information the board recommends a return to the Federal Bureau of Prisons. Additionally, federal placement offers the greatest potential for Mr. Doherty's eventual reintegration into a maximum custody general population where programming and work opportunities are available."

The following "Key Issues" were cited as justification for their recommendation.

a.   "Serving 1st Degree Life Sentence for Murder of inmate Perrotter [sic] at MCI Walpole, 1976."
b.   "Transferred to the Federal system due to his participation in a planned hostage taking and takeover of MCI Walpole."
c.   "Extensive disciplinary record with three years served in D.S.U. Also

charged with the murder of inmate John Stokes in 1979. However this was not processed when a witness recanted testimony."

d. "Generally good adjustment to USP Marion although program and work was limited. No incident reports."

I responded to each of the above. In response to:

a. "This conviction is under appeal on three separate issues. Two of these issues were personally discovered by plaintiff and show that crucial evidence was suppressed by the Mass. D.O.C. and the prosecutor's office. In fact, it is plaintiff's contention that the actual reason for both his illegal 1982 transfer and the current transfer attempt was and is to impede him in his efforts to perfect his criminal appeal."

"It is also interesting to note that although several other inmates have been convicted of inmate murders at Walpole, the only one who is currently being held against his will in the federal prison system is plaintiff's co-defendant (Keigney) who coincidentally discovered the third issue under appeal." fn1

b. "Plaintiff has never been charged with this allegation. In fact, although this incident purportedly took place in February of 1982, plaintiff was not informed of his alleged participation until April of 1984."

"Because he was never charged with this alleged misconduct plaintiff has never been given an opportunity to answer, or defend himself against it. Plaintiff vehemently denies any knowledge of, or participation in, any alleged hostage taking incident. For the D.O.C. to sidestep the disciplinary process and later rely on the alleged disciplinary infraction as the basis for a higher custody transfer is a blatant violation of due process of law."

"It is curious to note that of the 22 prisoners originally transferred to the F.B.O.P. because of this unsubstantiated allegation (and subsequently returned by court order) the only one(s) who the Mass. D.O.C. are attempting to involuntarily transfer back are plaintiff and his co-defendant, (Keigney)."'"

---

* Shortly after the board recommended that I be returned to the feds, I filed a request for a temporary restraining order (TRO) asking that the DOC not be allowed to ship me back out until the appeal of my murder conviction was heard. I had been confidentially informed that the DOC had clandestinely arranged for me to be arbitrarily shipped back to the feds. I immediately filed a TRO. The court granted the motion. Keigney was being held in a different prison (MCI Concord)

c. "First, the three years served in D.S.U. was the result of the murder con-
    viction currently under appeal. (See above, "a")

    "Second, when the only witness to implicate plaintiff in the mur-
    der of John Stokes recanted his statement, he admitted that he'd lied
    in order to get out of Walpole (which he accomplished). Further-
    more, as the D.O.C. is well aware, another inmate has subsequently
    confessed to, and been convicted of, the murder of John Stokes. The
    D.O.C.'s disgraceful attempt to distort and manipulate the truth in
    such a serious matter is not only wicked in substance but is also a
    clear example of the extremes to which they are willing to go in their
    attempt to remove plaintiff from the state and thereby continue to
    thwart his legitimate attempts to process his criminal appeal."

d. "The D.O.C. has virtually placed plaintiff in a no-win situation with a
    classic example of Orwellian double-think. Plaintiff's documented re-
    cord of good conduct while at U.S.P. Marion is now cited by the D.O.C.
    as a reason for exiling him to the F.B.O.P. for an alleged incident of mis-
    conduct over two years ago. In effect, they are saying that plaintiff is be-
    ing sent to the F.B.O.P. for being bad and that plaintiff is being sent to the
    F.B.O.P. for being good. A classic Catch-22."

Lynn's appeal to the commissioner was more detailed. It concluded by
pointing out that "Mr. DiPaulo was unable to render an impartial decision
as evidenced by his conduct at the hearing as well as his past decision to
transfer Mr. Doherty out of state ... [and that the decision] ... flies in the face
of the United States Constitution and the Declaration of Rights of the Massachusetts Constitution as interpreted by the United States Supreme Court
and the Massachusetts Supreme Judicial Court as well as the Department of
Correction's own regulations. Such a blatant disrespect for the law cannot be
allowed to stand as it is clearly an arbitrary abuse of discretion on the part of
the Board."

The commissioner, of course, denied the appeal.

---

and hadn't filed a motion. They snatched him out of Concord a few hours after my
motion was granted and shipped him back to the feds the same day, (USP Lewisburg).

fifty-seven

For the next year and a half, my criminal appeal bounced back and forth between the Superior Court (Keating) and the single justice/gatekeeper (Wilkins). After each shift, I had to renew the TRO that was keeping them from shipping me back out.

However, after the first year, they made a tactical error. Even though they had kept me locked in the hole, in Nine Block, apparently it wasn't enough. Almost a year to the day after I was returned from Marion, they officially classified me to the DSU and moved me to Ten Block.

Enough was enough. I had put up with being kept in the hole, without even being charged with anything, because I did not want to get into a big brouhaha over it and get sidetracked from the murder appeal. But this was too much. To actually DSU me, without even the semblance of a charge against me, was way over the line.

Even though Nine and Ten Blocks were both segregation units, there were many differences. Ten Block was worse, by far.

One example—certainly the most important to me—was access to the law library. When I first returned from Marion and was placed in Nine Block, they would not allow me access to the law library. In response to my vehement protests that I was illegally being denied meaningful access to legal material, they initially used a number of bogus excuses to justify their denial. Each time, I would respond and invalidate their duplicitous pretext(s).

It took a while but, in the end, they had the civilian law librarian come to see me in Nine Block. She told me that it was not necessary for me to go the law library. All that I had to do was to submit a list of any cases that I needed to her and that she would guarantee that I would promptly receive a copy of each of them.

I tried it once. It took about a week and a half to get a few cases. Not all that I had requested, just some.

I then submitted another request. I requested that *Wolff v. McDonnell* be Shepardized and that I be sent a copy of every case that had cited *Wolff*. At that point in time, *Wolff*, a United States Supreme Court decision, was the controlling case for most prison issues.

The librarian showed up at my door the next day. She was slightly frenzied. She practically screeched, "YOU WANT ME TO SHEPARDIZE WOLFF VERSUS MCDONNELL AND SEND YOU A COPY OF EVERY CASE? THERE'S ELEVEN THOUSAND CASES. CAN'T YOU NARROW IT DOWN A BIT?"

I said, "Not really. How can I know what cases I need until I read them?"

That was how I got access to the law library. They finally acceded to my rightful demands and allowed me to be brought to the law library for a couple of hours every Friday night after it had been closed to the inmates in the general population.

My being illegally placed in the DSU eliminated even this token access to the law library. I filed a motion with the court challenging the legality of my DSU placement and asking that I be placed back in general population. They stalled as long as they could, typical DOC procedure.

The volume of civil actions being filed out of Walpole, due to mistreatment and illegal lock ups, had reached the point where they didn't even take you out to the courthouse any more. Once a month, a judge would come into Walpole and hear the cases. The hearings would be held in the visiting room.

In August 1985, I appeared in front of Judge Harry Elam. Judge Elam heard both sides' arguments and then took it under advisement. On August 27th, he issued an eight-page ruling. He ordered the DOC to place me back in general population. He gave them three days to do it.

Two days later, an Institutional Classification Board recommended that I be placed back in general population.

However, the superintendent's yes-man, Tim Hall, overruled the board's recommendation and ordered that I be seen by a different classification board.

I found out about it at a hearing on October 4, 1985, at the hearing for the DOC's motion for stay (of Judge Elam's order). The motion was heard in front of a different judge, Judge Porada.

The DOC's lawyer, Assistant Attorney General (AAG) William Luzier, told the judge that they had asked Judge Elam if he would stay his order and allow a different classification board to release me into population administratively. He said that Judge Elam had stayed his order and that I would be seeing a new classification board. The implication being that it was just a matter of form. Judge Porada accepted Luzier's story and granted a continuance.

When two more weeks went by with no action taken, I filed a motion for contempt.

On November 1, over two months after I had been ordered released from the hole, I finally saw the board. The hearing began at nine o'clock in the morning. Although AAG Luzier had told Judge Porada that they were going to release me from segregation "administratively," prior experience with the DOC persuaded me to have a lawyer present. Attorney Steven Rappaport appeared with me at the hearing.

The DOC's idea of releasing me from the DSU was to offer me a transfer to DSU Phase Two. DSU Phase Two was situated at the RB, the segregation unit at MCI Norfolk. The RB was Norfolk's version of Ten Block. Actually, in many ways, it was worse than Ten Block.

Of course, I refused the offer.

The battle was on. First them. Then me. Then them. Then Rappaport. On and on, back and forth, it went on all morning, like a tag-team match.

Finally, a little after noon, the board chairman, whom I believe came into the hearing expecting to be out of there in a few minutes, threw his pen onto the desk and said, "THAT'S IT. YES OR NO? EITHER TAKE IT OR DON'T. WHICH IS IT?"

Very carefully, I said, "Well, if—as I understand it—you are giving me an ultimatum that I either accept your offer of Phase Two or you are going to ship me back to Marion, then of course I'll choose Phase Two."

He pointed at the contract that was lying on the table. "Sign that."

One of the terms of going to Phase Two was that you had to sign a contract that you would abide by certain conditions, some of them quite unconstitutional.

I picked it up and looked at it for a moment. Then I said, "I want to read this over again before I sign it."

He was packing up his papers, obviously in a hurry. Shaking his head impatiently, he said, "Just sign it."

I said, "I'll tell you what I'll do. I'll take it back to my cell with me and once I go over it again, I'll sign it and either mail it to you or give it to the guards to give to you. But I want to read it again before I sign it."

Preoccupied with getting out of there, he said, "All right."

As soon as I got back to my cell, I sat down and wrote to Judge Elam. I explained to the judge exactly how they were trying to get around his order that I be released from the hole. I also enclosed the contract that they were trying to coerce me into signing.

The contract had a number of outrageous concessions. One of them sticks in my mind to this day. If you went into DSU Phase II, you had to agree to speak with the mental health staff and you had to waive your constitutional right to confidentiality for anything that you told them. The letter went as follows:

To: Judge Elam
Fr: Stephen Doherty

Dear Sir,

On 10-30-85 my 'Motion for Contempt' was heard at MCI Cedar Junction. The case was continued due to Assistant Attorney General Luzier's claim that you had informed him orally that the D.O.C. did not have to abide by your decision of 8-27-85, (ordering them to place me back into general population within three days). The purpose of the continuance is for A.A.G. Luzier to draw up an order, for you to sign, stating that you have rescinded your previous decision.

Your Honor, I don't know what Mr. Luzier told you that made you change your mind, but the only change in my situation is in my favor.

On 8-29-85, an institutional Classification Board recommended that I be placed in general population. The reason for this recommendation was that "*Mr. Doherty does not pose a substantial threat to the security of the institution.*"

This is significant for a number of reasons.

First, according to the D.O.C.'s own rules and regulations, this finding calls for me to be placed back in general population. (Please see CMR 103 421.08 (3) and, by extension, CMR 103 421.07 (1).

Second, the staff member who made this finding, Lynn Woodford, Director of Classification), is the same person who recommended my initial placement (4-85) in DSU. If her opinion carried the weight to put me into DSU it should carry the weight to take me out of DSU.

Third, and most telling, is found in A.A.G. Luzier's "Memorandum in Support of Motion for Stay Pending Rehearing or for Reconsideration", where defendants claim that their opposition to your order placing me back into general population is "because of the opinion of correctional officials that he poses a threat to the secure running of the institution". Since this memorandum was filed eleven days after I was found **not** to be a threat to the security of the institution it is obviously based on an invalid premise.

Furthermore, the classification board's recommendation, that I be placed in general population, was illegally denied by a designee of the Superintendent in violation of agency regulations. (Please see 103 CMR 420.13 (2) (m), (n), (o), (p) and/or 103 CMR 420.14 (8), (9), (10), (11).)

Upon being denied return to General Population I was immediately scheduled to see another classification board. This board recommended, over my most strenuous objections, that I be placed in a program called "D.S.U. Phase II".

This program, although purported by the board to be an opportunity to "decompress", in a less restrictive atmosphere, before being placed back into general population, is, in fact, simply a device by which the D.O.C. may keep me in segregation for at least another six months in an atmosphere which, in actuality, is much more restrictive (e.g. less visits, less telephone access, less canteen, **NO** inmate legal assistance).

Although this program is ostensibly "voluntary" I am told that I must sign a contract which, among other things, obliges me to meet with mental health staff with the understanding they will be permitted to release their evaluation of me and that I must further agree to release the D.O.C. from any and all liability and legal responsibility arising from the release of this information.

Incidentally, the move is described, in the contract, specifically as "a lateral transfer within the Departmental Segregation Unit." (Please see enclosed copy of contract.)

Your Honor, it is now six and a half years since I've had a serious disciplinary report and almost four years since I've received even a minor disciplinary report. I have no problems with either inmates or correctional officers. (In fact, the D.S.U. Correctional Officers were willing to come to the classification hearing and testify that I should be placed directly in general population, but the board said that it was not necessary.) My point is that you made a correct decision, on 8-27-85, when you ordered me back into general population, and for you to change your mind now, because of misrepresentations made by the D.O.C., would be a grievous error.

As you said, in your earlier decision, if I am released into general population I will still be in custody and closely supervised by prison officials. Furthermore, there is nothing to prevent them from placing me back into D.S.U. in the event of a future disciplinary violation.

Thank you very much for your time and your consideration.

Sincerely,
Stephen J. Doherty
cc. A.A.G. Luzier

Judge Elam responded to my letter by writing to Commissioner Fair. The letter was dated November 8. It was concise and to the point.

Michael Fair, Commissioner
Department of Correction
100 Cambridge Street
Boston, Massachusetts 02114

Re: Stephen Doherty
vs. Commissioner of Correction and others
Norfolk Civil Action No. 85-1847

Dear Commissioner,

On August 27, 1985 after a hearing was held in the above entitled matter, this court enjoined the defendants from holding Stephen Doherty in the Departmental Segregation Unit and ordered that he be returned to an appropriate cell block in the general population. Shortly thereafter, Assistant Attorney General William Luzier, who represented the Department of Correction, asked that I stay my order to allow the Classification Board to reconsider this matter. I agreed to do so and have learned since that the Institutional Classification Board, after reconsideration of August 29, 1985, recommended that Mr. Doherty be returned to the general population. I am then given to understand that the Superintendent or his designee failed to follow this Board's recommendation and put the matter before another classification board, which recommended that Stephen Doherty be placed in "DSU Phase II", a procedure that does not return him to the general population as ordered.

This letter is to advise you that this court at no time rescinded its order but merely stayed it as requested by Assistant Attorney General Luzier to allow a classification board to reconsider the matter. Further, I never agreed to be bound by its decision.

Once again I am ordering your department in accordance with my decision of August 27, 1985 to release Stephen Doherty to the general population forthwith.

Very truly yours,

Harry J. Elam
Justice of Superior Court

I received my copy on Saturday, November 9, the day after it was sent. As the commissioner's office is not open on weekends, I was reasonably sure that the DOC had yet to receive it.

When the guard came by, I showed it to him and, as it was a legal document that I would probably be using as an exhibit in upcoming filings, requested that he bring it to the copying machine and make me ten copies.

He said that he would.

He came back a while later. He had the original and one copy. He said that his commander had laughed at it and said that it wasn't even signed and that it wasn't worth the paper it was printed on.

The following night, a senior officer, "Chicago Al" came by making a round. He stopped at my cell and, smiling, said, "I hear you typed up some kind of a phony letter. Supposed to be from a judge. I'm told it's not worth the paper it's printed on."

Al and I got along okay so I just smiled back, and he continued on his way, shaking his head.

The following Tuesday I was having a visit. Monday had been a holiday, Veteran's Day. Therefore, it had been a long weekend and the earliest that the commissioner would have received the letter was that day.

In the middle of my visit, Chicago Al came to the visiting room door. He nodded to me. Then he said to my visit, "I'm afraid that we're going to have to end this visit. You can no longer visit in Nine Block."

My visit said, "What? Why not?"

"Well, that's the good news. If you'd like, you can finish this visit in the visiting room in population," he said.

I asked, "This wouldn't have anything to do with that letter that wasn't worth the paper it was printed on, would it Al?"

Raising his hands and looking at me with a slight grimace he said, "Don't start. You're outta here."

"Look Al, how 'bout ya let us finish the visit here? Ya can move me after," I said.

Shaking his head, he said, "Uh uh, you're outta here now. We just got a call from the commissioner's office. They were screamin' on the phone. 'Put him in population. *Now!*'"

My visit said, "That's okay. The visit's almost over anyway. I'll come back tomorrow."

A half an hour later, I was moved back into general population.

fifty-eight

I n September 1986, I was in the process of finally filing my criminal appeal with the federal court.

I was living in the minimum end and keeping my head as far down as possible. I'd only been out of the hole for ten months. I wouldn't even have been in population if Judge Elam hadn't forced them to release me from my illegal lock down in the hole. So, I was well aware that they were looking for any opportunity to get me out of general population and away from the law library.

Then a stabbing happened in the block where I was housed. A couple of guys, call them Clay and Tony, had some kind of a personal beef going. I have no recollection as to just what it was over. I don't even know if I knew then. It was not my business. But, I did know that the beef was coming and, as I did not want to give the administration any opportunity to implicate me, I made sure that I was situated in a quite visible position. I was on the telephone, talking to my daughter. The telephone happens to be on the wall at the front of the block, about five feet from the guard's desk. You can't do much better than that for an alibi. One would think.

The beef went down at the back of the block, in the last cell on the right-hand side of the second tier. I couldn't have been any farther away from them without leaving the block. Shortly after that, they locked down the whole block.

The next morning, when they opened the cell doors, my door did not open. They fed four or five of us in our cells.

At some point that morning, Clay showed up at my door, accompanied by two guards.

He said, "They just called me down the IPS office."

The inner perimeter squad (IPS) were the guards who investigated any incidents that occurred inside Walpole.

Looking slightly abashed, he said, "They're sayin' you and me stabbed Tony."

"You gotta be shittin' me," I said.

223

"It gets worse. They say I'm a hit man for Charlestown," he said.

At that, we both started to laugh. Clay was from Maine.

I asked, "When did we start hiring?"

He just smiled and nodded his head.

Then, with a half smile, half regretful look on his face, he said, "Sorry, man."

I just shrugged. It wasn't his fault.

A few days later, we were both placed in Ten Block and charged with the stabbing. They also charged a third guy, call him Repo, who happened to be in the middle of appealing his murder conviction too.

Then they had to drop the charges on Repo, because it turned out that the block logs showed that he wasn't even in the block at the time that they finally claimed that the stabbing happened.

They originally claimed that it happened between 9:00 and 9:15. But, when I produced my daughter's telephone bill and the block cop told them that I was down at the front of the block after I got off of the phone, they changed the time of the incident to ten minutes before nine. It turned out that that wasn't going to work either, because the block logs showed that both Repo and Tony were out of the block until nine o'clock. That automatically brought the time of the stabbing back to after nine o'clock.

So, reluctantly, they dropped the charges against Repo. I guess that they wanted to kill my appeal more than his—which worked out for Repo, as he overturned his conviction about six months later.

When I went to the disciplinary board, I found out to my surprise that the evidence implicating the three of us allegedly consisted solely of a statement attributed to the victim. I say "allegedly," because, when they told me that Tony was the witness, I requested that he be called as a witness at the hearing. They just laughed at that.

According to the investigating officer, Nelson Julius, Tony *said* that I grabbed him on the back stairwell and held him while Clay stabbed him. They didn't even have a signed statement from Tony.

That didn't make any sense at all. First off, I didn't. But, beyond that, he didn't even get stabbed in the stairwell. He got stabbed in Clay's cell.

In the end, there were all kinds of witnesses, both black and white, who came forward, attesting to the fact that I had nothing to do with it. Tony happened to be black, and the black guys that came forward to testify that I was not involved were his friends—some of whom had actually seen what happened.

The final straw came just before my hearing when Clay gave me an unsolicited affidavit swearing that he was the one who had had the beef with Tony and that he had acted solely on his own.

It also came out that the first screw that Tony talked to at the hospital had turned in a report that Tony had told him that he had had a beef with one inmate, but he didn't name the inmate.

To get by the multiple discrepancies in their claims of just what time they said that the incident happened, the d-board declared that their own block logs were wrong! What? The block cop couldn't tell time?

After all that, the disciplinary board found me guilty.

They sentenced me to thirty days on the boards, and recommended that I be placed in Ten Block.

A guy I know told me later that when the disciplinary board members came out of Ten Block, a deputy warden (who went on to become the warden) named Duvall was waiting for them. He immediately stopped the chairperson and said to her, "Did you do what I told you to do? Did you find him guilty?"

Duvall and I had a history. He had worked in Ten Block for a while. The funny thing was, that some guards—not many, but some—were afraid to walk the tiers in Ten Block. Duvall was one of them. I asked another guard why we never saw Duvall on the tier. He told me that Duvall had a deal with the block supervisor. If Duvall would do all of the block paperwork, he didn't have to go on the tier.

About a month or so after they found me guilty, I received a letter in the mail from Tony. He was being held at Bridgewater. He said that he had just heard that I'd been found guilty of stabbing him and that the cops had said that he had said that I was the one who did it. He included an affidavit attesting to the fact that I had nothing to do with his being stabbed.

I sent a copy of the affidavit to the disciplinary board, asking that they reconsider their decision. They ignored it.

I then sent a copy of the affidavit to the warden, Michael Maloney, appealing the d-board's decision. Denied.

His initial response was that he thought that I had raised some interesting issues, that he had contacted the DOC legal department for their opinion, and that he would get back to me.

His next response was, in essence, "So what?"

They gave me two years in Ten Block, with the possibility of being transferred to the feds after one year.

It gets better, or worse, depending upon your point of view.

I filed a civil action in court, asking that the board's guilty finding be overturned and that I be placed back into general population. The case was heard on April 2, 1987, in front of Judge Volterra. On the morning of my hearing, I was waiting in the lobby outside of the visiting room. From where I was sitting, I could see the trap door through which outsiders entered the prison. Here comes Judge Volterra and a half a dozen or so other people. Volterra was at the head of the crowd talking and laughing with a blonde girl. Unfortunately, when they called me in for my case to be heard, the blonde turned out to be the lawyer for the DOC, named Conway.

When I presented all of my evidence, she did not respond to any of it except for Tony's affidavit. She claimed that the investigating officer, Nelson Julius, had gone to Bridgewater to see Tony and that Tony had said that he didn't write the affidavit.

I responded with an affidavit from Tony's best friend, who was in Walpole, which stated that he'd known Tony since they were kids, that they wrote each other all of the time, and that he had read the affidavit and would swear that it was Tony's signature.

Ms. Conway said that she was not talking about the signature. She admitted that it was Tony's signature. She said that her argument was that Tony didn't write the affidavit itself—and sat down.

I could not believe that that was the entirety of her argument.

I got up and said to Judge Volterra, "Your Honor, it's obvious that he didn't write the affidavit. It was typed. I've just submitted a half a dozen motions that were typed and I didn't type any of them. Does that make them invalid, even though I signed them?"

Volterra responded by saying, "Well, I think what she's saying, Mr. Doherty, is that someone forced him to sign the affidavit."

I was totally caught off guard.

I said, "I didn't hear her say that, Your Honor. When did she say that?"

When he didn't respond, I turned to Ms. Conway, who was sitting about five feet to my left, and said, "Did you say that? I didn't hear you say that?"

She was sitting there, ostensibly involved with some papers in front of her, and refused to respond or even look up.

I repeated myself, "Excuse me, Ms. Conway. Did you say that?"

When she still wouldn't look up, Judge Volterra intervened, saying, "That's enough, Mr. Doherty."

When I tried to press the issue, he interrupted me, saying, "I said that's enough. I promise you that I will view this evidence with a jaundiced eye. Now, let's move on."

Reluctantly, I did. I had some other motions and affidavits that I wanted to introduce.

But shortly after I started, Judge Volterra interrupted me, telling me again, that that was enough.

I tried to continue, but he repeated himself, with a little more emphasis, saying that that was enough.

I really didn't want to stop. I still had some more paperwork that I wanted to submit. But, in a way, his manner reminded me of Judge Elam, in the civil action that I'd filed two years earlier. Judge Elam had basically told me in the same manner, politely but firmly, to shut up.

At the time that he said it, I had thought that Judge Elam was riding roughshod over me. It turned out that when he told me, "That's *enough*, Mr. Doherty," he was speaking quite literally. He was saying that I had made my case. "That's enough."

Now here was Judge Volterra telling me, "That's enough, Mr. Doherty."

So I sat down. I was clinging to Volterra's promise that he would "view this evidence with a jaundiced eye." I guess that I was counting on him to exhibit the same kind of integrity that Judge Elam had displayed.

That was on Thursday, April 2. Two days later, on Saturday, I received Volterra's ruling. It was a slip of paper that simply said, "denied."[9]

After sitting in my cell in Ten Block for a while, cursing Volterra for being a weasel and myself for being stupid enough to have bought his "I'll view the evidence with a jaundiced eye" malarkey and persuading myself that he was going to make an honest ruling, I reread the little, maybe 3-inch by 8-inch, slip of paper for probably the tenth time. I finally saw what I'd missed all of the other times.

The date. It was dated April 1, 1987. Volterra had denied my motion on the day *before* the hearing—on April Fool's Day. He'd certainly made a fool out of me.

Afterward, I kept going over the hearing in my head and kept coming back to one thing. There had been nothing said in that courtroom that even implied that Tony had said that someone had forced him to sign the affidavit. That hadn't come from the DOC. That had come from Volterra.

So where did he get it? Was it from the conversation with Ms. Conway as they entered the prison? Maybe. I would guess that it was before that. Otherwise, why would he have denied the motion on the day before the hearing?

I tried for years after that to get a copy of the transcript of the hearing. Fat chance. They stalled me. They ignored me. They passed me off from one "clerk" to another. They lied to me, telling me that no transcript had been taken at the hearing. Finally, well into the nineties, I responded to their lie that no transcript had been taken in such a manner that the clerk responded and admitted that there was a transcript taken on the day of the hearing.

Eventually, after being shunted about some more, I was directed to write to a Mary Stanton, at the State House. I wrote to Ms. Stanton again and again. She never responded.

Years later, after I came home, I called Ms. Stanton on the telephone. Ms. Stanton was quite courteous. She sincerely sounded like she would have helped me if she could have, but, "oops! Sorry, too late." They only keep transcripts for so many years, and then they destroy them. I guess that I waited too long.

Oh yeah, one other thing. During the two years that they kept me in the hole, the federal courts turned down my appeal (on procedural grounds because of an error/oversight on the part of a former attorney).

One good thing that did happen during those two years was that two of the best lawyers in the state got involved in my case. I got a letter from a friend of mine from Charlestown, named Joe Murray. He wanted to know if there was anything that he could do for me, as he was about to begin serving a federal sentence (for trying to smuggle guns to Ireland), and wasn't going to be around for a while. I returned his letter telling him that, as I had just fired my lawyer, I needed a new one.

A few days later, Attorney Anthony Cardinale came to see me. The next time that Tony came, he brought Attorney Robert Sheketoff with him. As anybody in the legal system in Boston will tell you, you're not going to do much better than Bob and Tony.

fifty-nine

After two more years in the hole, I was released back into general population, in September 1988, and immediately began drawing up a new trial motion. I had uncovered more new evidence. Inmate Joseph Yandle, who had been housed outside of Walpole in a medium-security institution for years, had sent me an affidavit attesting to the fact that he was the inmate who CO Peter McGuire had identified as having gone into Perrotta's cell that night, because McGuire asked him to tell Perrotta that he had a visit. He swore under oath that Perrotta was in bed and already dead.

So, they locked me up again, without charging me with anything.

On Thanksgiving morning, there had been a beef between two kids in the block in which I was living. One was black. One was white. It sounds racial. It wasn't.

The black kid had woken up the block, singing loudly, about 6:30 in the morning. Guys all over the block—black, white, and anything in between—were yelling at him to shut up. Unfortunately, he was wearing headphones and between the music in his ears and his own singing, he just didn't hear anyone.

When the cell doors cracked at seven o'clock, it happened to be a white guy, who lived in the cell next to me, that confronted him first. Words were exchanged. It quickly turned physical. After a few minutes, a guy named Matt and I intervened. We spoke to my neighbor, and he relented and let up on the other guy. He was a good kid, and if the beef had gone any farther, it could have turned serious and he could have gotten into trouble. Real trouble. Not just a few months in the hole for a fight.

Unfortunately, it all happened out in plain sight, in front of a number of guards. Consequently, they locked the block down for a few hours. When they opened the doors, they kept four of us locked in (my neighbor, myself, Matt, and a fourth person who happened to lived next door to us).

After a week, Matt and I were released. Like me, Matt had grown up in Charlestown. During the week we were locked up, word had been spread all over Walpole that it had been a racial beef between townies and blacks. The rumor had been spread by the guards.

Matt and I went to the yard on the first movement after we were released from lock up. Word had spread that we'd been released. When we got to the yard, there were about fifty black guys standing on one side of the yard and about fifty white guys standing on the other side. They were all waiting for us.

The kid who'd gotten the beating had an uncle in Walpole at the time. Call him Dom. Dom was younger than me and was living down the minimum end. I really didn't know him, but Matty did. He liked him and said that he was a good guy. I think that they'd been in reform school together.

Understandably, Dom was angry. But, by the end of the conversation, he realized that it hadn't been a racial beef. He still wasn't happy, but at least the racial aspect was gone. If he should run into the guy who had had the beef with his nephew, there most likely would be a personal beef. But, as long as it stayed one on one, it would remain personal.

Still, as the following weeks went by, the rumors of racial tension continued. They were all false, and they were all started by the administration. By Christmas, it was obvious to me what was coming—a ship-out.

On the night of December 27, shortly before lock up time, Matt and another friend of ours named Danny stopped by my cell. I had a stack of warm clothing piled neatly on a box by my cell door. When they asked what the clothes were for, I told them that that was what I was going to wear when they came to lug us. They spent the next few minutes joking with me about being paranoid. Then we locked in for the night.

The cops woke me up around six o'clock the next morning. It was time for the move. They transferred a number of us, black and white, to various prisons around the state. I was taken to the Old Colony Correctional Center (OCCC) in Bridgewater, along with a black youngster named Stacy, where we were placed in the hole. I was assigned upstairs on the second floor. Stacy went downstairs.

Inmates were allowed to go to the law library one night a week, both upstairs and downstairs inmates, except Stacy and me. It soon became apparent that no matter how often we requested it, we were not going to be allowed to go to the law library at the same time.

The recreation area at the hole in OCCC was a slight improvement on the hole at Walpole. Walpole had cages. OCCC had a yard. One of the features of the yard was that you could talk to some of the guys downstairs through their windows.

One day, I was out in the yard for rec', and Stacy called me over to his window. He said, "Man, you ain't gonna believe the shit they just told me."

I said, "What's up?"

He said, "You know I been tryin' to get down the law library the same time as you?"

I nodded in response.

We had both been trying to get down there together. As we had both been locked up and shipped out without being charged with anything, we were going to be coplaintiffs in a civil action to get back out into population.

He continued, "Well, I got a response back from that letter I wrote to the warden askin' that we be allowed to go together. He denied it. So now I'm arguin' with the cops down here about it. You know, askin' 'em, 'How come? Why can't we go together? Everybody else can. We got legal work we gotta do.'"

"So this one cop says to me, 'Whatta you wanna be with Stevie Doherty for? We know you got problems with him.'"

"I told him, 'I ain't got no problems with him. Whatta ya talkin' about?'"

"The cop says, 'C'mon man, the guards from Walpole told us what happened when they brought you guys in. Stevie killed your brother, and then you knocked him out. They told us to keep you two separated.'"

I stared at him through the window screen for a moment, not quite sure what to say about his brother. I said, "Look Stacy, I'm sorry about your brother. I didn't know nothin' about him gettin' dead, but I had nothin' to do with it."

Shaking his head, in a half frustrated, half humorous tone, he said, "Man, my brother ain't dead; my brother's on the street. My brother's a *citizen*."

Laughing, I said, "Oh yeah? Then what the hell d' ya knock me out for?"

He laughed and said, "Man, ain't that some shit."

Sixty

I have one closing note on Knothead. At some point in the eighties, after the courts had ordered me back to Massachusetts, I'd heard that, after Knothead tipped his case and got out, he'd gotten busted for a skin beef. I didn't get the whole story, but, supposedly, he'd raped some girl.

I felt bad about it. Although we weren't all that close, and we didn't hang around together, I still liked him. On top of that, as much of a bug as he was, I never considered him to be a skinner.

I never ran into him again. But, in 1989, while I was at OCCC waiting to be shipped back to the federal system, I ran into a guy that I had been in Walpole with years before. He was a good guy and when they let our tier out for recreation, we walked the small yard together swapping updates on what was happening in the different places that we had each been in since the last time that we had seen each other (a.k.a. gossiping). In the course of our conversation, Knothead's name came up.

"Man, I gotta tell ya, Stevie. They bum beefed his ass. I know them bitches who ratted on him. They's 'ho's. He was partyin' with them for a couple a days. They was partyin' in Dorchester. Then they went down to Lynn. Then they came back to Boston, just partyin'," he said.

"Afterwards, the cops grabbed the two bitches. Told 'em they'd fuck their asses up if they didn't give 'em Knothead."

I heard that Knothead died from AIDS, or Hepatitis C, sometime in the nineties. He never got out again.

As I've said, I'm not the only one who ever got framed.

sixty-one

I n February 1989, I received a NOTICE OF CLASSIFICATION MEETING. The notice stated that the "classification meeting will be held … to consider your placement in a Federal or Out of State Facility."

"This meeting is being convened for the following reasons:

"As a result of an investigation it has been determined that you were a group leader responsible for instigating tension with other groups. In so doing yaou [sic] created a climate which enhanced the potential for violence in MCI-Cedar Junction. It was also determined that you were a principal in the struggle for control of drug traffic within MCI-Cedar Junction. You were also observed making remarks which can be directly attributed to increasing racial tension in the Essex 2 Unit."

When I first read these "reasons," I immediately assumed that they were pulling a swindle like the one that they had pulled on me the last time I'd discovered new evidence, when they shipped me to Marion. Namely, that while they were obviously alleging that I had violated a number of the rules and regulations of the disciplinary code, they were not officially charging me with them.

Therefore, I was not going to be given a disciplinary hearing. Instead, they were going to use these "allegations" as justification for holding a classification hearing to send me out of state.

One reason for their doing it this way was that there were different standards regarding the introduction of evidence at a classification hearing as opposed to a disciplinary hearing. The DOC had such a history of holding fraudulent disciplinary hearings, and railroading people, that the hearings had become widely known for being nothing more than star chambers. Consequently, after a number of court actions brought this to light, the DOC was compelled to institute certain disciplinary rules and regulations that at least gave the appearance of fairness.

One of these was the "credibility checklist" regulation.

This was only applicable to disciplinary hearings in which the evidence was attributed to an "unidentified reliable informant." The informant, and his information, had to measure up to a certain standard, albeit, not a very high one. Still, it was certainly better than the carte blanche with which they had previously been allowed to introduce "evidence" that had allegedly been given to them by an unidentified informant.

When they had pulled a similar chicanery on me a few years earlier, the Honorable Harry Elam had firmly slapped them on the wrist. At one point in his decision, dealing directly with this particular issue, Judge Elam stated:

"The use of informant information in disciplinary hearings has been the topic of recent court opinions... The restrictions on the use of informant information in the disciplinary process detailed in those cases should apply with equal force to the classification process... It would be ludicrous if the inmate were afforded protections in the disciplinary process but lost those protections in the classification process when the ultimate sanction... is the same."

Another reason that they wanted to avoid the disciplinary regulations in a case like this, was the "substantial evidence" standard.

Again, as a result of the DOC's history of automatically finding inmates guilty at disciplinary hearings, on little or no evidence, a line had been drawn. There was now a regulation requiring that, in order to find an inmate guilty, "substantial evidence" had to be presented against him.

So, as a result of their prior history, plus the fact that, in seventeen straight years of incarceration I had no racial incidents, nor drugs, on my record, my immediate reaction to the bogus allegations that I was *not* being charged with was that they were going to try to run their old swindle.

However, on page two of the notice, while confirming my suspicion that the "evidence" against me was going to be from an "unidentified informant," they also specifically stated that, "A summary of that evidence will be provided at your hearing consistent with the standards set forth in [the Disciplinary Rules and Regulations]."

I interpreted this to mean that they were going to abide by the disciplinary rules and regulations, i.e., a credibility checklist and the substantial evidence standard.

Also on page two of the notice was a question asking if I wished to call other witnesses to the classification hearing. I checked "Yes," and listed the names of the witnesses that I wished to call. Seeing as I was being charged with starting racial problems, a number of them were black.

It was over three months after I was placed in the hole before I received my counterfeit disciplinary hearing, i.e., pretending to be a classification hearing.

During that time, I prepared as well as I could. As to the preposterous accusation that I was going to take control of the drug traffic in Walpole, there really wasn't that much that I could do until I heard the explicit allegations.

However, the equally absurd charge that I was causing racial problems took a different course. At some point, I started receiving affidavits from black inmates. These affidavits were totally unsolicited. They ranged from older guys that I'd gotten to know well over the years to younger guys that I didn't know all that well but whose paths I had happened to cross. The one thing that they did have in common was that they were all black.

These were fellows that had nothing to gain by coming forward. A number of them were Muslims who, for the most part, kept their dealings with white inmates to a bare minimum. One of the affidavits actually came from the head of the Muslims.

The essence of the affidavits was that, whatever else I might be, I was not a racist. Some of them made note of the fact that, not only did I *not* cause racial problems but that, to the contrary, I was known for defusing them.

One of them even pointed out how I had taken the time to assist him with certain mathematical problems that resulted in his not being swindled into serving more time than he was supposed to do.

He had come into Walpole as a youngster with a life sentence, without parole. Eventually, he overturned his conviction and was given eighteen to twenty years. Shortly after it happened, he mentioned to me that they had just told him that he only had five or six years left. It didn't sound right, so I asked him if he had lost a lot of "good time." He said that he hadn't lost any. So, I told him to get the paperwork that determined his release date. When he got it, twenty years worth of good time numbers were jumbled up, in miniscule figures on one piece of paper. It took the better part of a night to unravel them. By morning I had figured out what they had done and had rewritten the figures, in large clear print, on a half dozen sheets of paper. When he gave the figures to the DOC representative, who had given him the original figures, they didn't even argue. They simply "apologized" and told him that "someone out front" must have made a mistake. He went from owing them five to six years down to two to three.

By the time of the hearing, I had received over twenty affidavits from black inmates.

I also made the DOC aware of the fact that a highly regarded television program on the local Public Broadcasting Station (PBS), called "SAY

BROTHER," had once done a show on the conditions in Ten Block. They had asked me to appear on the show.

"SAY BROTHER" was a program for black people, by black people, and about black people. The hostess of the show, who extended the invitation, told me that she wanted to have at least one white inmate's thoughts on the conditions in Ten Block. She also told me that my invitation to appear had come about as a result of the advocacy of black inmates. She said that she asked a number of black inmates to recommend a white inmate in Ten Block to be interviewed for the show. Each of them had referred her to me.

The hearing finally took place on March 30, 1989.

Right from the start, it was a farce. They broke just about every rule that there was.

Their entire case was, of course, based on "reliable informant information" allegedly from an unidentified informant.

Unfortunately, when we requested a credibility checklist, they refused to give us one. Despite the courts' rulings on the matter, they simply stated that this was not a disciplinary hearing, but that this was a classification hearing. Therefore, we were not entitled to a credibility checklist.

My attorney, Tony Cardinale, requested that the evidence be evaluated in accordance with the substantial evidence standard. This too was denied.

The notice had specifically stated, in accordance with the rules, that the "evidence will be presented by Investigators Charpentier and Gordon." Moreover, just to be safe, we had officially requested their presence as witnesses. In obvious violation of the rules, the board members neither would allow them to testify nor would they allow any of the other witnesses, whose testimony I had requested on the form, to testify.

Instead, a different staff member, CO McGonigle presented the evidence. His testimony could be broken down into two parts.

First, he testified that two unidentified informants had said that I was going to cause violence with the blacks—twice. Each of these alleged anonymous informants described a separate, impending incident. Each of them gave a different date when this alleged violence was supposed to happen.

It was the first that I had ever heard of it, and, as it turned out, neither of their predicted incidents had ever even occurred.

Despite this, the board found both informants to be reliable and their information to be credible.

Following that, McGonigle recited a vague series of second-hand anecdotes, taken out of context and twisted to imply that I was a racist. I'll describe a couple of them to give you an idea of how they do things. The following is an affidavit that I filed, in my appeal to the Commissioner, clarifying one of these alleged incidents. It should be self-explanatory.

AFFIDAVIT
OF
STEPHEN DOHERTY

1. At my federal transfer hearing (3-30-89) CO McGonigle testified that:

2. "On 11-16-88 a black inmate attempted to "cut" in front of inmate Doherty to use the telephone."

3. "Inmate Doherty shouted at the black inmate."

4. "Groups of blacks and whites quickly formed."

5. "The block officer was able to resolve the incident without violence erupting but tension remained in the block."

6. Of the above statements the only one that is accurate is # 3 - I did shout at an inmate who happened to be black.

7. What actually happened is as follows:

8. Nobody "cut in front of me". I was already using the telephone when the incident occurred. In the middle of a conversation, I had to leave the phone for a moment to get something from my cell. My cell, like the telephone, is on the flats. My cell is approximately sixty (60) feet from the telephone. As I stepped back out of my cell I saw that another inmate was standing by the telephone holding it up to his mouth as if speaking to someone. I had left the receiver hanging straight down. This is an accepted signal at Walpole that the phone is in use. At this point I shouted at the inmate that I was using the phone. I shouted because I was sixty (60) feet away from him (in a cell block with forty-five (45) inmates and a commensurate noise level). If I hadn't shouted he wouldn't have heard me. I quickly proceeded to the phone and the inmate gave me the receiver explaining that he didn't think that anyone was using the phone. The incident ended at that point.

9. At no time did "groups of blacks and whites" form. There simply wasn't time. The incident only lasted a few seconds.

10. The block officer did not "resolve the incident". There simply

wasn't time. Though the telephone is only about five (5) feet from the officer's desk the entire incident was over before he even got out of the chair.

11. There was no "tension remaining in the block" after the incident. In fact, the inmate and I discussed it shortly after I got off of the phone and he stated that he would've reacted the same way had our positions been reversed.

12. The inmate happened to be black.

13. If he were white I would've reacted exactly the same way.

14. The incident was about respect and manners, not race.

Signed under the pains
and penalties of perjury
this 18th day of April, 1989

The above is an example of the way that they will take something out of context and portray it as something altogether different from what actually occurred.

I'll give you another instance where they took it to a different level by flat out lying. But, in this particular case, there happened to be an element of which they were unaware.

Another one of the "antiblack Doherty is a racist" stories that McGonigle recited for the board went as follows:

> "On 10-20-88 due to problems with the heat in Essex II block and requests from blacks that it be turned up, inmate Doherty approached the Essex II block officer and complained about the black inmates 'playing games' with the heat, stating 'I'm telling you... unless things get straightened out, we're going to have problems with the niggers...'"

First off, I did say something to the block officer about the heat. I told *him* to stop playing games with the heat.

The truth of the matter is some guards like to cause problems between inmates—not all, but some. However, this time, they picked the wrong issue.

Years earlier, when I had first gotten out of Ten Block in January 1980, after the Perrotta lock down, I was placed in Block B-3 (that's Three Block in the max end). There were four or five youngsters from Charlestown in the block. Plus, they were running around with a bunch of other kids from South Boston and East Boston. All were good kids, but they were still a little rambunctious.

A couple of days after I got out, a black guy that I'd known for years, D.Z., came to me. D. was a good guy, a capable fellow, and a gentleman. He was doing life.

"Listen Stevie, I think we got a problem comin'. I'd like to head it off, if we can," he said.

I said, "What's up?"

"Ya know how there's always been arguments about the heat. Y'know the brothers want it hotter. The white dudes think it's too hot. Well, it's been goin' on. But since you got outta Ten, some a' them youngsters—'specially the Charlestown kids—been gettin' kinda pushy," he said.

I thought about it for a minute, and then I said, "Well, I'll tell ya, Z. I gotta go along with them on the heat. It's drivin' me nuts, too. But how about this? How about if we have the cops leave the heat on all day, but have 'em turn it off when we lock in at night? That way, you guys'll be warm during the day and when you go in at night you can always put another sweatshirt or somethin' on. Or get another blanket. And *we* won't be suffocatin' after we lock in. That's when the heat really bothers me."

He thought about it for a moment. Then he smiled. He said, "Man, I like that. The brothers'll go for that. You think the white boys'll go for it?"

Getting up from the table, I said, "I dunno'. It's just an idea. Lemme go talk t' them. While I'm talkin' t' them, why don't you go an' talk to your guys?"

The upshot was both sides liked the idea. It quite literally eliminated the problem in that block for the rest of the winter, not to mention that everybody was happy to avoid the beef.

The point is McGonigle had raised a black/white problem, which everyone knew occurred every winter, and tailored it in such a manner so that he could falsely quote me as having said, "We're going to have problems with the niggers."

One common theme that seemed to run through the twenty-two affidavits that I received from black inmates was that I was regarded by blacks as someone who would avert problems rather than start them. The following are examples.

"I know that Steve has helped de-fuse potential racial activity that had the potential to erupt into something very serious."

"I have seen him in action during crisis and he has always acted to head-off any confrontations between blacks and whites."

"I know from my own personal experience that Steve has actually acted as a peace-maker in incidents that could have blown up into something bigger and more explosive."

These are just a few of the remarks that were made, in different affidavits, regarding the subject of my fomenting racial problems. I have no doubt that some of them were actually references to the time that D.Z. and I worked out the heat problem. Likewise, I have no doubt that if the guys that sent me the affidavits had known about the fabrication that McGonigle brought up about the heat problems *before* the hearing, some of those affidavits would have specifically recalled the *real* heat incident.

|||||||||||||||||||||||||||||||||||||||||||||||||||||||||||||||||||||||

Not only would they not allow me to have the reporting officers, or the staff member(s) who professedly spoke to these alleged "unidentified informants," appear as witnesses, they also refused to allow any inmate witnesses to testify. Their justification for not allowing me to call any inmate witnesses, i.e., to present a defense, was that the "DRB did not call ... any inmates ... as it was accepted as fact that they would testify that he had no involvement in illicit activities."

When Attorney Cardinale cross-examined McGonigle, McGonigle admitted that he had not even spoken to the alleged unidentified informant. He stated that the informant information had been given to a different staff member. The board would not allow us to question this alleged staff member.

The cross-examination soon took on an apparent pattern. Attorney Cardinale would ask a question.

McGonigle would respond, "I don't know."

Over and over. Sometimes, after an, "I don't know," Tony would turn and ask the board members if they could answer the question.

They couldn't or wouldn't.

At one point, during the cross-examination, in an obvious attempt to bolster his clearly shallow testimony, McGonigle maintained that I had a gang. He said that it was known as the "Charlestown Crew."

When Tony pressed him to identify the members of this "Charlestown Crew," McGonigle came up with five names. Out of the five inmates that he named, only one of them was even from Charlestown, Matty. And he had moved out of town when he was fourteen or fifteen years old!

Tony Cardinale did an excellent job in cross-examining McGonigle, not that it did any good. I mean, it would have been swell if it had been in front of a jury, but not in front of a hand-picked lynch mob. Their decision was as follows:

"The DRB recommends, by a 3-0 vote, that inmate Doherty be placed in the custody of the Federal Bureau of Prisons. The DRB believes that inmate Doherty played a major role in the instigating tension and conflict at MCI-CJ between 10/88 and 12/88. As a result the DRB believes that his continued placement in the Mass. DOC would disrupt the security and orderly running of its institutions, hence the recommendation for FBOP placement. The inmate was advised of his right to appeal."

That sort of sums up the DOC. They can allege anything, attribute it to a nonexistent source, and declare it to be true. Yet, you cannot call a defense witness even if that witness can prove that you did not commit the alleged offense. I'll bet the Norfolk County DA's office would love to be able to use that one.

sixty-two

As ludicrous as the hearing was, the appeal was just as bad.

The rule is you have five working days to submit your appeal. However, in this case, there was going to be a slight delay. Before the hearing, we had requested (as was our right) that the hearing be tape-recorded.

After the hearing, Tony Cardinale asked for a copy of the tape. They told him that they would make him a copy and send it to him that day.

The hearing took place on a Thursday. This meant that the appeal had to be sent to the commissioner of corrections by the following Thursday. On Wednesday, when Tony still hadn't received the tape, he called the DOC. He told them that there was no way that he could have the appeal in on time. He needed the tape before he could do the appeal.

They told him, "No problem. We'll waive the time limit. You'll have five days from the day you get the tape." And then it just dragged on.

Finally, a couple of weeks later, my paranoia got the best of me. I submitted my own appeal. It went as follows:

To: Commissioner Fair
From: Stephen Doherty
Re: Federal Transfer Recommendation
Date: April 18, 1989

The only reason given by the DRB to justify their recommendation was that they "believed" that I "played a major role in instigating racial tension and conflict at MCI-CJ between 10/88 and 12/88." Therefore, I shall confine my appeal to that issue, (along with procedural objections).

First, the hearing was unlawful, as was the three months confinement in segregation which led up to the hearing. The transfer to OCCC Segregation was unlawful because the Commissioner did not sign off on it "PRIOR TO ITS OCCURENCE." (103 CMR 420:09

(3), (a).) The hearing itself was unlawful because it was not held "within twenty (20) working days of such a transfer." (103 CMR 420:09 (3) (b). The exceptions to this rule (See id) are not applicable in this case, as the investigation had been completed and all necessary information compiled prior to 12/28/88.

Furthermore, the procedure at the hearing was in violation of the DOC's own rules and regulations. The reporting staff person(s) were requested, but not called. No determination of unavailability was made. (103 CMR 430:14(5).) All of my witnesses were denied. The reason given, (that their testimony would be cumulative and repetitive), is verifiably untrue. A review of the transcript of the hearing will show that there were a number of questions that neither the staff member (CO McGonigle), nor the board members could, (or would), answer, that could've been answered by some of the requested witnesses.

My attorney requested that evidence be judged in accordance with the <u>substantial</u> <u>evidence</u> standard (See inter alia *Wightman v. Supt.* etc, 475 N.E.2d 85). This request was denied.

We requested a credibility checklist in regard to the unidentified informant. This too was denied.

As to the issue itself, that I instigated "racial tension and conflict at MCI-CJ between 10/88 and 12/88", it is patently absurd. I've been incarcerated for the last seventeen (17) years and have absolutely no history of "instigating racial tension" nor of ever having been involved in a "racial conflict".

To the contrary, I have, on more than one occasion, defused racially tense situations and prevented racial conflicts (Please see Affidavits (22) of Black inmates, submitted at hearing). Furthermore, if I were at all bigoted or in any way inclined towards creating racial problems, I would certainly not have been invited to appear on the television program "SAY BROTHER". 'SAY BROTHER' is a program for blacks, by blacks, and about blacks, and the invitation to appear was extended on the recommendation of a number of black inmates. (Please see S. Doherty Affidavit submitted at hearing.)

In regards to the credibility of informant # one: How plausible is it that when seventeen years of close professional monitoring in a controlled environment produces an excellent record of race relations, and no record of drug trafficking, that, within the space of thirteen days a single informant should discover that I am both the head of a drug ring and the leader of a group devoted to racial violence? Not merely implausible, but preposterous - certainly not credible!

As to informant # two, he "did not specifically identify" me but merely "alluded" to my "involvement". This statement is so vague as to be meaningless. Furthermore, both of these alleged informants were referring to two discrete incidents separated by more than three weeks in time, yet the unavoidable fact is that, in neither case, did the predicted racial violence take place. By definition, the alleged informants' information was not credible. Racial violence did not occur on 12-1-88 as informant # one said it would. Racial violence did not occur when the food packages ended as informant # two said it would. For that matter, to the best of my knowledge, there were no incidents of racial violence at any time while I was in General Population at MCI-CJ in 1988, (i.e. 9-7 to 12-28).

In addition to the alleged informants the staff member (McGonigle) also listed five 'incidents' which, when viewed in the particular manner in which they were presented, tend to make me appear to be anti-black. At the hearing, I explained each of these incidents and in no case was my explanation rebutted or challenged. The truth of the matter is that the incidents in question were simply misperceived, misinterpreted, or taken out of context, and gained significance only in retrospect. (Please see attached affidavits).

I would like to point out that Key Issue # 2 describes me as a "serious adjustment problem during this ... sentence". In the last <u>decade</u> I have received one serious disciplinary report (i.e. D-Report # 86-8330), which is presently being challenged in court. I will not dispute that I was a somewhat less than model inmate in the 1970's but, there can't be too many inmates who have been lock up all of the 1980's (as I have) who have less D-Reports than I do.

I would also point out that I am presently in court on a number of matters, including a PRO SE appeal of my first degree murder conviction, and certain Civil Suits against the Mass. DOC (The DOC also has a subjective interest in opposing my criminal appeal). A transfer to the FBoP at this time would deprive me of meaningful access to the courts. Such meaningful access is a fundamental right. (Bounds v. Smith, 430 U.S. 817, 828 (1977). Your office has been aware of this since, at least, 1984, when the federal court, Caffrey, CJ), stated, "I rule that by 1980 ... The Constitutional Right of prisoners to have meaningful access to the courts had been clearly established by the United States Supreme Court." Blake v. Berman, 598

F.Supp. 1081 (1984).Therefore, for all of the reasons stated above I'm requesting that you allow me to remain in Massachusetts, preferably at a medium security institution where there will be less turmoil and consequently less chance for my name to be thrown into things that I have nothing to do with.

Stephen Doherty

The Commissioner's response, dated May 9, was the epitome of the manner in which the DOC dealt with legitimate appeals.

For the most part, he confined his limited response to procedural issues. Then he misrepresented them by ignoring the actual facts.

"I am in receipt of your letter dated April 24. 1989, appealing the recommendation of the March 30, 1989, Departmental Review Board (DRB) that you be transferred to the custody of the Federal Bureau of Prison (FBOP).

"*Pursuant to 103 CMR 420.10(c), you had five (5) working days to submit such an appeal. Therefore, the deadline for its submission was April 6, 1989. I am thus denying your appeal since it was submitted approximately two and one-half weeks late.* "In any event, I find no fault with the procedures utilized in your case ... Determinations regarding the witness requests were within the DRB's discretion. The "substantial evidence standard" and "credibility checklists" concern disciplinary proceedings and were not relevant to your classification hearing."

"The substantive determinations by the DRB are clearly supported by the evidence indicated in the DRB report, and I see no reason to disturb these findings."

||||||||||||||||||||||||||||||||||||||||||||||||||||||||||||||||

APPARENTLY NO ONE told the commissioner that they had waived the time limit until we received a transcript or a copy of the tape of the hearing, which, when we finally did get it, had about twenty minutes missing. They said that the recorder had stopped working for a while.

||||||||||||||||||||||||||||||||||||||||||||||||||||||||||||||||

BY MAINTAINING THE facade that this was not a disciplinary hearing, Commissioner Fair neatly sidestepped the real issue. That this was actually a disciplinary hearing, in the guise of a classification hearing, and was shown not only in the NOTICE OF CLASSIFICATION MEETING, which specifically stated that the evidence would be heard in accordance with the disciplinary regulations, but also in the allegations themselves. If these allegations had any validity whatsoever, they could have, should have, and certainly *would have* been rendered into at least twelve separate violations of the DOC's Disciplinary Code of Offenses—something of which Commissioner Fair was well aware. That is why he deftly avoided the issue.

sixty-three

I n light of the DOC's prior history of illegally shipping inmates out of state, with no forewarning, I decided that it would make sense to get my new trial motion filed before I found myself on a bus back to the hinterlands. The problem was I couldn't get in touch with either of my lawyers, Tony Cardinale or Bob Sheketoff. For some reason, both of them were out of state. I think Bob was in China.

So, I filed the new trial motion pro se, from the hole, where they kept me for another year and a half before sending me back out of state again—again without charging me with anything.

It took that long for them to ship me out, because I fought them in court. It was obvious that the only reason that they were shipping me out was to interfere with my access to the courts. The court finally ruled that they had the right to ship me out of state, but only under the condition that they would promise to bring me back to Massachusetts for any court hearings that I might have.

Once again, I was off to the BOP.

sixty-four

I n April 1990, they shipped me out. Coincidentally, they also shipped out the jailhouse lawyer who was working on my case, and we both wound up in Leavenworth.

Shortly before I was sent out of state, Superior Court Judge Roger Donahue had denied my new trial motion on the grounds that, "The present motion for a new trial presents no issue which has not already been adjudicated."[10]

He must have missed Joey Yandle's affidavit that stated, quite explicitly, for the first time, that Bobby Perrotta was dead before I was ever placed at the scene of the crime.

I wonder if this was the same Judge Donahue that helped them in getting Carden out by throwing out the prison sentence from which he'd escaped?

Bob Sheketoff and Tony Cardinale drew up the appeal of Donahue's denial. They sent a copy to me, out in Leavenworth. I liked it, but I wanted to add a few issues and the jailhouse lawyer did too.

So we drew up a supplemental brief, with excellent assistance from my wonderful daughter, Chris, who is a paralegal.

After Bob and Tony read it, they really didn't have any problems with it. But Bob told me that he wouldn't be arguing the other issues that we raised. He was just going to argue the points that they had made in their brief.

"No problem. But, I want you to tell the SJC that even though you're not arguing the pro se issues, that I am not waiving them. That I want them to consider them and rule on them," I said.

"No problem," he said.

During the oral arguments, that was the first thing that Bob told the SJC, which was a good thing and necessary. If the SJC should deny the appeal, the issues that were raised in the pro se brief would remain procedurally viable and could not be barred. If necessary, we could raise them in an appeal to the federal court, which, of course, we did when the SJC eventually denied my new trial motion in 1991. By the way, this was the second time that they shot me down on my birthday. Despite the denial, they were forced to admit that the judge's instructions to the jury were unconstitutional. But they ruled that the error was "harmless."

However, there was a dissent. The Honorable Justice Francis O'Connor strongly disagreed. After emphasizing the lack of evidence against me, he dissected the issue of Keating's blatantly unconstitutional instructions to the jury, gave an articulate analysis of the issue and of why he dissented, and concluded by stating that, "The error was far from harmless. I would reverse the order denying Doherty a new trial."

Interestingly, Justice O'Connor was a widely respected conservative. But, he was known for coming to each case with an open mind and for getting passionately involved in cases where he wrote a dissent, yet could not persuade the other SJC justices (in my case, Wilkins et al.) that they were wrong. In this case, he *was* right, and they *were* wrong.

One thing about the SJC's ruling that was rather ironic was that, like Judge Donahue, they never dealt with any of the pro se issues that I raised—particularly Joey Yandle's sworn statement that he had seen Bobby Perrotta's dead body before I was ever placed at the scene. When the gatekeeper (Wilkins, of course) ruled that he was granting me leave to appeal, he did not specify any issues. So, by definition, he granted me leave to appeal all issues. However, when the SJC made their ruling, they avoided the Yandle issue by stating, in a footnote, that "We do not consider other issues that the defendant argues in his pro se brief as to which no leave to appeal has been granted."

The pure irony is that Wilkins not only wrote the gatekeeper decision, in which he specifically granted appeal, he also wrote the full SJC decision in which he said that no leave to appeal had been granted!

The ruling did clear the way for me to file a Habeas Corpus Petition with the federal court. Fortunately, it was before Congress passed the deceptively named *Anti-Terrorism and Effective Death Penalty Act* (AEDPA).

If AEDPA had been in effect when I filed my petition, the court would have dismissed it as having been filed too late. This, in turn, would have precluded the evidentiary hearing that resulted in the long-overdue disclosure of the most egregious of all of the evidence that they had hidden over the years.

Under AEDPA, newly discovered evidence is sort of like that tree that falls in the forest. If there's no one there to hear it, is there really any noise?

If you discover new evidence that proves that you are innocent, but there's no court there to hear it …?

It is ironic that, by and large, proponents of AEDPA are also proponents of the death penalty. They do everything that they possibly can to impede and interfere with inmates' attempts to appeal their convictions. Then, when the conviction is overturned, they cite the reversal as proof that the system works.

Such a lovely Catch-22. Such hypocrites.

sixty-five

Despite the DOC's promise to the court that they would bring me back to Massachusetts for my civil court matters, the Commonwealth's attorneys spent the next seven years fighting my attempts to be brought back to Massachusetts, not only for my criminal appeal, but for trials in various civil actions that I had filed regarding the illegal ship-outs and lock ups to which they had subjected me.

When I first got to Leavenworth, Bob Sheketoff and Tony Cardinale were really too busy doing criminal cases to handle the civil stuff. So, after a year or so, I engaged a young lawyer named Rosemary Scapicchio to handle them, two that were filed in Norfolk County and two in Suffolk County.

Initially, she was somewhat confused. When we talked on the phone, she told me that she couldn't find the court documents. Eventually, though, she tracked them down. They were in the closed case file! Somehow they had all been dismissed after my departure to the federal system. I wonder who had that done?

The court quickly reinstated them.

In response to my requests to be returned for a civil trial, the DOC responded that: "I was too dangerous to be housed in any prison in Massachusetts."

I wrote directly to the judge who was handling the case. I told him that that argument was ridiculous.

I said, "I'm fifty-two years old and I weigh one hundred and forty-seven pounds. They've got twenty year old kids coming in there every day, about the size of a Buick, and they handle them just fine. I'm sure that they can handle me. Especially as we all know that I am going to be locked in the hole all the time that I am there."

So, they went to Plan B. They changed their story to: "They didn't want to take a chance on moving me because I was an escape risk."

I wrote to the judge again.

I said, "I've been locked up for twenty years and I have no escapes, nor even any escape attempts, on my record. They have a policy here in Leavenworth whereby all inmates who are classified as escape/security risks have to wear a certain type of identification card. I am not one of those inmates. Therefore, by definition, I am not an escape risk."

They went to Plan C. They told the judge that: "Whereas I was convicted of a prison murder, that I would be a threat to the inmates who testified against me."

Again I wrote to the judge.

I said, "There was only one inmate who testified against me and he's already dead. What else can I do to him?"

At which point, with no explanation why, the judge ruled against me and denied my motion.

I guess that that was Plan D.

sixty-six

I n 1997, a federal court granted me an evidentiary hearing. I was finally scheduled to appear in front of a judge who had the integrity and the guts to order that I be returned for a court hearing, the Honorable Justice Nancy Gertner. At the court's order, the Commonwealth reluctantly returned me to Massachusetts for the hearing.

The evidentiary hearing was ordered, in part, because of Joey Yandle's affidavit. In May 1997, at my hearing in federal court, Joey Yandle—who had been out on parole for a few years by then—testified that on the night of the murder, he'd been walking along the third tier returning from the shower when he heard C/O McGuire call Perrotta's name. Yandle looked down at McGuire who asked him if he would check Perrotta's room to see if he was in there, as he had a visit.

Yandle said, "Sure." He knocked on Perrotta's door and yelled his name. When he got no response, he looked through the cell door window and saw Perrotta lying in his bed. He knocked and called his name again, still no answer.

The bed was along the back wall. Perrotta was lying on his left side, with his back to the door, and he was wearing headphones. So, Yandle opened the door, walked into the room, and yelled his name again. When he still got no response, he walked over to the bed and touched him on the shoulder. Perrotta just rolled over on his back. Yandle could see that there was something wrapped around his neck and what he believed to be his tongue hanging out of his mouth. And he knew that he was dead.

Remember, when Officer McGuire made the five o'clock count, Perrotta's room was so dark that he had to open the door and step into the room, just to be able to see flesh (which Judge Keating would not let Attorney Caplan question McGuire about). He only went one step into the room. Bobby was in the same position then that he was in when he was found dead. When Joey went into the room, even with the light on, he couldn't tell that Perrotta was dead, until he walked over to the bed and actually touched the body.

He took one look and rolled Bobby right back into the position in which he'd found him. He turned around and walked out. As he was closing the door, he wiped his fingerprints off of the door handle with his towel. He then yelled down to McGuire that Perrotta wasn't there and immediately left the scene.

The fact that he even went into the room, as CO Peter McGuire testified at the trial, is proof that Perrotta was in his cell, already dead. Otherwise, there was no reason for Joey Yandle to go into the cell. If Bobby had not been in the cell, Joey would have known it the minute he looked through the window. This would have been obvious to the jury, if they had been allowed to view the murder scene.

Yandle's reason for not reporting the body was self-preservation. He was already serving a life sentence and, as he said, the last thing in the world that he needed was to be the one to find a body. The other inmates would label him as an informant, and the administration would try to pin the murder on him.

During cross-examination, First Assistant Attorney General Frances McIntyre asked him what his state of mind was when he found the body.

Yandle replied, "I was in deep shit."

When she asked him to elaborate, he said, "I was in serious trouble. I just found a dead body. Somebody just got killed, and I either got to deal with the people who killed him or I got to deal with the administration. Either way I'm screwed."

He also pointed out that it was common knowledge at Walpole that prisoners who testify for the defense, in cases that concern crimes occurring inside of the prison, would suffer retaliation from the administration. (Just as the opposite is true—that prisoners who testify for the prosecution are rewarded.)

Yandle's testimony made it clear that Carden's testimony was irrelevant. It meant nothing, because Bobby Perrotta was already dead before Carden placed me at the scene.

sixty-seven

On the second day of the hearing, we were sitting in the courtroom, waiting for the session to begin. The courtroom was full, but Judge Gertner had yet to appear. Bob Sheketoff was standing off to the side talking to AAG McIntyre. He then approached me and handed me a sheet of paper. He asked, "Have you ever seen this before?"

It was a handwritten letter.

I quickly read it and, looking up at him totally astonished, said, "I never saw this before in my life … I …"

He interrupted me. "Shhh. Don't say anything."

He walked over to the witness stand where Alan Caplan was already seated, waiting to testify. As he handed Alan the letter, Alan was putting on his reading glasses.

Alan read quietly for a moment. Then, eyes widening as he looked up glaringly around the courtroom, he said, in a spontaneously angry voice, "No, I never saw this before. If I had this at trial, there wouldn't have been a trial!"

He was staring directly across the room at AAG McIntyre as he spoke.

In response, she nodded her head slightly toward him, silently acknowledging her agreement. She said, "I just received it."

On the night of the murder, Carden had written a letter to another inmate in the block, obviously a friend of his. In the letter, he described just how Perrotta had been murdered—and mutilated for being an informant—and how Carden had found the body. It contained a number of other details relevant to the murder. It even identified the person that Carden claimed was responsible for the murder, the guy who supposedly ordered the hit from outside of the prison.

But it never mentioned me (nor Campbell or Keigney).

It also initiated the theory that Perrotta's penis was torn off and placed in his mouth, because he was suspected of being an informant. This isn't something that I have ever heard of happening to someone, because they were an informant. On the other hand, it is something that I could see happening to

255

someone who had grievously offended a female member of someone's family. Like Carden's sister?

The letter had been found in Carden's cell on the day after the murder and given to State Police Lieutenant William Bergin.

If we had been shown this letter at trial, as the law required, it would have destroyed the Commonwealth's case. To prevent this from happening, Bergin hid the letter.

THE CARDEN LETTER

"DEAR J. W. POST.

"As you already know what happened to Bobby, well it came from the street, Remember our co-defendant well he's carzy [sic] and put a jacket on Bobby. So [indecipherable] happened."

"We were warned the same day at about 4:30 so we kept together. Then after the six o/c count I went up and check on him. And he was alright so I went to put the betting slip in and left Tom to stay out on the teiar [sic] until I came back. So when I was over Three Block putting the slip in They yelled Perrotta, visit, So I knew something must have happened, I then ran over to "2" block and saw his door opened I then knew something happened, I got in to his room and there he was with the belt of his bath robe around his neck, and I got crazy when I looked at his mouth and found his penis in his mouth. I then got the srew, [sic] but before that I checked his pulse and heart beat but there was nothing his was kill like they kill informores [sic], all because of that son of a betch you know who I mean."

Write Bakt
The <u>SKULL</u>

When Fran McIntyre first turned the letter over, Sheketoff asked her where it had been all these years.

She replied that it had been found in Lt. Bergin's files.

Sheketoff said, "Let me guess. He's dead."

McIntyre responded, "That's right."

It's funny how people can see the same thing, yet see it entirely differently. When Fran McIntyre first turned over the letter, Bob Sheketoff took it at face value, describing her in the newspapers as "one of the finest opponents I have ever had the pleasure of dealing with." He was even quoted as calling her "the hero of the case." Everyone agreed with him.

Except me. I didn't see it that way. Right from the start, I thought that it was a stall. Maybe I wouldn't have felt that way if she had turned the letter over on the first day of the hearing, before Joey Yandle testified. Before it became obvious to everyone who heard him testify that, even if Carden had been telling the truth (which he wasn't), it didn't matter, because Bobby Perrotta was already dead before Carden ever placed me at the scene.

But she didn't. She waited till the second day. Then, and only then, did she turn over the letter.

On the other hand, I cannot avoid the fact that I have become, shall we say, slightly paranoid in regard to the Commonwealth's employees.

sixty-eight

When testimony resumed on the second day of the hearing, Al Caplan's testimony was helpful and Fran McIntyre, while cross-examining him, tried to diminish his effectiveness by implying that his testimony was influenced by his personal feelings for me.

McINTYRE: "Mr. Caplan, can you describe what your relationship is with Mr. Doherty, please?"

CAPLAN: "I would say a personal friend and also a client."

Q: "And your friendship and your association with Mr. Doherty has extended since 1976?"

A: "Absolutely."

Q: "And you have a strong feeling for him?"

A: "I have a very strong feeling for him."

Q: "And strong concern for him and his future?"

A: "An extremely strong concern. Can I explain?"

McIntyre ignored Alan's request to clarify.

Q: "And you have great feelings for the verdict, great feelings regarding the verdict in this case; isn't that right?"

A: "Absolutely."

At that point, she called for a pause in the proceedings. When she resumed her questioning, she went to a totally different subject, thereby denying Alan the opportunity that he had requested to clarify his remarks.

Upon redirect examination, Bob Sheketoff allowed him to finish what he had been trying to say.

Q: "Now, the assistant attorney general asked you whether or not you had strong feelings for Mr. Doherty, correct?"

A: "Yes."

Q: "Do you remember that question?"

A: "I do."

Q: "And you said you do have strong feelings."

A: "That's correct."

Q:"He is not only—he not only was a client, he's also become a close personal friend?"

A: "That's fair to say."

Q: "And why did that happen, sir? Why do you have these strong feelings for him?"

A: "Because of all the cases I've handled since I started practicing criminal law, this case has haunted me more than any other..."

Ms. McINTYRE:"Objection, Your Honor."

THE COURT:"I'll allow it for what it's worth."

A: "I felt that there was absolutely no evidence to tie Mr. Doherty to this case. I thought that the matter—very respectfully, I'm talking to a judge about other judges. I thought that the manner in which the state court judge handled this case was a total perversion of justice."

"And I feel that Mr. Doherty has been sitting in prison for twenty years for a crime he didn't commit. And I have been trying to work with everybody I can to help him for the truth to come out and get him released. I think it's an atrocity, and I am appalled."

Q: "Is that why you refused to speak to the assistant attorney general?"

A: "That is why. I didn't want to do anything to cooperate with anyone who is keeping Stevie in jail."[11]

sixty-nine

T wo weeks after the hearing, Fran McIntyre sent Bob Sheketoff a letter that offered the Commonwealth's justification for hiding the letter for over twenty years. It went as follows:

Dear Attorney Sheketoff:

I write to provide you with the following particulars.

In March, 1997, I, along with Assistant Attorney General William Duensing, undertook the handling of the evidentiary hearing in the above-captioned matter on behalf of the respondent. As you know, this was scheduled for May 12 and 13, 1997.

Preparatory to the hearing, AAG Duensing sought the files from the Norfolk County District Attorney's Office. Pursuant to his request, that office provided several file folders of photocopied material to this office.

On May 12, during a final review of the materials provided by the Norfolk District Attorney's Office, I examined a stapled three-page document and recognized what the document purported to be. This document was provided to you as Mr. Doherty's counsel on May 13, 1997, and has been characterized as the "Carden letter".

On May 12, I spoke to the trial prosecutor, John Prescott and faxed to him a copy of the document. Mr. Prescott told me that he had no memory of the document's existence, and had no memory of ever seeing it. He said it appeared to be in Carden's handwriting. Specifically, he had no memory of providing it in pre-trial discovery or during trial.

On May 12 and 13, I spoke to the assistant district attorneys who handled Mr. Doherty's case post-trial. Judge Charles Hely had no memory of the specific document. Assistant D.A. Stephanie Glennon wrote the S.J.C. brief regarding a motion for new trial, and never transmitted any discovery. Assistant U.S. Attorney James

Lang argued the motion for new trial before the S.J.C., and never transmitted any discovery.

On May 13, it was reported by Sheila Craven, an administrative employee in the Norfolk District Attorney's Office that this document was found in a file maintained by the State Police at the D.A.'s office at 360 Washington Street in Dedham.

On May 23, I spoke to First Assistant D.A. John Kivlan who indicated that the original letter had been located in a State Police file, and that it had apparently been in that same file during the entire pendency of this matter.

The investigating State Police officer, William Bergin, whose initials apparently are on the envelope, died several years ago.

These seem to be the pertinent circumstances regarding the document.

Thank you for your courtesy in this matter.

Sincerely,
Francis A. McIntyre
Assistant Attorney General
Chief, Criminal Bureau.

I wonder why McIntyre didn't ask the guy who did their oral argument in front of the First Circuit Court of Appeals, in 1987, AAG William Gottlieb. He was the one who admitted that Carden *had* had a bank robbery charge pending at the time of our trial; after all of the other "honorable" ADAs had denied it. Of course, at that point, it was to the Commonwealth's advantage to change their story. So Gottlieb did.

Obviously, the essence of the letter's history is, "Nobody knows anything, except Bergin, and he's dead."

At least on its face, but then Delahunt admitted that he knew about the letter. This raises an interesting question: "How could all of these other prosecutors, each of whom handled the case personally, while Delahunt was still the district attorney, not have been aware of its existence?"

This raises the next question: "Just who is fibbing?"

Let's see; John Prescott prosecuted the case. He was, by definition, Delahunt's conduit to the paperwork. Ergo, how could Delahunt have seen the letter and Prescott not have seen the letter?

As I see it, we're left with two choices. Assuming that Delahunt finally decided to tell the truth, then either Prescott really did see the letter and just flat out lied, or Bergin bypassed Prescott and took the letter straight to Dela-hunt. But, if that's what happened, the implication would be that Delahunt told Bergin to hide the letter and not show it to Prescott. Otherwise, why wouldn't Bergin show it to Prescott?

Hmm, a rather anomalous situation; obviously, someone fibbed. It must have been Prescott or Bergin. They're dead, they can't deny it.

As to the others, the rest of the prosecutor mob, ADAs Glennon and (now Judge) Hely, and (now Assistant U.S. Attorney) Lang, did they simply not request all of the paperwork when preparing for the case or did they re-quest it and just conveniently ignore the letter? Or, did Delahunt not turn the letter over when they did request it? Who knows?

Are they all fibbing? Who knows?

The only thing that we do know, for sure, is that the first time that any Commonwealth lawyer ever admitted to knowing of the existence of the let-ter, just happened to be the first time that the case was heard after Delahunt was no longer the DA.

It also came out after more than twenty years—when, at the order of the court, the DA's office finally turned over Perrotta's institutional file to us—that Bobby Perrotta and Johnny Stokes had had a fight *shortly before Stokes was killed*. Keating and the Delahunt mob had made sure that neither we nor our jury ever knew about that.

One can only wonder just what else did the DOC, the state police, and the DA's office hide and/or lie to us about?

seventy

Shortly before being returned to Massachusetts for the hearing in 1997, I had, once again, filed requests for jury trials in some of the civil actions that I had pending against the DOC. So, after the evidentiary hearing, while waiting for Judge Gertner's decision, I decided to file a Request for a Preliminary Injunction asking the court to prevent the DOC from sending me back out of state until I was given a trial on my civil actions. They had used my being out of state for so many years as an excuse for not giving me a trial that I felt that this was my one opportunity to actually have my cases heard. It was about time. The two in Norfolk County were ten and twelve years old. I kept it quite simple in each case.

In regard to the two years I did in the hole for the bogus stabbing case, I filed the following.

COMMONWEALTH OF MASSACHUSETTS
NORFOLK, SS.
SUPERIOR COURT DEPARTMENT
NO. 87-419
Stephen Doherty, pro se v. Michael Maloney, et al, *
Defendants

REQUEST FOR PRELIMINARY INJUNCTION

Now comes the plaintiff, Stephen Doherty, pro se, and petitions this Honorable Court, pursuant to R.Civ.P.65, to grant him a preliminary injunction preventing the Massachusetts Department of Correction (DOC) from transferring him out of state until after the instant action has been brought to trial. In support of this motion please see the attached Memorandum and Affidavit.

Respectfully submitted,
Stephen Doherty

MEMORANDUM IN SUPPORT OF
REQUEST FOR PRELIMINARY INJUNCTION

This action is now more than ten years old and should have gone to trial long ago. The reason it hasn't is Plaintiff's out of state placement. Plaintiff is a Massachusetts state prisoner who, for the last seven years, had been housed in the Federal Bureau of Prisons where he was sent by the Department of Correction (DOC) in order to impede his access to the courts.

Plaintiff's attempts to be brought back for trial on this, and other, civil actions against the DOC, have been vigorously opposed by the DOC. However, Plaintiff is presently being housed in Massachusetts, at MCI Cedar Junction, pending a hearing, on unrelated matters, in the Federal District Court.

In light of the DOC's consistent refusal to return plaintiff to Massachusetts for trial, Plaintiff contends that this temporary housing at MCI Cedar Junction will be his only opportunity to obtain a trial in the instant action.

As proof that this action is ripe for trial, Plaintiff refers this Honorable Court to Plaintiff's earlier filings and to the Court's decision (Jacob, J.) of 9-21-87.

Therefore, Plaintiff prays that this Honorable Court, for the reasons stated above, issue a Preliminary Injunction preventing the DOC from transferring him out of state until after the instant action has been brought to trial

Respectfully submitted,
Stephen Doherty

AFFIDAVIT

I hereby depose and state:

1. 1. My name is Stephen Doherty and I am serving a life sentence for the State of Massachusetts.
2. I am the named Plaintiff in *Doherty v. Maloney*, Norfolk C.A. NO. 87-419.
3. In 1988, shortly after having filed a motion for a speedy trial, in a separate civil action against the Department of Correction

(DOC), I was removed from general population and placed in segregation preparatory to being transferred out of state to the Federal Bureau of Prisons (BOP).

4. I challenged this transfer in court, (Suffolk C.A.NO. 89-2437-B).

5. In 1990, I was transferred into the BOP, with the understanding that I would be brought back for any trial in the case.

6. In 1992, during settlement negotiations involving C.A 87-419, and three other actions against the DOC, my (then) attorney requested that I be brought back for trial.

7. The DOC refused to return me for trial.

8. I was recently returned to Massachusetts, by court order, for an evidentiary hearing in an unrelated matter in Federal Court.

9. I am presently being housed, temporarily, at MCI Cedar Junction.

10. I am being held in Ten Block, i.e., segregation.

11. A rule has just been implemented which effectively eliminates meaningful telephone contact between Ten Block inmates and attorneys.

12. Norfolk C.A NO. 87-419 is ripe for trial.

13. Based on the DOC's past behavior, and present attitude, I firmly believe that, if I do not receive a trial, on Norfolk C.A. NO. 87-419, before I am returned to the BOP, this action will never come to trial.

Sworn to under the pains and penalties of perjury this 12th day of June, 1997.

Stephen Doherty

Their response was ludicrous.

DEFENDANTS' OPPOSITION TO PLAINTIFF'S REQUEST

FOR A PRELIMINARY INJUNCTION

Now come the defendant, through counsel, and herein submit their Opposition to plaintiff's Request for a Preliminary Injunction.

As grounds therefore counsel submits there are only two issues remaining in this case pursuant to Judge Jacobs September 21, 1987 Order (attached Exhibit 1).

The first issue is whether the witness/victim was coerced into testifying against the plaintiff. The defendants submit the attached affidavit from Officer Julius dated March 31, 1987 answers this query (attached Exhibit 2).

The second issue raised relates to witness request or waiver at the plaintiff's disciplinary hearing.

This issue is minimal at best, especially in light of the fact the plaintiff fails to raise this as an issue in his appeal of the disciplinary board's finding (attached Exhibit 3). Since it is unclear whether the issue was raised previously the plaintiff should not be permitted to make this claim now.

The plaintiff was deemed a danger to members of the prison population in Massachusetts and was transferred to federal custody. The plaintiff's custody status has not changed since 1986 and the fact the plaintiff now wishes to pursue his claim after many years of disinterest should not be rewarded.

Based upon the attached documentation and the aforementioned arguments, the plaintiff has no likelihood of success on the merits of his claim, therefore his Request for Preliminary Injunction should be denied.

> Respectfully submitted,
> NANCY ANKERS WHITE
> Special Assistant Attorney General

The epitome of a DOC lawyer's response, pure deceit; after spending years trying to be brought back for trials on my civil actions, only to be thwarted by lying DOC lawyers, now that I was back, AAG Ankers White hypocritically tells the court that "*after many years of disinterest*" I should not be allowed to have a trial.

Moreover, this hypocritically disingenuous mendacity was based on the flat-out lie that my custody status had not changed since 1986. For the record, my "custody status," in the relevant time period, i.e., 1986 to June 20, 1997, went as follows:

1. From January 1, 1986, to October, 1986, I was in "General Population, Massachusetts;"
2. In October 1986, it changed to "Segregation, Massachusetts;"

3. In September 1988, it changed to "General Population, Massachusetts;"
4. In December 1988, it changed to "Segregation Massachusetts;"
5. In April 1990, it changed to "General Population, BOP;"
6. In (circa) December 1990, it changed to "Segregation BOP;"
7. In (circa) January 1991, it changed to "General Population BOP;"
8. In March 1997, it changed to "Segregation, Massachusetts."
9. This is where I was on June 20, 1997, when AAG Nancy Ankers White told the court that my custody status had not changed since 1986.

I filed a response listing the facts and the lies that they told—all for naught. On July 31, 1997, Judge Chernoff denied my request that the Commonwealth not be allowed to ship me back out of state until they allowed my ten-year-old civil action to be brought to trial. Graciously, he did tell them to put me on the trial list.

> "Motion denied. Case to be placed on available trial list. The Department of Correction, through counsel, to be notified that plaintiff is expected to be produced for trial. (Chernoff, J.)"

As Yogi Berra said, it was déjà vu all over again. It immediately brought to mind the court's 1990 ruling that said that they could ship me out of state (for no reason) but that they would have to bring me back to Massachusetts for any court hearings that I might have.

Once again, they were able to respond, with a straight face, "Of course we'll bring him back." They didn't. Despite Judge Chernoff's order, the case was never even placed on the trial list.

seventy-one

On September 17, 1997, Judge Gertner issued her ruling.[12] She found that I had made the required showing of being actually innocent. However, she could not rule on my issues because of the Commonwealth's turning over the letter, which meant that I had to go back to the state court.

"At some point, notwithstanding all the changes in habeas, this process should make sense. Habeas is "at its core, an equitable remedy." [cite] But for the Court's evidentiary hearing, the letter would not have come to light. This is certainly not a case where the delayed discovery is the fault of the petitioner. As a result, I find a stay to be the most appropriate resolution. Doherty may return to state court and file a motion for post-conviction relief on the Carden letter. After he has exhausted that claim in the state courts, and fairly presented it to the SJC, I will grant him leave to amend his petition and add it as another ground for relief. I realize that this adds another delay to this process, but is the most equitable and efficient solution.

"Doherty's case raises substantial issues. In addition to the new testimony given by Yandle, an entirely new piece of evidence, the Carden letter, has surfaced. These circumstances distinguish this case from frivolous, multiple filings which occasion pointless delays. While I have not resolved the petitioner's erroneous instructions claim, I note that intent was the central, pivotal issue in Doherty's case. His guilt hinged on whether the jury believed he shared Campbell and Keigney's intent to murder Perrotta. The SJC conceded that [t]he question of whether the defendant shared the intent of Campbell and Keigney was a very live, important and seemingly close question for the jury." [cite] The trial court's instructions on this issue were less than perfect, and I am unconvinced that Doherty's trial was untainted by constitutional error."

"CONCLUSION"

"For the foregoing reasons, I ORDER that the petition be STAYED

268

pending the petitioners state proceedings. The case will be administratively closed during this period, and counsel shall keep the Court advised of any developments in these proceedings."

"SO ORDERED"

"Dated September 17, 1997"

"NANCY GERTNER, U.S.D.J."

seventy-two

One morning, a few weeks after Judge Gertner's ruling, as we were preparing to file my motion for a new trial, two transportation officers showed up at my cell door in Ten Block. I was told that I had a court hearing scheduled and to get dressed. For some reason, I was under the impression that this court appearance was in relation to one of the civil actions.

As we were driving down the road, they suddenly swung off of the road into a tiny airfield. There were two state police pilots waiting for us. They were taking me back to Lewisburg in a little four-seater plane. In essence, they were kidnapping me.

I did not want to go. While the four of them were discussing procedures, I considered resisting. I had no doubt that I could put a stop to it. Short of rendering me unconscious—and keeping me that way for the entire trip—there was no way that they could safely fly a plane that small if they were in the middle of the commotion that would ensue from a physical struggle.

At the same time, I also knew how they would twist it for the news media. "DERANGED KILLER TRIES TO CRASH PLANE;" "KILLER TRIES TO ESCAPE," yadayadayada. This was not the time to give them anything to twist into something else. So, against all of my better instincts, knowing that it was just another way for them to stall the case, I bit my tongue and went with them, peacefully. As much as it killed me, I knew that it was the sensible thing to do.

Despite the federal court's actual innocence finding, and the discovery of the hidden letter, the DOC quickly sent me back out of state again before we could get my Motion for a New Trial filed with the state court.

This was the third time that they had sent me out of state to a federal penitentiary. Each ship-out was subsequent to the discovery of new evidence. Not one of these transfers was the result of any wrongdoing on my part. (Except, of course, from the Commonwealth's point of view. They felt that it was absolutely wrong for me to keep finding concealed evidence, thereby violating their right to hide it.) As with the first two ship-outs, I was charged with nothing. And, once again, I was in the process of filing for a new trial because of newly discovered evidence. Another coincidence?

The Commonwealth was always aware that I was the driving force behind these appeals. Therefore, it should come as no great surprise that, in the twenty-three years between Bobby Perrotta's death, in November 1976, and my release in November 1999, I only got to spend about three of those years in general population in Massachusetts. The rest of the time they either kept me in the "hole" or out of state in a federal penitentiary, about ten years in each. In hindsight, it's obvious that this was due to my discovering evidence and bringing it to the court's attention, as opposed to any misbehavior on my part. This is borne out by my disciplinary record—or lack of one—throughout the eighties and nineties.

||||||||||||||||||||||||||||||||||||||||||||||||||||||||||||||||||||

WHEN THE NEW trial motion was finally filed with the state, the Commonwealth began their usual stalling tactics. So, I also requested bail, which was not an unreasonable request. The hiding of the letter alone was such an egregious violation that even Fran McIntyre described it as the "heart of the case."

More importantly, I knew that it would interfere with their stalling.

The case was assigned to Judge Charles Grabau who ordered me returned for a bail hearing on the following Friday, to no avail. The Commonwealth did not bring me back.

At the hearing, I was told that, when Judge Grabau asked why I was not present, the Commonwealth responded that they had not gone to get me, because the order had not included a specific date for my return. The clerk of the court pointed out that the order had specified "Forthwith." The court then heard arguments and took it under advisement.

On Tuesday, the court granted bail under conditions of house arrest. I would also have to wear an ankle bracelet. Judge Grabau ordered that I be returned on Friday for a hearing to set conditions. The hearing was scheduled for 9 am.

I was brought back on the day of the hearing, unfortunately, not until 3:30 pm, which was too late. They had to put the hearing off till the following Tuesday. I was taken straight to Walpole.

On Monday night, the news broke about Joey Yandle having lied about serving in Vietnam, and all hell broke loose. It was an election year and the politicians, including the Norfolk County DA who was running for reelection, couldn't find enough cameras, or reporters, to be appalled in front of.

In another front page story,[13] the *Herald* implied that it was Joey Yandle's testimony that convinced the court to release me on bail. That was typical of the *Herald*; they never mentioned the truth—that the real reason that I was granted bail was the letter that the Commonwealth had hidden for over twenty years.

The Tuesday hearing was canceled, and my bail was revoked shortly thereafter. It also just might explain why they sent me back out of state despite the court's actual innocence finding and then flaunted Judge Grabau's order(s) to bring me back on two separate occasions. Timing really is everything and, in this case, not just for me.

Although their wanton manipulation of the news media allowed them to stall my release for over two more years (and then keep me under house arrest for almost two more), they screwed Joey Yandle even worse.

He'd been a young kid who'd been in the service in the late sixties, was stationed in the Far East, and came home addicted to drugs. After he came home, he got involved in a drug robbery where someone, unfortunately, was killed. He did not do the killing. He was outside in the car. He was sentenced to life. After he went to prison, he cleaned up his act, quit drugs, and, for over twenty years, was a model prisoner—a fact that even his most ardent opponents did not deny. Joey was not only a model prisoner, and the personification of what the rehabilitation process is supposed to accomplish, he was also a model parolee. While he was home, he had reunited with his family and worked two and sometimes three jobs at a time. It didn't matter. Even though the governor's actual letter of recommendation that Yandle's life sentence be commuted made no mention of Yandle's military service and the recommendation from the Advisory Board of Pardons mentioned Yandle's military record only in passing, they still revoked his parole.

When the initial hullabaloo died down, it came out that the Commonwealth had been aware of Joey having lied about Vietnam long before they chose to make it public. This makes it obvious, on its face, that they all knew that it was irrelevant to his having received a parole. Otherwise, they would have revoked his parole way back when they first found out about it.

There are just too many self-righteous politicians displaying their indignation for the media and pointing fingers at each other. (I find a certain amount of irony in a politician being indignant about somebody else telling a lie. We all know that politicians don't lie, *right?*)

So Joey went back to prison. They gave him the maximum setback—five more years before he could even request that his parole be reinstated. Bottom line? Joey didn't go back to prison for lying. He went back for telling the truth about me. A truth, unfortunately for Joey, that they had hidden for over twenty years and did not want uncovered.

seventy-three

n October 1998, Judge Grabau heard our new trial motion. The Norfolk DA's office argued against it. Their position, basically, was, "Well, maybe Carden did write the letter and maybe State Police Lt. Bergin did hide it, but there's really nothing new there, *except that he never mentioned Doherty, Campbell, or Keigney.*"

If a defendant made a similar argument, it would be considered laughable and dismissed out of hand as frivolous. But, because it was the Commonwealth making the argument, it was given serious consideration.

They called John Prescott to testify. His latest claim of ignorance, of course, was of the Carden letter that his right-hand man, Bergin, had hidden. Like all of the other things that were hidden in this case, Prescott just didn't know about the letter either.

At one point though, while being questioned on the transcript of the first transcribed interview with Carden after the murder, the one that Keating had allowed him to "edit," Prescott was forced to own up to the fact that he had removed too much information.

After being shown a copy of the original document, which he had edited by drawing a yellow "X" across every page that he did not want us to see, and instructing his secretary to redact all of the pages that were marked with an "X," he admitted that, "There is a great deal of yellow redactions. I can only say that they must indicate redactions."

At which point, Judge Grabau injected, "In other words, you weren't too generous?"

PRESCOTT: "I'm sorry?"

GRABAU: "You weren't too generous?"

PRESCOTT: "No. I took out a lot of stuff I wish I left in."[14]

The Commonwealth also argued that the letter really wasn't that important, as it was cumulative. Obviously, Lieutenant Bergin didn't think so. Otherwise, he wouldn't have hidden it.

seventy-four

Judge Grabau took the case under advisement. Then things got a little out of hand.

After he had ordered me back to Massachusetts in 1998, I was held, as usual, in a segregation unit, Nine Block.

After a few months, as a result of the numerous protests that I sent to everyone—from the warden to the commissioner of corrections—about the illegality of my being kept in the hole—I hadn't received a disciplinary report in eight years—I was finally transferred out of Nine Block to a another lock down block.

However, shortly after that, I was told to pack up my stuff and was escorted to a new block. As I walked into the block, the wall to my right was lined with guards dressed in their Darth Vader outfits, all carrying clubs. On my left were the cells, three tiers, fifteen cells on each. I was told that I was going to cell thirteen on the flats. As I was walking toward the cell, I heard an inmate call out to the guards, "Hey, are we gettin' out for recreation today?"

A guard responded, "No rec."

Another inmate yelled from his cell, "What about showers?"

A guard answered, "No showers."

As I entered cell 13, I realized from the yelling that was going on around me just what was happening. They were creating a new lock down block and, like me, everybody else in the block had just been brought here. As I laid on my bed and listened to more guys being brought in, I knew what was coming.

War.

The block quickly looked like a garbage dump, which, for whatever reason, was exactly what the administration wanted. It was unavoidable, and they knew that from *Jump Street*. A little known fact, at least to the public, is that not all prison disturbances are initiated by the inmates. Sometimes, for various reasons, it is to the administration's benefit to attract the news media's attention (e.g., an increase in prison funding, an attempt to pass new prison rules that would be considered outrageous under normal circumstances, an opportunity to influence voting on a prison bill that is before the legislature)—thereby giving the DOC the means to promote their agenda by influencing public opinion.

It's real simple. You take forty-five guys and place them in a lock down block. Don't let them out for anything (no showers, no recreation, no law library, no visits, no phone calls, and no nothing), just give them three meals a day, and you know that you're going to get a reaction. Then, intensify the situation by refusing to tell anyone why they were being locked down, and you have a very explosive situation. And it exploded.

It started with the food. After the meals, they wouldn't come by to pick up the garbage, so the garbage went out on the floor—not in the cells, out on the flats.

It rapidly became obvious, through the guards' attitudes and lack of responsiveness to questions, as to what this was all about; that it wasn't going to change. After a few days, all hell broke loose. In total frustration, guys blocked their toilets and sinks and flooded the block.

By this time, they had taken all of our property, including food that we had purchased from the canteen. They had also cut the meals in half, right from the start, and then turned off the water in the cells.

The flats, by the way, are not the best place to be housed when a block is flooding out. As gravity requires water to flow downward, it all winds up in the cells on the flats. Augmented, of course, with urine and embellished with garbage and feces.

At one point, a captain whom I'd known for years was making a round. As he was going by my cell, he looked in and I saw the surprise register on his face. He stopped and said, "What the hell are you doing in here?"

I just shrugged and said, "I have no idea. I haven't had a ticket in years. I keep asking, but nobody seems to know."

"I'll check into it," he said.

A few days later, I was being escorted to the hospital, and I ran into the captain in the corridor. I asked him if he'd found out why I was locked up and if I could get moved to a normal block.

Looking uncomfortable, he said, "Nobody wants to talk about it. I was pretty much told to mind my own business." I believe he was actually embarrassed.

At the time, I was taking pain medication—some kind of an NSAID—for arthritis in my neck, medication that I was supposed to take with food and lots of water. My complaints that I did not have sufficient food or water fell on deaf ears.

After a few more weeks of this (although the water had been turned back on by this time), I suddenly passed out. It was about 11:30 on a Saturday night. I'd just stood up when all of a sudden I knew that I was going down. And I did. I didn't lose consciousness, but I couldn't get up. After about five minutes, I was able to pull myself up on the bed. Then I passed out.

On Sunday morning, I requested to see a doctor. I was taken down the corridor to the hospital where I was told that I had the flu and sent back to the block.

The rest of the day is rather blurry. When I woke up on Monday morning, I could barely get out of bed. I took a few steps and had to sit back down.

I was sitting up in my bed with my back against the wall when another inmate, who was out on the tier, stopped in front of my cell. He took one look at me and ran down the tier. By this time, I had been moved to cell 30, the last cell on the second tier.

The next thing I remember, I'm speeding down the corridor in a wheelchair. At the hospital, they gave me a glass of water. I drank it right down, and it came right back up. Only it came up black. I was promptly rushed to an outside hospital, the Shattuck, in Boston.

It turned out that the pain medication had burned a hole in my stomach, through which I'd been bleeding internally. They immediately administered two pints of blood intravenously. They then hooked me up to another IV and rehydrated me, twenty-four/seven, for the rest of the week.

They kept me in the emergency ward, on a heart monitor, for twenty-four hours. A doctor told me that he'd never seen anyone as dehydrated as I was. The doctor said that I was so dehydrated that they couldn't tell whether I had had a heart attack, was having a heart attack, or was going to have a heart attack. They almost got what they sentenced me to—my life.

On Tuesday, they took me out of the emergency ward, slid a camera down my throat, and took a picture of my stomach. That's when they discovered the hole.

Transportation arrived soon after to take me to a prison hospital, up in Shirley, where they kept me in a twenty-four-hour-a-day lock down cell, with one whole wall made of glass, sort of on display. They kept me there for the rest of the week, all the time still hooked up to the IV.

On Friday, they removed the IV, returned me to Walpole, and placed me back in the same block.

seventy-five

Judge Grabau kept the case under advisement for almost a year before he finally issued his ruling. In September 1999, he reversed my conviction and ordered a new trial.

The Commonwealth immediately applied for leave to appeal.

Supreme Court Justice, Neil Lynch, was the sitting single justice (i.e., the gatekeeper) in November 1999, who heard the Commonwealth's appeal. At one point, during oral argument, he asked the DA if he knew of any cases where the SJC had overturned a lower court decision under similar circumstances. ADA Robert Cosgrove admitted that he did not.

Bob Sheketoff was unable to be there for the hearing, so his partner, Kim Homan, sat in for him. When it became clear during argument that the Commonwealth would be unable to retry the case, the judge said to Kim, "So, basically what you're looking for is a get-out-of-jail-free card."

To which Kim responded, "Well, seeing as my client has done over twenty years for a crime, which he did not commit, I'd hardly call it getting out of jail free."

At the end of the hearing, Justice Lynch took it under advisement.

Within a week, he denied the Commonwealth's appeal. For all intents and purposes, it was over. As I stated above, by law, there is no appeal from a gatekeeper's denial of leave to appeal.

A superior court judge granted bail. Unfortunately, he simply reinstituted Judge Grabau's earlier order (which had been granted before the conviction was overturned). While the order did grant my release, it was a partial release, which required confinement under house arrest, while wearing an ankle bracelet. This also included my being breathalyzed twice a day (after twenty-seven years without a drink). Twice a day was the DOC's interpretation of the court's order that allowed them to breathalyze me *randomly*!

But all the bracelets in the world couldn't have diminished the sensation of walking out of the courthouse and down the stairs to the street—unattached to anyone else, able to move my arms and hands, able to walk in whatever direction that I chose—with no walls in sight.

The fact of the matter is, though, while this was the best thing that had happened to me in over a quarter of a century, the Commonwealth turned it into a totally frustrating stall tactic. They knew that they could not retry the case. So, as they had done over twenty years earlier, they offered to let us plead guilty to a lesser charge in exchange for time served. I declined the offer. I wanted a new trial.

seventy-six

After the gatekeeper denied the Commonwealth's appeal and we refused their offer to plead guilty to a lesser charge and accept time served, we filed a motion in Superior Court asking that the Commonwealth not be allowed to use Carden's testimony from the first trial, as we would be unable to cross-examine him on the hidden letter.

On March 28, 2000, Judge Malcolm Graham, while admitting that the prosecution's behavior was "reprehensible ... undermining the integrity of our system of constitutional protections," still denied our motion. He ruled that the letter was "cumulative."

We naturally appealed his ruling. When the Commonwealth responded to our appeal, they added a shocker. They also filed a motion for reconsideration of the gatekeeper's denial of their earlier appeal. They based their motion on Judge Graham's finding that the letter was cumulative.

The Commonwealth's motion was so out of line on so many levels that it was mind-boggling. In essence, it was a disingenuous ploy, attempting to appeal a decision that, by law, cannot be appealed. So, they didn't call it an appeal, they called it a motion for *reconsideration*.

This was a rather duplicitous play on words that, while conceivably conforming to the letter of the law, does slither around the law's intent. Nonetheless, it is still an outright contradiction of the Commonwealth's—and specifically the Norfolk County DA's office—long-standing position on this issue. In this very same case, when the circumstances were reversed, when *I* attempted to appeal a gatekeeper's denial, some fifteen years earlier, the Commonwealth's position was quite explicit: In their opposition, they stated that, "*Re-review of the identical issues decided by the single justice—is barred by principles of res judicata and is not permitted by G.L.C. 278, s. 33E. See Leaster v. Commonwealth, 385 Mass. 547 (1982),*" COMMONWEALTH'S MEMORANDUM IN OPPOSITION TO PETITIONER'S MOTION FOR RELIEF, COM. V. DOHERTY, CAMPBELL & KEIGNEY, NO. 84-167.

The SJC then adopted that position with the succinct, stringent ruling that; *"That decision is not appealable... defendant's remedy, if any, lies with the federal courts."* Com. v. Doherty, S.J.C. No. 84-167 (March 4, 1986, Abrams, J.)

This time, however, when the shoe was on the other foot and it was the Commonwealth that had been denied leave to appeal to the full bench, this same DA's office filed a motion for reconsideration. Reconsideration, by definition, is "re-review." For example:

(1)WEBSTER'S DICTIONARY, 1990 Edition; p. 457. One definition of "review" is "reconsider";

(2)AMERICAN HERITAGE DICTIONARY ROGET'S II: The New Thesaurus (electric/battery); a synonym for "review" is "reconsider"—and vice versa.;

(3)The Thesaurus in Microsoft 98 identifies "review" and "reconsideration" as synonyms of each other; and last, but far from least;

(4)BLACK'S LAW DICTIONARY, 6TH EDITION CENTENNIAL EDITION, 1891 TO 1991, p. 1320 *"review"*-"To reexamine judicially or administratively. *A reconsideration;"* [emphasis added]

The Commonwealth had blatantly reversed their position, deliberately flaunting the doctrine of judicial estoppel. "The doctrine of judicial estoppel provides that a party may not gain an advantage 'by taking one position and then seeking a second advantage by taking an incompatible position.'" [cite] It is quite clear, by definition, that the Commonwealth did gain just such an advantage, both times.

The timing was so apropos. We were scheduled to be heard on our appeal of Judge Graham's denial on Wednesday, May 3. ADA Cosgrove filed their response two days before the hearing. Bob Sheketoff received it the day before the hearing. On the same day, before he could even respond, he was contacted by a clerk from the SJC who told him that the May 3 hearing was canceled, because Judge Lynch was going to grant the Commonwealth's motion for reconsideration and that that month's gatekeeper, Judge Ireland, felt that, if that was the case, it made the present hearing moot.

Sheketoff was flabbergasted.

He said to the clerk, "You're telling me that Judge Lynch is going to allow a motion for reconsideration of a six-month-old decision that's already been back to Superior Court on other matters, and he's not even the sitting single justice?"

The clerk said, "That's right."

After hanging up, Sheketoff quickly drew up an opposition to the motion for reconsideration. It was filed before noon on Thursday. Although the

Clerk had said that Judge Lynch was going to grant the motion, he hadn't actually done it yet.

Sheketoff confined his argument to the issue at hand. A petition for reconsideration may not be considered by a single justice, because it is procedurally barred. After specifically pointing out exactly why, Sheketoff wrapped up his motion as follows:

"Should this Court conclude that it will consider and grant the Commonwealth's motion for reconsideration, the respondents request that the Single Justice report to the full bench the issue of whether the motion for reconsideration could be considered by the Single Justice."

This was a very nice way of saying, "Okay, you've been turning down defendants' appeals for years, on these very grounds, now please tell me, publicly, why the law does not apply to the Commonwealth?"

On May 19, Judge Lynch granted the Commonwealth's motion. In doing so, he carefully avoided the issue that Sheketoff raised as to whether Lynch even had the authority to rule on a motion for reconsideration. He also carefully avoided the law.

Then he retired.

Apparently, what's sauce for the goose is not always sauce for the gander.

Ironically, a couple of months after they allowed the Norfolk DA's office to challenge the gatekeeper's denial in my case, the SJC ruled, in a different case that a "[d]ecision of [a] single Justice ... who acts as gatekeeper ... in [a] first degree murder case ... is final and unreviewable; thus, it may not be appealed to the full Court and is not subject to collateral attack on the merits."

Of course, that ruling was against the defendant, not the Commonwealth.

|||||||||||||||||||||||||||||||||||||||||||||||||||||||||||||||||||||||||

ALLOWING SUCH AN inapposite finding as Judge Graham's to be employed as a reason to override a gatekeeper's denial of leave to appeal in a first-degree murder case would be tantamount to allowing a defendant who'd been acquitted of a first-degree murder charge to be retried, because he was subsequently found liable for the murder, in a civil action, by a different judge.

O. J. Simpson better stay out of Massachusetts.

|||||||||||||||||||||||||||||||||||||||||||||||||||||||||||||||||||||||||

AFTER I ASKED some other lawyers that I knew, besides Bob, to explain to me how Lynch had done what he had done, none of them could explain the reason. I asked Bob, "If the Commonwealth can file a motion for reconsideration of a six-month old gatekeeper's denial, then, apparently, there is no time limit. So, can we file a motion for reconsideration of a fifteen-year-old gatekeeper's denial of a pro se motion that I filed in this same case?"

Bob just laughed and said, "No, we can't. What they filed was improper and should have been dismissed out of hand."

I realized that he was right, but the fact was it had *not* been dismissed out of hand. It infuriated me. Why should they be allowed to do something that no defendant had ever been allowed to do, that I had been specifically told that I could not do?

In 1985, when the gatekeeper, Judge Wilkins, denied me leave to appeal Judge Keating's denial of my motion for a new trial, I had attempted to appeal his denial, pro se. The Commonwealth replied with (what was then) their stock response: "Re-review is not permitted by G.L.C. 278, s.33E." The sitting single justice/gatekeeper completely agreed with them. Her entire decision read: "The petitions are dismissed. The defendant filed a motion for new trial which was denied. The Single Justice denied leave to appeal. That decision is not appealable. (cite) *The defendant's remedy, if any, lies with the federal courts.*" (Abrams, J.) [emphasis added]

Now, fifteen years later, it would appear that the law was changed. Words have a specific meaning. Justice Abrams' unambiguous ruling that *"defendant's remedy, if any, lies with the federal courts,"* by definition, eliminates any more state court filings and should have been applicable to the Commonwealth. It wasn't.

So I did it pro se. On July 19, 2000, citing Justice Lynch's decision, I filed a pro se Motion for Reconsideration of Wilkins' 1985 denial, augmenting it with subsequently uncovered evidence that cast grave doubts upon the grounds on which the denial had been based. I limited it to two major issues that he had enabled them to avoid: Prescott's lying to the jury about Carden not being rewarded for his testimony and staff member David Powers' sworn statement that Perrotta had told him that Carden had given him a black eye just a few days before the murder occurred.

As to Prescott's lying about Carden being rewarded, I simply pointed out how obviously Keating had completely distorted Judge Sullivan's STIPULA-TION. Moreover, at one point after Wilkins' denial, I had written directly to Judge Sullivan, exhibiting how Keating had misused his STIPULATION. Judge

Sullivan responded, admitting that number nine was "ambiguous." I included his response in my motion.

As to the gatekeeper's adoption of Keating's skirting the issue of Carden giving Perrotta a black eye, Wilkins' justification was that, "There is no evidence that the prosecutor or the police knew of this statement at the time of trial."

So, I included the following: Long after trial, it came to light that, in Bergin's initial report, which was kept from us at trial, Bergin admitted that he'd confiscated and reviewed Perrotta's file on the day after the murder. While he made no mention of the Powers' memo, he was forced to mention Powers in regard to an unrelated matter. However, he immediately went on to say that Powers was no longer working for the DOC but that he, Bergin, was attempting to locate him.

Bergin lied. Eight years later, when Powers testified at defendants' hearing, *he was still working for the DOC.*

Why would Bergin tell such a blatant lie, except to deflect attention from Powers and to keep us unaware of him? And, by extrapolation, unaware of the fact that the only witness that the Commonwealth had who implicated us, had actually been the one to give the victim a beating shortly before he was murdered.

I then put side by side the similarities between the circumstances surrounding the missing Powers' memo and the hidden Carden letter.

On the night of the murder, Carden wrote the letter. On the day after, it was discovered and given to Lt. Bergin. The letter then disappeared and was not seen again for twenty years, when it was found in Lt. Bergin's file.

Also, on the day after the murder, Walpole staff member David Powers placed the "black eye" memo in Perrotta's file. That night, Lt. Bergin took possession of the file, and the memo was never seen again. Lt. Bergin then flat out lied by saying that Powers no longer worked for the DOC.

By the way, while preparing this motion, I attempted to review the motion that I had initially filed in response to Wilkins' 1985 denial. When I requested a copy from the SJC, I was told that the requested filing was missing and that it was not even listed in the docket entries. The Commonwealth's response, however, *was* listed in the docket entries! The SJC clerk then graciously offered to request a copy from the Norfolk DA's office on the theory that, where they had filed a response to it, they must have a copy in their files. Unfortunately, the DA' office claimed that they couldn't find their copy either. As with so many other crucial documents over the years in this case, they too were "missing."

||||||||||||||||||||||||||||||||||||||||||||||||||||||||||||||||||||

IT HAS BEEN my experience that, more often than not (or, to be more accurate, whenever they can), prosecutors and AAGs simply ignore pro se filings. However, this time, shockingly, they were given a date to respond, which they did on July 31, 2000.

The Commonwealth's response to my motion was, in all honesty, gibberish, not, mind you, that it wasn't well done. Bob Cosgrove, the assistant district attorney who drew it up, did a brilliant job. He created a seemingly meaningful brief, based on nothing more than a hodgepodge of half-truths, innuendo, statements taken out of context, and flat-out lies.

OOPS! I'm sorry. That's probably politically incorrect of me. Prosecutors don't lie. For the most part, when a court catches them in unequivocal acts of mendacity and falsification of the truth—and they cannot avoid commenting on it—the worst that a court will generally say is that the prosecution "misstated the facts." Of course, if I did that, the same court would call it perjury.

He basically avoided the real issues. His main argument was that I should not be allowed to proceed pro se, because I was represented by Bob Sheketoff and that I was attempting to lead the court into error by advocating contradictory positions simultaneously.

I loved it. It gave me the opportunity to show just how fallacious Bob Cosgrove's arguments were. On August 18, 2000, I filed a reply that opened with the following first-page exposition of the factual history of the case and the issue.

DEFENDANT'S RESPONSE TO COMMONWEALTH'S OPPOSITION

TO DEFENDANT'S PRO SE MOTION FOR RECONSIDERATION

"The Commonwealth's assertion that defendant "should not be allowed to proceed pro se ... [because he is] represented ... by Attorney Robert L. Sheketoff, [and that he is] attempt[ing] to lead this court into error [by] advocating contradictory positions simultaneously" is somewhat disingenuous. Defendant has been placed in this position precisely because the Commonwealth has done exactly what they are accusing defendant of doing, i.e., "advocating contradictory positions".

"Some fifteen years ago, in this very case, the Commonwealth, in opposing *defendants'* attempt to appeal a Gatekeeper's denial of Leave To Appeal, stated unequivocally that "Re-review of the identical issues decided by the single justice—is barred by principles of res judicata and is not permitted by G.L.C. 278, s.33E'"A Single Justice (Abrams, J,) concurred, stating, "That decision is not appealable... defendant's remedy, if any, lies with the federal courts."

"Now, however, *the very same Norfolk County District Attorney's office has requested that a Gatekeeper's decision be re-reviewed* and a Single Justice (Lynch, J.) has granted that request."

"The utter lack of congruity in these filings, and rulings, *has* led to an interesting anomaly. The Commonwealth, complains that defendant and Attorney Sheketoff have filed petitions which contain "contradictory positions". This is true—for the following reason—Attorney Sheketoff insists that defendant's request for reconsideration of a Gatekeeper's denial is procedurally prohibited and, basically, preposterous."

"However, with all due respect to Attorney Sheketoff, he said the same thing about the Commonwealth's motion for reconsideration. The one that Judge Lynch allowed."

"As a result, defendant is totally baffled as to whether to believe his attorney, Judge Abrams, and all prior case law on this issue—(not to mention the Commonwealth's own filings), or, alternatively, to believe the *present* Norfolk County District Attorney and Judge Lynch."

"Accordingly, in the event that defendant's remedy no longer lies exclusively with the federal courts; that an appellant (other than the Commonwealth) is now allowed to request that a Gatekeeper's denial of Leave To Appeal be reviewed, defendant respectfully requests that this Honorable Court grant his Motion For Reconsideration. What's sauce for the goose, should be sauce for the gander."

||||||||||||||||||||||||||||||||||||||||||||||||||||||||||||||||||||||

AFTER WAITING AROUND six months, I filed a motion asking that the court consolidate my pro se motion with the motions that the lawyers had filed. According to the law, as mandated by the United States Supreme Court, if the issue under appeal is evidence that was hidden by the state (e.g., the Carden letter), then it must be considered collectively along with any other suppressed evidence that was uncovered after trial, which is exactly what all of the issues are that I raised in my pro se filings.

And there it sat. Although it took the single justice just one day to respond to the Commonwealth's motion for reconsideration, my reconsideration motion languished for more than another year.

The SJC finally scheduled us for a hearing, on September 6, 2001, for the appeal that the lawyers had filed, *not* for my pro se motion for reconsideration. The mere act of doing so showed that they were tacitly giving approval to Lynch's decision. I renewed my request that my pro se appeal be consolidated with the others.

My request was ignored.

Sometime in August, Bob Sheketoff asked me if I had given any thought to accepting the Commonwealth's offer that I plead in to a lesser charge in exchange for time served.

I told him, "No. Why would I? They've got to deny the Commonwealth's motion. You know that there's no appeal of a gatekeeper's denial."

He nodded and then said, "Right. But they're hearing it anyway. Doesn't that scare you?"

Before I could respond, he said, "Look, I'm not telling you to take the offer. I'm just saying that you should think about it. That's all."

So I did. For the next couple of days, I went back and forth. In the end, I just couldn't do it. I couldn't quit. In the first place, I did not commit the crime. More importantly, their motion for reconsideration was preposterous and shouldn't even have been allowed to advance as far as it had gone. And, most importantly, with all of the evidence that we now had, which had been hidden from us at trial, I welcomed the opportunity to present it to a jury.

Moreover, I could not help fantasizing about getting a fair trial, in front of an impartial judge. Actually, I'd settle for a judge that would simply allow the jury to view the murder scene.

On the other hand, I could not help remembering the original offer that they had made, before trial, when the autopsy report showed that their only witness was lying. My feelings then were exactly the same. The case was over.

That was almost twenty-five years ago, and the case still wasn't over.

I shared my thoughts with very few people, probably because I knew how they felt. Everyone in my family had been in favor of my taking the offer from the day it been proffered.

I discussed it with a friend of mine, who happens to be a lawyer. We'd been friends for a lot of years, and we'd always stayed in touch, even during the ten years that I'd been out of state in federal prisons. He said, "Look, I really do understand. And you're right. But you were just as right twenty-five years ago when you refused the offer the first time. And they screwed you. If you want my opinion, they'll do it again. This is not a good SJC. They're totally political. And, for whatever reason, this case is political and always has been."

"You know, with all the shit they've pulled in this case, if you do go in front of the SJC, the state could ask that bail be 'temporarily' revoked while the decision is under advisement. And this SJC just might allow it and then keep it under advisement for a year or so. All of which time you'd be locked up."

Then, as if he were reading my mind, he said, "And if you're figuring that, even if they do screw you, you can go back up to the federal court, where a judge has already made an actual innocence finding, don't be too cocky. If the state appeals it, which you know they will, you'll wind up dealing with the First Circuit, which is about as bad a First Circuit as I've ever seen. For different reasons, but they're still not good in your circumstances. And, if the SJC rules against you, your bail will almost certainly be revoked. So even if you do eventually win in the federal court, with the way that they've been stalling this case, it could take another five years or so. And they'll keep you locked up all that time."

"And you know," he said. "Best case scenario? Even if you were to win it at the SJC, Norfolk County could still stall it as long as they wanted, which would mean that many more years under house arrest."

As I was approaching my third year under house arrest, I really couldn't dispute the point.

He was silent for a moment, obviously pondering something. Then he said, "You know, there's something else you might want to consider. I know you intend on filing a major civil suit for all the years you did. And you should. By all rights, with all the stuff that's come out, you should win. And if you do, what would Sheketoff have coming? At least a million or so, probably a lot more. Whatever it was, it would be a good piece of change. Yet he's telling you to think about taking the offer. Think about that. You're lucky to have him. A lot of lawyers wouldn't even consider telling you to take the offer, just for the money. Being a lawyer, I really shouldn't say that. But it's the truth."

|||||||||||||||||||||||||||||||||||||||||||||||||||||||||||||||||||||||||||

SHEKETOFF WAS GOING away on vacation, so I had a week or so to make up my mind. Needless to say, I really did not think of too much else that week.

One day, the weirdest thing happened. I was in the car, driving to a hospital appointment. The radio was on and a song happened to catch my ear. I had never heard it before, but it had a nice sound to it, and I started to listen to the lyrics. It turns out that the name of the song was "I Hope You Dance" by Lee Ann Womack and, as I was listening to the lyrics, some of them were so on point, it was as if she was telling me not to plead in.

Whenever one door closes, I hope one more opens
Promise me that you'll give faith a fighting chance
And when you get the choice to sit it out or dance
I hope you dance
I hope you dance
I hope you never fear those mountains in the distance
Never settle for the path of least resistance
Living might mean taking chances. But they're worth taking
Don't let some hell bent heart leave you bitter
When you come close to selling out, reconsider
And when you get the chance to sit it out or dance
I hope you dance

But now is when it gets weird. I'd never heard the song before. Then I heard it five days in a row, right in the middle of the week that I'm seesawing back and forth, trying to decide whether to "dance" or to throw in the towel.

When it came on, on the fifth day, I literally yelled at the car radio. "WILL YOU KNOCK IT OFF!"

I think I might have been a little nuts by that time. I don't think that I have ever been as conflicted about anything as I was about that decision. And now, between Bob Sheketoff (who'd stuck by me for thirteen years, and is far more than my lawyer, he is also my friend), and my other friends and family members, who all just wanted it to end, I was finally leaning toward taking the Commonwealth up on their offer/threat and pleading guilty to manslaughter. Now here comes Lee Ann Womack telling me that I should 'never settle for the path of least resistance' and that if I was considering "selling out I should reconsider" and when I got "the chance to sit it out or dance, that I should dance."

The worst part of it was I liked the goddamn song. Not to mention that I agreed with her. There was no way that I did not want to "dance." It went far beyond the fact that I was legitimately not guilty of the crime. The sad truth is, in the real world of law, actual innocence doesn't make a damn bit of difference.

If you think I'm kidding, check out a United States Supreme Court decision, on a case out of Texas, where they killed a guy named Herrera. Herrera
was on death row for allegedly killing a cop. After he was sentenced to die,
somebody else admitted to committing the murder. So Herrera filed an appeal. Of course, the Texas courts shot him down. So he took the appeal to the
United States Supreme Court. In essence, what they said was, "Well, yeah,
you might actually be innocent but, unfortunately, actual innocence is not
a constitutional issue. So, you can die." Well, not exactly. They did let him
know that he had another alternative. They said that it wasn't as if he didn't
have any other options. He could always file a request with the governor for
clemency. In Texas?

Beyond my innocence, case law on the relevant issues that we had raised in
front of the court clearly established that numerous Constitutional violations
had been committed by the state and that the case was, and should be, over.

And so it went on. Everyone who I knew that honestly cared about me
wanted me to take the offer. And yet I couldn't. In the end, I think it came
down to the quitting. I'd been fighting to prove my innocence for over twenty
years. I'd done it, and I just couldn't quit.

I decided to dance.

Then I got a phone call that changed everything. My doctor called me
to tell me that the results of some tests that I had taken were in and that she
wanted "to take a closer look."

When I asked her what she meant by a closer look, she said, "From the
inside." The bottom line was that I might have cancer.

The earliest that the procedure could be performed was almost three
weeks after the hearing was scheduled. What would happen if the SJC revoked my bail?

I was all too familiar with the medical treatment, or lack thereof, at Walpole. My near death, after I'd been brought back from Lewisburg was, in good
part, because of the deplorable lack of meaningful medical treatment at Walpole.

So, with that episode still fresh in my mind—to this day, I still feel the
aftereffects of the dehydration caused by the hole that was burned in my
stomach—the thought of my being returned to Walpole, while possibly in
need of medical treatment for cancer, was the deciding factor. I acceded to
their offer/threat to plead guilty to a lesser charge, manslaughter, in exchange
for time served.

If the Commonwealth's threat was to retry me, as opposed to Judge Gra-

bau's decision going in front of the SJC, I would not have given in to their co-
ercion. I would have danced—in public, in front of a jury. It would have been
a lot different this time. With all of the new evidence that we now had that
had been hidden from us at trial, I would have welcomed the opportunity to
present it to a jury. And the Commonwealth knew that. So they kept it behind closed doors, where the option was the possibility of the SJC reversing
Judge Grabau's decision. I just could not chance it, not with the way that the
SJC had handled my case for so many years.

The one thing that I did insist upon was that it be done under an Alford
plea. Although I did plead guilty, I preceded the plea by specifically stating
that I did not commit the crime.

On September 6, 2001, I appeared in front of the judge. Things started
off smoothly enough. It was agreed that the charges would be reduced and
that we would receive time served.

The judge then entered the basic facts concerning Jackie and I into the
record, e.g., age, place of birth, education, mental stability, etc.

He then stated that everyone had agreed that the charges would be reduced to voluntary manslaughter.

He then had ADA Cosgrove recite the facts that the Commonwealth
would rely upon in a retrial. The entirety of the evidence was what Carden
had testified to at the original trial.

When Cosgrove was finished the judge asked Jackie and I if we had both
heard what Cosgrove had said about the underlying facts of the case.

We confirmed that we had.

The judge then asked us, "And do you -- did you in fact commit those
acts as I have heard them or, alternatively, are you willing to concede that
the Commonwealth's facts are sufficient to ground a guilty finding in a trial
before you, but for whatever reason, through lack of memory or lack of voluntary understanding at the time the acts were committed, you don't wish to
admit that you are guilty of those acts.

"Is that what I understand, sir?"

I replied, very carefully, "First, there's two separate things there, your
Honor. The first one: Did I commit it? No, I did not."

The judge said, "All right."

I then started to continue, "Do I believe they have the evidence to convict
me?"

At which point, the judge interrupted me. "You better discuss that with
your counsel, because if you don't, then I'm not going to take this plea."

I said, "Okay."

Sheketoff came over to me and said, "The question the judge has asked you is do you believe that the Commonwealth has sufficient evidence that if presented to a jury, a jury could believe that evidence and return a guilty verdict against you. That is the question.

"Now you sat through a trial. And you saw this evidence unfold, the first time, so you know what the evidence is that they have. Or at least with one witness having died, it is—more than one witness—there is prior recorded testimony.

"So the question is, are you making a decision to plead guilty with an understanding that the Commonwealth has sufficient evidence that they could convince a jury to convict you of the crime charged?"

I said, "I'm under oath so let me be truthful..."

The judge interrupted, "I can't hear you, sir."

I said, "I'm under oath so let me be truthful."

Again, "I'm sorry, sir, I can't hear you."

I raised my voice slightly and, quite clearly, stated, "I am under oath, so I'm trying to be truthful. I believe if that were all of the evidence, that I would agree with you, that because it happened before, they could convict me on it."

The judge said, "All right. Well, that's all I need, sir. Now all I need from you is if you wish to change your plea -- that's up to you -- if you, sir, wish to change your plea, all I need to know from you is that you agree that the Commonwealth's evidence, as recited to you, and on the elements of the offense that underlies the indictment against you, that the two of those will be sufficient, if the jury believed it, to find legally that you are guilty of the offense.

"Do you understand that?"

I said, "Yes, I do, sir."

He said, "And do you believe that that is the case, sir?"

I said, "If the case were limited to that, yes."

After that, things moved on rather quickly.

Jackie and I stated that we wanted to plead guilty to voluntary manslaughter and that it was up to the court to determine the sentence that we were going to be given.

Then the judge said, "And you understand that what I could do in this case is to sentence you to twenty years in jail starting today on this offense, if I wanted to."

I said, "No, I didn't, sir."

"All right." He said. "Well, why don't you just take a minute with your counsel and he will explain to you what I am saying."

Sheketoff said, "What the judge is saying is that the maximum penalty for this charge is twenty years. Do you understand that?"

I said, "Yes."

The judge joined in, "And further, that I can give you twenty years?"

I said, "Yes sir."

He went on. "Starting now. Do you understand that I can do that?"

I wasn't too comfortable with the fact that, technically, he could give me twenty years starting that day. On the other hand, it was already on the record that the purpose of this hearing was for us to plead in to a lesser offense and receive time served.

So I answered, "Yes."

He then explained that by pleading guilty we were waiving numerous rights that come with a trial.

When we agreed that we understood that, he asked one last question. "Have any promises, other than the recommendation that you heard that the district attorney and your counsel have agreed may be presented to the court -- have any promises been made to you which would have induced you to plead guilty to this crime?"

I said, "Yes sir."

He asked, "What were those promises, Mr. Doherty?"

I replied, "Time served."

The judge said, "Other than the recommendation, that is the recommendation that the Commonwealth and your counsel are making to me, Mr. Doherty, do you understand that that is a recommendation that is being made to me?"

I answered, "Yes".

He then said, "That is not a promise in the sense that I have to go along with it. Do you understand that?"

I said, "I didn't until right now, Sir.

He said, "Well, do you now?"

I answered, "Yes, I do."

He then asked me if I still wanted to plead guilty.

I did not immediately respond. I just stared at Bob Sheketoff. Bob was sitting at a desk that was a few feet in front of me, off to my left. He was not looking in my direction and the silence suddenly became tense.

The judge seemed to be straightforward enough. But I really wasn't familiar with him. A few minutes earlier, he had told us that, technically, he could sentence us to twenty years, starting from that day. Now he was telling me that he did not have to abide by our agreement with the District Attorney. Enough. I'd been screwed by too many judges and prosecutors over the years.

Finally, a court officer who was standing close to Sheketoff, whispered something to him, as he nodded in my direction.

Bob got up and came over to me and started to explain just what would happen if the judge should decide not to accept the prosecutor's recommendation of time served.

The judge interrupted him, saying, "I was going to get to that."

Sheketoff said, "Okay. But the problem is that he didn't realize that you were going to get to that."

The judge said, "All right. Well let me put it to you this way. Your counsel points out something that I would have brought up to you which is that if you do not receive the sentence which is recommended, I am going to permit you to withdraw your guilty plea."

At that point, I said, "Thank you very much, your Honor. I understand now."

Shortly after that, the judge accepted the plea and sentenced us to nineteen to twenty years, time served.

It was over.

||||||||||||||||||||||||||||||||||||||||||||||||||||||||||||||||||

A POSTSCRIPT.

Eight months after I pled in, I read a piece in the paper[15] about a guy named George McGrath who had overturned his murder conviction, about a year or two earlier, after serving almost thirty years; he was out on bail awaiting a new trial.

The SJC had just reversed the superior court judge's decision that the trial judge's instruction on reasonable doubt had been constitutionally defective and reinstated the conviction. McGrath was going back to prison for the rest of his life.

The trial judge had actually told the jury that, "If reasonable doubt or a mere possibility of innocence were sufficient to prevent a conviction, practically every criminal would be set free to prey upon the community."

"Such a rule would be wholly impracticable and would break down the forces of law and order and make the vicious and lawless supreme."

As I read the article, I actually got goose bumps.

Without even getting into the rule's practicality, the rock bottom foundation of criminal law in the United States, at least to my limited knowledge, was always that a jury must be convinced of guilt, *beyond a reasonable doubt*.

No more. At least not according to the SJC. I now have no doubt that, had I pursued my appeal, I would be back in Walpole serving the rest of my life in prison for a crime that I had nothing to do with.

Not that my issues were even remotely close to McGrath's issue. But, if the courts are now able to find that the standard of "beyond a reasonable doubt" no longer exists, then no principle of law is exempt from their attack.

I sat there for a little while, just thinking about the decision and its ramifications. Then I got up and went to the telephone and called Bob Sheketoff at his home. It was a Saturday, and he was probably gone away for the weekend, so I left him a message.

I just thanked him, from the bottom of my heart, for convincing me to plead guilty. I can honestly say that that morning was the first time that I was without reservations regarding my decision to plead guilty to a crime that I did not commit.

I was truly happy.

would like to make one point. Don't get the impression that I am saying…"Woe is me, poor innocent me." I was never an innocent person. I
was a bank robber. So, to a certain degree, it was, at least partly, my own
fault that I got framed for killing Bobby Perrotta. I put myself in the position
where a politically ambitious politician saw an opportunity to make political
hay and took advantage of it. But does that make it appropriate for him to do
that? Does that give them the right to frame someone for a horrific murder
that they had nothing to do with?

They seem to feel that it does. I'm far from the only person that the "justice system" has framed, wholly aided and abetted by the court system. And
neither are guys like Peter Limone and Joe Salvati who just did over sixty years
between them for a murder for which they were purposefully bum beefed. I
suppose the silver lining in that case is that, finally, after all of the years that
the government got away with covering up what they pulled, it has become
public knowledge just how disgracefully the government will act when they
want to frame someone and the lengths to which they will go to cover it up.

One of the government's favorite ploys that is played up by the media is
the phony propaganda that "everyone in prison claims that they didn't do it."
That's such a lie. But, because the media trumpets it, the public automatically
accepts it as common knowledge. Unfortunately, as we all know, a lie told often enough—especially by Big Brother—becomes accepted as the truth.

Now that the decision in the Limone case (by Judge Gertner) has pulled
the curtain back and exposed the truth, maybe some people will open their
minds and accept the fact that some people really are framed. Who knows
how many?

There were guys like Louis Greco and Henry Tameleo, who died in
prison after being framed for the same murder as Peter Limone. Or, there
is George McLaughlin, who they all spent time on death row with after he
was framed by the same FBI agent that got them. He's got over forty years
in now. If the death penalty hadn't been abolished, they all would have been
fried, like Sacco and Venzetti. Or they might've died on death row like Billy

Kelley, who waited on death row in Florida for over twenty years. The list just goes on and on. Remember Leonard Peltier? He's got over thirty years in, and they still avoid his case. Or Ricky Costa and Dennis Daye, but they've only got about twenty years in.

One of the classics was a guy named George Reissfelder. He got grabbed for an armed robbery with a guy from Charlestown named Silky Sullivan. They didn't even know one another. A guy had to introduce them to each other in the Charles Street Jail, where they were held while awaiting trial. Unfortunately, someone got killed during the stick up and they both got life.

A couple of years later, in Walpole State Prison, Silky got cancer and died. However, on his death bed, he told the priest that Reissfelder was innocent. The priest knew Silky well enough to know that he wouldn't lie in confession, especially in his deathbed confession. So he got involved.

The priest's quest to discover the truth took a number of years. Eventually, he tracked down a retired former homicide detective, who'd been involved in the case. The cop admitted that they'd known, way back before the trial, that Reissfelder had nothing to do with the armed robbery. The problem was they hadn't found out that he was innocent until after they had charged him, and they felt that if they dropped the charges against him, it would hurt their case against Silky. And they wanted Silky off the street. So, they let the charges stand.

What makes it classic is that, after the guilty verdict came in, they still tried to get the death penalty for Reissfelder, *even though they knew he was not guilty.*

It took about fourteen years before Reissfelder was cleared and finally released.

Another classic, of course, is Willie Bennett. When they busted him for killing a nine-month-pregnant woman, everybody knew that he did it. The media said so daily and, for a couple of months, everybody knew that Willie was an evil baby killer. Not only did the woman's husband, Charles Stuart, identify Willie, but, according to the media's "reliable sources," the cops had witnesses that Willie admitted that he'd done it. Until Stuart's brother gave him up, and the witnesses admitted that they lied.

Is there anyone who doesn't believe that if Stuart's brother hadn't given him up for being the real killer and if the alleged witnesses hadn't admitted that the cops threatened them into saying that Willie told them that he'd done it that Willie wouldn't be doing multiple life bits right now for killing a pregnant woman and her unborn baby? And you know that the proponents of the death penalty would be screaming his name outside of the State House.

In Judge Gertner's decision, in the Limone case, she cited a report that was written by the United States House of Representatives, which was the result of a lengthy investigation into FBI misconduct in the case. She described the report as "A stinging rebuke of federal law enforcement officials for tolerating and encouraging false testimony, for taking 'affirmative steps' to ensure that the individuals convicted would not obtain postconviction relief and would die in prison."

Like shipping me out of state every time that I discovered new evidence that I was framed?

By the way, in light of Justice Gertner's scathing decision in the Limone case, Congressman Delahunt said that he plans to file a bill that would impose criminal sanctions against federal authorities who fail to produce information or evidence that "implicates crimes of violence."

I wonder if he'll file one that would impose criminal sanctions against *state* authorities who fail to produce information or evidence that implicates crimes of violence? You know, like DAs who lie and hide evidence, or state police who lie and hide evidence, or judges who allow them to lie and hide evidence.

seventy-eight

The bottom line is I was convicted solely on the testimony of the one person that all of the impartial evidence pointed to—who just happened to be the only one that would tell the lies that could get Delahunt his badly needed conviction.

It was admitted that neither I nor the other defendants had any motive.

Carden had multiple motives.

Perrotta had just divorced Carden's sister and had a new girlfriend.

Carden and Perrotta were involved in an ongoing dispute over this problem.

Carden gave Perrotta a black eye just a few days before he was murdered.

Perrotta was murdered on the day that he was getting a visit from his girlfriend.

Perrotta's penis, which the girlfriend took from the wife, was torn from his body.

Perrotta testified against Carden at a federal grand jury.

Perrotta had a fight with Carden's best friend, Stokes, and then Stokes was killed.

Carden was the last person with Perrotta.

Carden found Perrotta's body.

Carden knew that he was going to get out of prison for testifying.

So, in the end, Delahunt's choice was, "Do I go after the one who all of the evidence is against or do I go after the ones that he said did it?" That is, "Do I go after justice or a conviction?"

I wonder if the rules are different for a congressman than they are for a DA when it comes to hiding evidence? This might be a good time to ask Delahunt about those forced inmate interviews. Maybe he'll tell us just what that "very productive, worthwhile, new information" was that he claimed to have uncovered (on the front page), but never revealed at our trial.

seventy-nine

There is one last item. Each of the civil actions that I filed against the DOC for keeping me in the hole, or out of state all those years, was dismissed for various "procedural" reasons. For example, after I was transferred from Leavenworth to Lewisburg, *and notified them of the transfer*, the Suffolk County Clerk's Office sent a document, which I had a deadline to respond to, to Leavenworth. So, of course, I never got it. When I didn't respond, they dismissed the case. Stuff like that.

There were actually two cases still alive when I was released—the one where Judge Elam ordered me released from segregation and the one for the stabbing that they bum-beefed me for that I tried to get a trial on when I was back in Massachusetts in 1997 and in which AAG Ankers White told her lies.

But, when the civil actions came up in court, this time, another AAG, Randall Ravitz, parroted Ankers White by claiming that it was me that stalled the case, for all those years that they kept me out of state. In keeping with his precursor's mode, Ravitz wove blatant, documented lies into his filings. When I responded, I clearly cited Ravitz' undeniable lies and specifically requested that the court address those lies.

Instead, the court dismissed the filings without addressing either the issues or AAG Ravitz' irrefutable lies. It turned out that the judge who dismissed the case, Judge Elizabeth Donovan, happened to have been an AAG herself for about fourteen years. Maybe the "code of silence" has moved from Charlestown to the "justice" system.

I have always maintained that the only reason that they kept shipping me out of state and/or keeping me in lock up was to prevent me from proving that they had framed me and to cover up the egregiously underhanded tactics that they used to accomplish, and maintain, that frame. And it's not just me. Over the years, I have come to realize that it is standard operating procedure for the "justice system" to stall and stall and stall until, in the end, so many guys get so fed up with so many courts blithely allowing their fellow Commonwealth employees to get away with anything, that they just give in

and quit trying. You can't quit. Just because, when you fight city hall, the ostensibly "liberal" state of Massachusetts turns into Nazichusetts doesn't mean
that you have to quit. You can't quit.

Ironically, the judge who dismissed the civil claim, which clearly depicted
how I was framed by Delahunt, was the same judge whose ruling made Delahunt a congressman. In 1996, when Delahunt lost the primary to Phil Johnston, by 266 votes, he got a recount that reduced the lead to 188 votes, but
he still lost. So, he took the matter to Superior Court where Judge Elizabeth
Donovan reexamined the ballots by hand. She changed almost 300 votes,
giving the election to Delahunt by over 100 votes, and ordered the secretary
of state to remove Johnston's name from the ballot and replace it with Delahunt's. Johnston did charge that Judge Donovan, who was a former AAG
under one of Delahunt's campaign strategists, then Attorney General Frank
Bellotti, had ruled indiscriminately. But, the SJC affirmed her ruling.

Wheels within wheels, life does run in circles.

THE END
(maybe)

postscript

Y ou may have noticed that I didn't really mention Arthur Keigney a lot in the second half of the book. After they shipped Arthur back out of state in 1984, we only got to see each other one more time. They had to bring him back for the evidentiary hearing in front of Keating in November 1984. That was the last time that we ever saw each other. After the hearing, they sent him right back to the feds.

Arthur died on Christmas Day 1995, less than a year and a half before they finally turned over the Carden letter.

Back in the late seventies, when we were in Ten Block, Arthur had gotten into art. He started with cartoons and carvings. He used to do these little carvings from double bars of Ivory soap. They were great. To this day, I still have one of the little carvings. He also started drawing (mostly cartoons) and eventually he got into painting. He was very good.

An eminently respected author, lecturer, art teacher, and expert in prison art named Phyllis Kornfeld put out a highly regarded prison art book titled *Cellblock Visions: Prison Art in America*. Of all of the artists' works that she had to choose from, she chose one of Arthur's paintings for the cover of the book.

At one point, in the late 1980s, Ms. Kornfeld arranged to have an art exhibit, consisting of inmates' paintings, displayed at the DOC headquarters in downtown Boston, at least one of which was Arthur's.

Sometime in the early '90s, Arthur discovered that they had one of his paintings hanging on the wall at the DOC's headquarters in Boston. (It's not really unusual for your property to disappear when you're inside, especially during shakedowns.) He asked a friend if he'd go up to the DOC and take a picture of the painting. He did, or at least he tried. When he got there, they recognized him as being a Charlestown guy that had been in Walpole, mobbed him, and wouldn't let him in the door. Their excuse was that he had a camera and that they were afraid that he was going to take pictures of the DOC employees. He assured them that that was not the case, that he just wanted a picture of Arthur's painting for Arthur. He then offered to give them the camera, and he would wait outside while they took the picture. No go, so much for the "security" pretext.

So, Arthur never got to see which painting that they had "confiscated." I wonder if they still have it?

They not only stole his life, but they stole his life's work.

endnotes

1 12/3/76 BOSTON GLOBE

2 1/18/77 BOSTON PHOENIX

3 12/16/76 BOSTON GLOBE

4 12/17/76 BOSTON HERALD

5 12/25/76 REAL PAPER

6 COMM. *v.* CAMPBELL, 378 MASS. 680

7 COMM. *v.* CARDEN, NOR. SUP. CT. 61726

8 COMM. *v.* CARDEN, SUF. SUP. CT 98006, 98093

9 DOHERTY *v.* MALONEY, NOR. SUP. CT. 87-419

10 DOHERTY *v.* COMM. OF MASS., NOR. SUP. CT. 68154

11 DOHERTY *v.* DUBOIS, C.A. NO. 93-12166-NG 3/13/97 Hearing Tr.

12 DOHERTY *v.* DUBOIS, C.A. NO. 93-12166-NG 9/17/97

13 8/26/98 BOSTON HERALD

14 COMM. V. DOHERTY, NOR. SUP. CT. 68154, 10/26/98 Hearing Tr.

15 5/25/02 BOSTON HERALD

CPSIA information can be obtained at www.ICGtesting.com
Printed in the USA
LVOW131559031212

309867LV00002B/792/P